# FORMS OF HEAVEN

*Also by Clive Barker*

Fiction

CABAL

WEAVEWORLD

THE BOOKS OF BLOOD, VOLUMES I-VI

THE HELLBOUND HEART

THE GREAT AND SECRET SHOW

IMAJICA

EVERVILLE

SACRAMENT

For Children

THE THIEF OF ALWAYS

Plays

INCARNATIONS: THREE PLAYS

# FORMS OF HEAVEN

THREE PLAYS

*BY*

## CLIVE BARKER

HarperCollins*Publishers*

HarperCollins*Publishers*
77–85 Fulham Palace Road,
Hammersmith, London W6 8JB

The HarperCollins World Wide Web site address is
http://www.harpercollins.co.uk/voyager

Published by HarperCollins*Publishers* 1997
1 3 5 7 9 8 6 4 2

First published in the USA by
HarperPrism 1996

Professionals and amateurs are hereby warned that this material, being fully
protected under the Copyright Laws of the USA, the UK and all other countries
of the Berne and Universal Copyright Conventions, is subject to a royalty. All
rights including, but not limited to, professional, amateur, recording, motion
picture, recitation, lecturing, public reading, radio and television broadcasting,
and the rights of translations into foreign languages are expressly reserved.
Particular emphasis is placed on the question of readings and all uses of these
plays by educational institutions, permission for which must be secured from
the author's agent: Adam Krentzman, Creative Artists Agency, 9830 Wilshire
Blvd., Beverly Hills, CA, 90212, USA, Tel: (310) 288 4545.
NB: it is the author's intention that any *amateur* or *non-profit* organisation that
wishes to mount a theatrical production do so with the *minimum* of contractual
or financial burden. Therefore, theatrical producers should plainly state their
amateur or non-profit status (if applicable) when attempting to secure
permission to produce any of these plays.

A catalogue record for this book
is available from the British Library

ISBN 0 00 225592 8

Set in Berkeley

Printed and bound in Great Britain by
Caledonian International Book Manufacturing Ltd, Glasgow

# Contents

FOR ANNA

Notwithstanding the notice posted on the copyright page of this book, alerting potential producers to the fact that the plays in this volume are fully protected under the Copyright Laws and thus subject to a royalty, it is my intention that any amateur or non-profit organization that wishes to mount a theatrical production (this does not apply to any other medium) do so with the minimum of contractual or financial burden. Plainly, if a company or a producer seeks to profit by one of these plays, then a royalty rate must be agreed and paid. If, however, an amateur or non-profit company is interested in mounting a production, write to me or my representatives at the address below, and let's see if we can make it work. Please note: the above does not mean I am offering a blanket sanction to any and all. I reserve the right to veto any production (if, for instance, a professional version is planned in the vicinity) but plays are written to be produced, and I will certainly entertain any reasonable approach from any organized source.

Please write to my agent: Adam Krentzman, Creative Artists Agency, 9830 Wilshire Blvd., Beverly Hills, CA, 90212, (310) 288-4545.

---

## http://www.clivebarker.com

# Laughter, Love, and Chocolate: An Introduction

Somebody asked me recently, while watching me paint a sizable canvas for a series of pictures I'm making, why I didn't make life a little easier for myself, and paint smaller pictures? I replied that I enjoyed the challenge of scale; the sheer physicality of covering large expanses of empty canvas, the satisfaction of ending the day spattered and smeared with paint. But that evening, after my visitor had left, I sat in my studio noodling over the successes and failures of my day's work, and I realized that there was another reason for my desire to paint big pictures: they envelope me. In the process of painting them I am immersed in the fields of color I'm laying down, lost, as it were, in a self-created wonderland. Sitting there, slumped in my chair puffing on a painted cigar, I was surrounded by an invented terrain, populated by invented people and creatures, and it was a blissful state. That's not to say I'd be happy blotting out the real world entirely, eclipsing it with canvas and retreating into a world of my own inventions. Reality excites my imagination too much with its spectacles and absurdities. When I see skies above me that are blue or pink or grey, I get an itch to paint a green sky, a red sky, a sky filled with faces, a sky filled with moons. But there is at the heart of the pleasure I take in making images and stories a desire to be lost in the imagined world awhile; to wander mapless in a place that doesn't work by the rules of the waking world.

So we come, via these musings, to the plays in this second collection. Unlike the three troubled dramas that were contained in *Incarnations*, these pieces are all comedies, which—despite the range of their settings and casts—have this essential quality in common: they explore and celebrate the strange territory that lies between the world of our imaginations and the world in which we live our daily lives. More particularly, the plays present us with a variety of dreamscapes: places where the impossible becomes plausible, and we can for a little time define our hopes for a new perfection. Hence the title of this collection. These are stories that all contain (indeed are constructed around) some of the shapes that heaven takes. A pair of pig-skin wings, a race of daughters, the beauty of a young man, the love of an adhesive gorilla, a sinking ship, an early spring. All of them, in these tales, forms of heaven.

For those readers familiar with my later novels (the books categorized as fantasy) some of the thematic material in these plays will be familiar. Just as *Weaveworld*, *Imajica*, the *Books of the Art* and *Sacrament* trace the journeys taken by ordinary men and women out of their recognizable lives into worlds steeped in the strange and miraculous, so these plays carry their protagonists (and hopefully the audiences who identify with them) into places charged with magic. In two of the three, those voyagers are duly returned, albeit shaken, to the comfort of their own reality. Only in *Crazyface* does one of the characters escape the gravity of his situation completely, and take flight, never to return; and even here it is the image of his blind mother sitting listening to the report of her son's ascent into the clouds with which we're left at the story's close. In other words, these plays are as much concerned with the transformative powers of the journeys their characters take as with the wonderments encountered along the way. When the journey is over, and the spectacle fades into darkness, the stories aim to leave their audiences a little changed. A little lighter spirited perhaps; perhaps, who knows, a little more loving?

Love is, after all, so often the motor of comedy; and these plays are no exception to that rule. Love stymied, love misused, love unlikely or undiscovered; love that will find its way, at last, into the light. In *Paradise Street*, Georgia loves Bonner, even though he's a sexist bastard, and Queen Elizabeth, Gloriana herself, falls for a wandering derelict of a man called Jack Mulrooney. In *Crazyface*, the sweet-natured, virgin fool Tyl Eulenspiegel takes an epic journey to Rome, but returns, at last, to the feet of the only soul who ever truly loved him, his mother. And in *Subtle Bodies*, which probably dramatizes the complexities and confusion of affection (sexual, familial and bestial) most elaborately, the entire story is predicated upon a series of problematical relationships. Carys loves Dex who loves Rob who fancies Sean who's an object of lust for Edward Lear who ends up marrying a gorilla, while Vince is in drunken pursuit of Rose who has deeply repressed feelings for Phoebe whose husband Lindberg once had an unforgettable night of lust with a transsexual in Bangkok. The way these passions—whether failed, frenzied, or simply foolish—shape the behavior of the characters is at the heart of the play; the fantasy elements are simply entertaining methods of revelation.

In literature, of course, fantasy has become a separate genre of its own, regrettably; more for the ease of marketing, packaging and stocking of books than for the edification of the reader. But it would be a pity to import such narrow classifications to theatre, which, long before the novel was invented, was a place where fantastical events and observations about the real world existed side by side. In classical drama, in medieval mystery plays and works of Shakespeare and his contemporaries, the supernatural world abuts and informs our own. In Noh and Kabuki, in Kathakali and Bunraku, in opera and ballet, magical events are central devices in the progress of the story. In our own time, Tony Kushner's *Angels in America* brilliantly weds heightened realism with fantastical splendors; glimpses of heaven, ice-floe visions, and of course the Angel herself, cracking the ceiling to make her presence known. Or consider the musical—that most popular of theatrical forms. Nobody bothers to dub *Phantom* or *Carousel* or *Into the Woods* fantasies, though they all use magical situations to move and excite their audience. I'd like to see the same freedom from the constraints of definition be granted my own texts, in time, and I certainly feel these plays will work best in production if their fantastic elements are not overly emphasized, but simply taken for granted.

A word or two here about the circumstances in which the plays were produced. *Paradise Street* was penned for the Dog Company, a troupe which mounted productions of a number of my plays, including *The History of the Devil* and *Frankenstein in Love* (there was also a production of a play of Joycean complexity, and length, called *Dog*, which may in the fullness of time find its way onto the printed page, and a piece of feather-light nonsense called *The Secret Life of Cartoons*). At the time of its first production, *Paradise Street* was neither a great failure nor a notable success. Amongst the critics in London—and later at the Edinburgh Festival—it had its supporters, if memory serves, but I fear of all the pieces the Dog Company mounted it suffered most from our absence of funds. It needs sumptuous costuming for the Elizabethan characters, who travel through time—in the midst of Gloriana's light—to visit the depressed streets of my native Liverpool. They bring with them a series of magical transformations and theatrical conceits, all of which, in addition to some glamor, required more casual bravura in their staging than I as director had the skill to provide. Nevertheless, the actors served the humor and the humanity of the piece well, and the outrageous nature of its interwoven plotlines—sexual revenge, visitations from the past, Elizabeth's search for a husband, etc.—pleased its audience mightily.

The other two plays were, like *Colossus* (a play about Goya contained in *Incarnations*), commissioned by a fine and far-sighted man called Alasdair Cameron, who was artistic director at the Cockpit Theatre in London. AIDS has since taken Alasdair from us, but I would like to think that these plays are some small testament to his faith in, and fiscal support of, writers and creators like myself. At a significant juncture in my life, before the books had started to earn me enough money to put bread on the table, he invited me to write a trio of plays as summer workshop projects at the Cockpit. *Crazyface* was the first of these, and after the constraints of writing for a small touring ensemble like the Dog Company, which regularly performed in tiny spaces above pubs, it felt wonderful to be *unleashed*; to be able to create stories that called for a large cast, and to write scenes that employed an ambitious range of lighting and scenic effects. Excited by the sheer scale of what I now had at my disposal—comparatively speaking—I wrote *Crazyface* as a kind of fool's epic, putting the character of Tyl Eulenspiegel at the heart of a picaresque that takes him through war, assassination plots, murderous sibling rivalry, an encounter with lesbian bandits and angelic intervention to end up at the feet of the Pope, all the while carrying with him one of the great, unlikely secrets of the Western world: *chocolate*. The result is a play that is part pageant, part circus and part meditation on the glory of clowns. I loved writing it, spiking its high spirits with sudden eruptions of violence and scenes of strange melancholy.

The following year, Alasdair commissioned me again, but this time he had a particular theme in mind: he wanted me to write about sexuality, particularly gay sexuality, in the context of the family. I pondered the problem, determined to write a piece that, unlike much of the politically driven gay theatre playing in London at the time, would offer the actors a chance for detailed character work. *Subtle Bodies* was the result. It takes some of its formal design from English farce—the cast of disparate characters converging on a hotel over one calamitous day and night; the manic concealing of secrets and the inevitable humiliations when the plots these people have laid against one another unravel—but to this familiar mix I added a few wilder elements of my own. Chief amongst them, the politely anarchic person of Edward Lear, whose romantic nonsense poem *The Owl and the Pussycat* had been a favorite from childhood. The truth about Lear's sexuality remains ambiguous; his biographers disagree vehemently as to whether he lived a life of repressed homosexuality or not. For the purpose of the play, I assumed that he was certainly living an *after*-life charged with such barely spoken feelings. And from those feelings—from the heart of his frustration—springs a rage, a poetry and finally a vision that drives the play far from the confines of the hotel. Lear, it turns out, is not simply a nonsense poet, passing his post-mortem span in shameful anonymity. He's an agent of a Dream Bureau, which has apparently taken to heart the challenge of shaping the imaginative life of the nation. Having volunteered for the task, however, Lear hasn't been enjoying himself.

"Most of the minds I peer into," he remarks, "are awash with trivia. . . . They make up shopping lists, and re-run soap operas. Its banality grinds me down."

The play finally liberates him both from his job and his repression, allowing him a perverse revenge upon the kinds of people whose triviality (and lack of common courtesy) so enrage him. He gives the warring hotel guests (who appear in pursuit of a missing bride and groom to be) a collective dream: the hotel transforms into a ship overnight, which promptly strikes an iceberg and sinks.

The play's not as polemical as some would like, I realize. It doesn't end with an unequivocal triumph of honesty over concealment. The characters are all left at the start of new paths, but it's by no means plain that those paths will lead to some brave new world. At the time, the play was criticized for what was perceived as a lack of political correctness; but I regret few of the choices I made. My first service was, and is, to the truth of the characters. I couldn't make the young, troubled lovers Dex and Rob end up in each other's arms, any more than I could pair Lear off with the youth he dotes on throughout the first two acts. At the close of the piece the gay best man goes swimming with Lear's object of affection, the confused bridegroom is probably heading back to the closet, and the poet, in a triumph of nonsense, marries a gorilla he's conjured up, to whom he's become devoted simply because the creature likes his nose. (Biographers report that Lear was obsessed with the size of his nose.)

The notion of a ship setting out on a voyage across a dream-sea may be familiar to readers of *The Great and Secret Show* and *Everville*. In those novels, this sea is dubbed Quiddity, and in *Everville* a character called Joe Flicker takes a leaky vessel called the *Fanacapan* out across its wastes, only to have the ship finally founder. Beyond this, there are few similarities of detail between play and book, but have no doubt, the first mention of Quiddity is here in *Subtle Bodies*, and appropriately enough, that mention comes from the lips of Edward Lear himself:

"Think of it. All of us on one final cruise into frenzical waters . . . " (*Filled with an almost visionary zeal*) "The sea, Treadaway, do you hear it?"

There is another connection between these plays, besides love and comedy, which may be of interest. All three employ theatrical artifice to create alternative realities within their established framework. In *Crazyface*, the relatively naturalistic tale of a wandering fool is constantly transfigured by formal elements that come from the circus, pantomime and silent movies. The horse is not a real horse, but a suit occupied by two warring actors. The

Pulcinellas are a grotesque chorus of identical creatures, a la Tiepolo. In *Subtle Bodies* the Dream Technicians operate as invisible stage-hands to mount a show of Lear's creation: the final voyage of the *Bear of Amsterdam*. And in *Paradise Street*, which opens with a dialogue between two masquers debating the very subject of the play, the line between "theatre" and "reality" is crossed, back and forth, without the audience being entirely aware of the fact, until the end. (The paradox here being that the most "realistic" scenes are in fact the theatre—that is, they're being watched by Gloriana—and the scenes that posit the most unlikely ideas—a time-traveling court, for instance—are presented without much razzmatazz.) In sum, all three plays are besotted with such games, and offer, I hope, considerable opportunities for actors, directors and designers to delight and amuse their audiences with visual tricks and spectacles. There's space for puppets and dance, mime and magic in these pieces; room for live music and (especially in *Crazyface*) interaction with the audience.

Like the texts in *Incarnations*, these plays are intended as invitations to companies who want to make their own, personal journeys into the worlds I have laid out on the page. The stage directions I offer are deliberately sparse, and finally inconsequential. Anything of mine that gets between interpreters and their pursuit of their own truth should be discarded. Respectfully, mind; but disregarded nevertheless. Every production, every assembly of actors demands, I realize, a different set of technical and artistic solutions. I ask only that you respect the words the characters speak. The rest—the sets, the costumes, and the stage business—is all ripe for invention.

Unlike the grim worlds of *Colossus*, *Frankenstein in Love* or *The History of the Devil*, however, these are overtly optimistic stories, their darker aspects finally overwhelmed by the sheer brio of their visionary characters. Queen Elizabeth and Jack Mulrooney, Tyl Eulenspiegel, and Edward Lear all carry the seeds of new worlds with them, and their passion to sow them will not be dampened. By the end of these tales, something bright and strange and promising has come into bloom, and the worlds into which these ideas have flowered will not be quite the same. In that sense, they are all plays about the act of making stories; all hoping, perhaps naively, that they will prove prophetic. That very naiveté is an essential element of their humor. Like fools entertaining us with the spectacle of their resilience (falling down and getting back up again, bruised but unbowed), these pieces set a dreamy idealism against hard-nosed cynicism, and they draw much of their comedic strength from depicting the unlikely victory of the apparently frailer force. In short, they have an unwavering faith in the essential goodness of things; a belief that with open eyes and ready hearts their characters will find everywhere signs of heaven's presence.

Clive Barker—Los Angeles, 1996

# FORMS OF HEAVEN

# CRAZYFACE

# Production Notes

I won't burden these notes with a detailed history of Tyl Eulenspiegel. The facts (those few that can be ascertained) and the legends that sprang up around the facts, have been well documented elsewhere. Suffice it to say that Tyl Eulenspiegel was a peasant trickster who dies in the middle of the fourteenth century, his pranks, many of which are cruel or scatological, carrying a distinct whiff of social anarchism. There have been numerous interpretations of his story. Strauss wrote a symphonic piece about the character, and Hauptmann penned an epic poem. My own introduction to the figure was a Belgian novel, which took ten years of its author's life to write, called *The Legend of the Glorious Adventures of Tyl Eulenspiegel in the Land of Flanders and Elsewhere*, by Charles de Coster.

How many of these works are strictly relevant to *Crazyface*? In truth, none. There's no necessity to read any of these texts in order to mount the play; though some of them may make an interesting bed of reference for a production that is particularly interested in verisimilitude. There again, perhaps the only kind of truth relevant to this tale and its telling is a clown's truth: the truth of laughter, though its source may be cruel and unsavory.

Certainly the play offers a broad canvas on which a company may daub their own particular follies. This, more than any play I've penned, lends itself to enrichment through improvisation and the use of a cast's particular skills. Like a circus, the play is constructed in a series of short performances—some of them barbaric, some of them farcical, some of them vulgar, some of them high-minded—but all, all in some way functions of, or reflections upon, the state of the fool.

Our Tyl Eulenspiegel is not the hard-hearted prankster of German folklore. He is a young Auguste clown, an idiot savant who will pass through a blizzard of horrors on his way to his own very particular salvation. Along the way he will encounter all manner of cruelty, arrogance, and stupidity, but his spirit remains unbowed, however grim the circumstances become.

That balance of sweetness and savagery is not as hard to strike as it may at first seem. After all, there is an element of cruelty in most comedy (we laugh at misfortune, not at victory). All this play does is push the elements to their extremes, so that one moment we are watching a pantomime horse, the next we are in a torture chamber of the Inquisition. Even these two examples contain elements of their contraries. The clown straddling the pantomime horse (who may or may not be Crazyface's father) is apparently dumb from the horrors that rage around him. And that torture chamber is run by a pack of hunched-back clowns, all of whom look to have been hatched from the same curdled egg.

The question is: how real should all this be, *could* all this be, given the bizarrities that occur in the tale? Perhaps it's best to view the play as a kind of alternative reality, in which historical fact (Spain *did* own the secret of chocolate), psychological realism (Lenny's envy of Tyl is what fuels his murderous rage) and clown-lore (the horse, the fish on a string, the cross-dressing, the chases, etc.) all co-exist on the same stage. The company's job is to make the elements sit so seamlessly side by side that this "other earth," part Breughel, part Freud, part circus, seems as consistent as a "naturalistic" drama.

Of course, there's no fourth wall necessary here. Like any clowns, the performers should work the audience wherever it seems appropriate. Indeed, part of the pleasure in mounting *Crazyface* is creating an atmosphere in which the audience feels complicit; drawn into the absurdities, and—hopefully—moved by Tyl's strange journey.

Though it may appear to be a tonally chaotic show—mayhem one moment, farce the next, sentimental scenes of parting or reunion the next—the story builds, as any good picaresque should, until towards the end, a number of narrative elements are tied together and resolved, leading Tyl to finish his trek unpursued. We have witnessed, we realize, a kind of life history. At the beginning of the play Tyl is still a child, innocent of self-knowledge. Then, once he's abandoned, he's given a quick, nasty education in the ways of the world. He is attacked, stripped, terrorized and humiliated, his situation worsened still by the presence of an itinerant angel who—far from offering celestial guidance—merely torments him. Our fool reaches his own version of sexual maturity at the wedding of a pig-breeder's daughter, and sets off again on his travels, now tracked by his murderous brother, Lenny. The story finally brings the brothers full circle. Lenny confronts his brother, and dies. Tyl meets the Pope, and realizes all in the Holy See is not what it's made out to be. At last, having viewed more of the world than most sensible men, he returns to his mother, and to the wings that will give him a glimpse of heaven.

It is a glimpse we don't get to share. Though the Tyl Eulenspiegel of *Crazyface* is a far sweeter and more *accidentally* anarchic character than his historical or anecdotal forbears, the two Tyls have this in common: they live in a dark, mud-splattered and superstitious world, in which joy is hard to come by, and revelation damned near as impossible. We watch the workings of the mighty from the point of view of the disenfranchised: the outcast fool and his family, wandering from place to place looking for somewhere to lay their heads. These are the lives lived on the verge of extinction; and if *Crazyface's* journey teaches anything, it is that the rich and the mighty are not any more secure than those they lord over. The laughter and the high spirits of the piece should never quite drown out the sound of the four fatal horsemen, coming to claim both the Kings and the Fools of the world.

Clive Barker—Los Angeles, 1996

# The Cast:

ELLA EULENSPIEGEL
CRAZYFACE: Tyl Eulenspiegel
SHEBA
IRVETTE
ANNIE
THE ANGEL
THE TOWNSPEOPLE OF LOON
CHEESBY
JINKS
ZELLER: a sometime scholar
WORMWOOD: the Birdman
THE PRIEST of Loon
ALVAREZ: the Spanish Spy
ALVIN: the English Spy
ALFONSO: the Italian Spy
ALLEGRO: the French Spy
ASSASSINS
PULCINELLA WITH SIGN
SPANISH DANCER
THE KING OF SPAIN
ATTENDANT
MENGO: a priest involved in the Black Arts
SECOND PULCINELLA
THIRD PULCINELLA
THE WITCH
THE OLD CLOWN
FIRST SOLDIER
SECOND SOLDIER
MARY TOLLER: the Bandit Leader
SECOND BANDIT
THIRD BANDIT
FOURTH BANDIT

LENNY EULENSPIEGEL: Crazyface's brother
FATHER: Bartholomeus, the Father of the Bride
SHIRLEY: the Bride
MOTHER: the Mother of the Bride
BRIDESMAID
FIRST GUEST
SECOND GUEST
THIRD GUEST
SERVANTS
BRIAN: the Bridegroom
FIRST VOICE (front end of Horse)
SECOND VOICE (back end of Horse)
FIRST CRIPPLE
SECOND CRIPPLE
THIRD CRIPPLE
BEGGAR
LA MOTA
FIRST CARDINAL
SECOND CARDINAL
FIRST CATAMITE
SECOND CATAMITE
THE POPE

# List of Scenes

### Act 1

Scene One: The Low Countries. Just beyond a forest.
Scene Two: The Low Countries. The outskirts of Loon.
Scene Three: The Low Countries. A crossroads.
Scene Four: Spain. The Palace Gardens.
Scene Five: The Low Countries. A wasteland.
Scene Six: The Low Countries. Another wasteland.
Scene Seven: Spain. The Torture Garden.
Scene Eight: The Low Counties. A forest road.
Scene Nine: The Low Countries. The pig-breeder's house.

### Act 2

Scene One: The Low Countries. A wasteland.
Scene Two: Spain. The Torture Garden.
Scene Three: The Low Countries. A town.
Scene Four: A prison.
Scene Five: The road to Rome.
Scene Six: The Vatican.
Scene Seven: A garden in Loon.

# Act 1

# Act 1:

## <u>Scene</u> <u>One</u>

### The edge of a forest

*THE SET IS IN DARKNESS. JUST A SLIVER OF MOON. NOW WE HEAR BIRDS. AT FIRST JUST A HESITANT FEW; THE CHORUS TUNING UP. THEY BUILD THROUGH THE SCENE, AS DOES THE DAWN-LIGHT, CREEPING ACROSS THE STAGE FROM THE EAST.*

*AT THE MOMENT, HOWEVER, THERE'S ONLY A DIM LIGHT. AND BY IT, A MELANCHOLY TABLEAU.*

*ELLA, A MIDDLE-AGED WOMAN, ONCE ATTRACTIVE, ONCE WARM-HEARTED, NOW TOO WEARY AND WOE-BEGONE TO BE EITHER; HER SON CRAZYFACE, AND TWO OF HER THREE DAUGHTERS-IN-LAW, SHEBA AND IRVETTE. ANNIE, THE THIRD, IS TRAILING ALONG BEHIND SOMEWHERE.*

*THE WOMEN ARE ALL LOADED DOWN WITH THEIR BELONGINGS: THEY ARE CARRYING ALL THEIR WORLDLY POSSESSIONS. IN ADDITION TO THE STUFFED BAGS AND*

*KNAPSACKS, EACH OF THEM CARRIES SOME TELLING PERSONAL POSSESSION. SHEBA CARRIES TWO BOOKS. IRVETTE CARRIES A STUFFED ANIMAL, STRAPPED TO HER BACK. ELLA, EVER PRACTICAL, CARRIES A SELECTION OF FRYING PANS, BLACKENED WITH USE. ONLY CRAZYFACE CARRIES NOTHING. ALL HE DOES IS TRAIL A LARGE SILVER FISH BEHIND HIM ON A STRING. THEY HAVE TRAVELED ALL NIGHT. NOW, JUST BEFORE DAWN, IT'S VERY COLD, AND THEY'RE EXHAUSTED.*

CRAZYFACE: I'm hungry.

*NOBODY ANSWERS HIM. IRVETTE PUTS DOWN HER BAGS, TIRED AND ANGRY. SHEBA DOES THE SAME.*

ELLA: No more midnight escapes! I'm too old. (*To Crazyface*) Next time we're leaving you to face the music.
CRAZYFACE: What music?
SHEBA: She means let you hang.
IRVETTE: Oh happy day.
ELLA: (*Stern*) Irvette.
IRVETTE: Or we could leave him to the lions.
SHEBA: Are there lions around here?
IRVETTE: Oh yes. And worse.
SHEBA: What's worse than lions?

*IRVETTE IGNORES THE QUESTION.*

ELLA: Where's Annie?
CRAZYFACE: I left her behind.
ELLA: Why didn't you say anything?
CRAZYFACE: I forgot.
SHEBA: (*Hisses the question to Irvette*) What's worse than lions?
ELLA: She's the only one who can read.
CRAZYFACE: So?
ELLA: Signposts! She has to read the signposts for us. Or else how do we know one turn from another?
IRVETTE: Makes no odds where we go. He'll end up having us thrown out.
SHEBA: (*To herself*) Nothing's worse than lions.

IRVETTE: Bandits are.

SHEBA: Bandits?

IRVETTE: They hang you upside-down and rape you.

SHEBA: Isn't that difficult? I mean upside-down.

ELLA: *(To Crazyface)* Retrace our steps. Find Annie.

CRAZYFACE: Suppose I get eaten by a lion?

SHEBA: We'll say a prayer—

IRVETTE: —for the lion.

CRAZYFACE: *(Taking a ball of string out of his pocket)* Take hold of the end. *(Gives the end to Ella)* If I pull on it, I'm being eaten.

*HE GOES TO EXIT.*

IRVETTE: Before you go I have to ask.

CRAZYFACE: What?

IRVETTE: It's been niggling me. What are you doing *pulling* that fish around?

CRAZYFACE: *(With a grin)* Well, I can't *push* it, can I?

*CRAZYFACE EXITS.*

IRVETTE: The world's his straight man. *(Under her breath)* Little bastard.

SHEBA: *(A little dreamily)* I wouldn't mind seeing a bandit.

ELLA: Don't tempt Providence.

SHEBA: Don't see that Providence can do us any more harm than it already has.

ELLA: We're alive. That's something.

IRVETTE: He'll be the death of us.

ELLA: Now, now—

IRVETTE: We have to get rid of him.

ELLA: He's my son, Irvette.

SHEBA: He's dangerous.

IRVETTE: *(Sternly)* Ella. He sees angels.

SHEBA: Or he *thinks* he does.

IRVETTE: Why would angels appear to him?

ELLA: He's a little simple. Maybe they like simple virgins.

SHEBA: *I'm* a virgin.

IRVETTE: No, you're not.

SHEBA: Once doesn't count.

IRVETTE: Of course it counts.

SHEBA: Not if you close your eyes!

ELLA: Stop it.

IRVETTE: You're a used woman! Admit it!

SHEBA: Don't say that!

ELLA: Stop it, both of you! Stop it! Or *go to Hell!*

IRVETTE and SHEBA: (*Both shocked*) Oh.

ELLA: I'm . . . I'm sorry.

IRVETTE: No, it's understandable. We're not your flesh and blood after all. We're your *daughters-in-law*. Not even that, I suppose.

ELLA: Now don't . . . you'll upset us all.

IRVETTE: Well, it's true isn't it? Lenny married three women. We were all charmed by his fancy talk.

SHEBA: I hope he rots.

IRVETTE: Quite a pair of sons you've got. One was a trigamist, the other's soft in the head. What was their father anyhow?

ELLA: That's for me to know and you to wonder.

IRVETTE: The Devil himself probably.

ELLA: Close.

*IRVETTE LOOKS AT ELLA, PUZZLING AT THE REPLY. THE DAWN'S COMING MORE QUICKLY NOW. SHEBA GETS UP AND LOOKS AT THE UNFOLDING LANDSCAPE.*

SHEBA: It's going to be another scorcher.

*SUDDENLY THE STRING IS TUGGED.*

ELLA: Boy?

IRVETTE: What's wrong?

ELLA: Oh God in Heaven!

*SHE STARTS TO HAUL IN THE STRING. IT'S NOW JIG-GLING AROUND AS THOUGH A FIGHT'S GOING ON AT THE OTHER END. THERE ARE ROARS OFF-STAGE.*

SHEBA: (*Yelling to Crazyface*) Just tell them you're not Christian!

ELLA: Hey, lion! Leave my boy alone!

*SHE PULLS AND THE STRING COMES FREE. THE FISH CRAZYFACE WAS PULLING BEHIND HIM IS ON THE END, HALF-EATEN.*

ELLA: *(Peering at fish)* Boy?

*FROM THE OPPOSITE SIDE OF THE STAGE, CRAZYFACE APPEARS WITH ANNIE. ANNIE IS COVERED IN MUD.*

CRAZYFACE: What?
ELLA: *(Jumps)* Oh! *(Turns)* You're there.
CRAZYFACE: I'm here. *(Sees the fish)* Oh. Look at my fish.
ELLA: What are you doing there?
CRAZYFACE: I left him on the end of the string to guard it.
ANNIE: I was a long way behind.
CRAZYFACE: Poor fish.

*IRVETTE AND SHEBA LOOK AT EACH OTHER IN DESPAIR AS CRAZYFACE CRADLES THE FISH.*

ELLA: *(To Annie)* Where are your bags?
ANNIE: I fell in a quagmire.
CRAZYFACE: She did.
ANNIE: He pulled me out.
CRAZYFACE: I did.
SHEBA: My prayer book was in your bag.
ANNIE: You couldn't read it anyhow.
ELLA: That was careless, Annie.
ANNIE: *(Casually)* It's done. No use complaining. By the way, I climbed a tree. There's a town over the brow.
IRVETTE: Always another hill.
SHEBA: *(Quietly to Annie)* Careless bitch.
ELLA: *(Business-like)* All right, let's not linger.

*ELLA PICKS UP HER BAGS, AND IRVETTE AND SHEBA DO LIKEWISE.*

ELLA: Now, don't get left behind.

*EXIT ELLA FOLLOWED BY IRVETTE AND SHEBA.*

CRAZYFACE: (*Without accusation*) You lost the bags deliberately.
ANNIE: Only a bit deliberately. They were heavy. And who cares about a prayer book?
CRAZYFACE: Do you think only half a fish is still a fish?
ANNIE: Is half a mind still a mind?
CRAZYFACE: What's that got to do with it?

*ANNIE LAUGHS, AND EXITS. AS CRAZYFACE IS ABOUT TO FOLLOW, A GOLDEN LIGHT POURS THROUGH THE TREES AND AN ANGEL APPEARS. IT PROFFERS A PACK OF CARDS.*

ANGEL: Crazy?
CRAZYFACE: (*He's seen this vision many times*) No. I told you before, I'm not playing.
ANGEL: Just a short game.
CRAZYFACE: Mama says you don't exist.
ANGEL: (*Outraged*) That's heresy. I'm an angel.
CRAZYFACE: How do I know you're telling the truth?
ANGEL: Because angels never tell lies. Come on, just a short game.
CRAZYFACE: (*Tempted*) I shouldn't. They don't believe you're real, you know.

*HE APPROACHES THE ANGEL.*

ANGEL: You have to touch me? Is that it? I can see it in your eyes.
CRAZYFACE: (*As though mesmerized*) Yes, I want to touch you.

*SUDDENLY, HE GRABS THE ANGEL'S ARM.*

CRAZYFACE: Got you!
ANGEL: (*Pained*) All right, you made your point.
CRAZYFACE: (*Yelling*) Mama!
ANGEL: Let go!
CRAZYFACE: *Mama*, come quickly! I've got proof. Once and for all!
ANGEL: (*A hint of threat*) Now don't be stupid!
CRAZYFACE: Quickly!
ELLA: (*Off-stage*) Who's shouting?
ANGEL: No!
CRAZYFACE: This way!
ANGEL: Don't be childish!

ELLA: (*Off-stage*) Where are you?
CRAZYFACE: Over here!
ANGEL: (*Breaking away*) One of these days—

*THE ANGEL BACKS OFF AS ELLA'S VOICE GETS CLOSER.*

ELLA: (*Off-stage*) Are you all right?
CRAZYFACE: It's all right Mama. I'm coming.
ELLA: (*Off-stage*) What's going on?
CRAZYFACE: It wasn't anything. Just a trick of the light.
ANGEL: That's a dangerous game, Crazyface. Your brother played
    that game, treading on angels' tails, and he was twice the
    man you are. He lives on a slow wheel now, and sometimes
    he passes through fire and sometimes through ice. Two years
    of perpetual torment. It's curdled his brain.
CRAZYFACE: Is he mad?
ANGEL: Well, he's not very pleased.

*THE ANGEL DISAPPEARS.*

CRAZYFACE: (*Looks at half-eaten fish*) Poor fish.

# Scene Two

## The outskirts of the town of Loon

*THERE COMES THE WHISTLING SOUND OF A BODY,
FALLING THROUGH THE AIR, ENDING IN A THUD. A
SILENCE FOR TWO BEATS. THEN A GROUP OF TOWNS-
PEOPLE ERUPT ONTO THE STAGE, ALL TALKING AT
ONCE. THEY ARE CARRYING THE BODY, ALMOST DEAD,
OF WORMWOOD. HE IS BLOODY, AND HIS HOME-MADE
WINGS, WHICH HE IS STILL WEARING, ARE DAMAGED.*

*HE JUST JUMPED OFF THE CHURCH SPIRE IN AN ATTEMPT TO FLY. THREE TOWNSPEOPLE DO MOST OF THE TALKING ABOVE THE BABBLE OF THE OTHERS. THEY ARE CHEESBY, JINKS AND ZELLER.*

CHEESBY: Can't bury him in consecrated ground.

JINKS: Fell like a stone.

CHEESBY: It's obviously suicide.

ZELLER: He didn't jump.

CHEESBY: Still a suicide.

ZELLER: He was trying to fly. That's not suicide. It may be a little over-ambitious, but it's not suicide.

JINKS: Shouldn't somebody fetch a surgeon?

*ONE OF THE TOWNSPEOPLE PRESSES FORWARD.*

FIRST TOWNSPERSON: The surgeon's away.

CHEESBY: (*Looking at Wormwood*) Much good it'd do him anyway. This is a dead man. You jump off the church spire, you're a dead man.

JINKS: We could try cutting off his legs. That might save him.

CHEESBY: He'll bleed to death.

SECOND TOWNSPERSON: And his arms are shattered.

JINKS: Well . . . we could cut them off too.

ZELLER: Doesn't leave him with much does it? I mean, what if his nose itches?

THIRD TOWNSPERSON: Shouldn't we put him down?

JINKS: He's had enough of the ground I shouldn't wonder. Daft bugger.

ZELLER: Pity he can't go in the family grave.

CHEESBY: No suicides in the churchyard.

ZELLER: I can't see why.

CHEESBY: In case it encourages others to do the same.

JINKS: We'll have to dig a hole at the crossroads.

FIRST TOWNSPERSON: That's hard ground.

SECOND TOWNSPERSON: Too damn hard.

CHEESBY: We'll find a volunteer.

THIRD TOWNSPERSON: He's waking up.

ZELLER: (*Squatting on his haunches beside Wormwood*) So . . . you came back to see us then.

*WORMWOOD TRIES TO SPEAK. NOTHING.*

JINKS: Sh! Sh! Will you all shush?

*THE CROWD QUIETENS.*

ZELLER: He's trying to say something.
CHEESBY: He wants to confess.
ZELLER: *(To Cheesby)* Ssh!
CHEESBY: He's probably broken his tongue.
TOWNSPEOPLE: *(To Cheesby)* Ssh!

*CHEESBY LEAVES THE SIDE OF WORMWOOD, DIS-GRUNTLED.*

WORMWOOD: *(Speaking through pain and blood)* Well . . . that was quite a flight!

*TOWNSPEOPLE CHATTER AND LAUGH.*

JINKS: You didn't fly, you fell.
ZELLER: Don't move.
JINKS: You've broken every bone in your body.
WORMWOOD: I wondered. And the wings?
ZELLER: Forget the wings. You won't be flying again.
WORMWOOD: I almost made it, you know. All I needed was a stronger up-draft. Next time . . .

*THE CROWD CLOSES ROUND THE BODY OF WORM-WOOD, AND THE CHAT GOES ON, AS ELLA, CRAZYFACE, SHEBA, IRVETTE AND ANNIE ENTER.*

*ELLA APPROACHES CHEESBY, WHO IS LIGHTING HIS PIPE.*

ELLA: What town is this?
CHEESBY: Loon.

*THE CROWD LAUGHS.*

ELLA: What's this? A cockfight?

CHEESBY: It's the town idiot. He jumped from the church spire, thinking he could fly.
CRAZYFACE: (Looking up) Where is he?
CHEESBY: (Points) There.
CRAZYFACE: Oh, he came down again.
CHEESBY: He fell like a stone. Should be a law against it. Suppose he'd fallen on somebody?
IRVETTE: That's true.
CHEESBY: (Sees the women) Well, who have we here?
ELLA: My daughters-in-law.
CHEESBY: (Appreciatively) Welcome to Loon.

*AN ARGUMENT ERUPTS IN THE CROWD. IT OPENS OUT AGAIN.*

ZELLER: He's not a heretic!
JINKS: How do you know?
FIRST TOWNSPERSON: Yes, how do you know?
JINKS: I say we fetch the priest.
SECOND TOWNSPERSON: Have him excommunicated before he dies.
ZELLER: Why do you treat him like this? Huh? You can't *bear* the idea of somebody who does something different, can you?
CHEESBY: (To Irvette) Zeller used to be a scholar, but it addled his brain.
JINKS: (To Zeller, contemptuously) What do you know?

*THE CROWD STARTS TO EXIT.*

CHEESBY: (To Irvette, Sheba and Annie) Would you ladies be interested in a tour of the town?
IRVETTE: Oh *yes.*
SHEBA: How nice.
ANNIE: Why not?
CHEESBY: We can leave the birdman here; he won't be going anywhere. Except in a bucket.

*IRVETTE LAUGHS. SHE FINDS CHEESBY VERY ATTRACTIVE.*

CRAZYFACE: What do you mean, "in a bucket?"
CHEESBY: I mean he's jam, boy.

*IRVETTE LAUGHS AGAIN.*

CHEESBY: Follow me, ladies.
ANNIE: *(To Sheba) What* a creep.

*THE THREE WOMEN FOLLOW CHEESBY OFF. ZELLER IS
LEFT ON STAGE, STARING AT WORMWOOD. ELLA IS SIT-
TING ON HER BAG, EXHAUSTED. CRAZYFACE WATCHES
THE BODY TOO.*

CRAZYFACE: *(Approaching Wormwood)* It's a pity about the
wings.

*ZELLER LOOKS AT HIM SUSPICIOUSLY, AND LEAVES.*

CRAZYFACE: *(To Wormwood)* You broke your wings. Still, they
could be mended.
ELLA: Let him alone.
CRAZYFACE: A bit of rope. A dab of fish glue.
ELLA: Boy . . . I'm too tired to argue. Will you *come away?*
CRAZYFACE: It's all right, I'm not going to catch his disease.
WORMWOOD: What disease?
CRAZYFACE: The falling sickness.
WORMWOOD: *(Laughs weakly)* Who are you? Clown, are you?
CRAZYFACE: My name's Tyl. Tyl Eulenspiegel. But I'm called
Crazyface. Good wings.

*HE HAS TO TOUCH THE WINGS. HE BENDS TO DO SO,
GLANCING BEHIND HIM AT ELLA. SHE'S ASLEEP.*

WORMWOOD: I flew, you know. For a while. But the ground
wanted me more . . .
CRAZYFACE: . . . than the sky did.
WORMWOOD: Yes. Do you want the wings?
CRAZYFACE: Well . . .
WORMWOOD: You do, don't you. I can see it on your face. Take
them.

CRAZYFACE: For me?
WORMWOOD: You look like a man with Heaven in his hair. Take them.

*CRAZYFACE STANDS UP.*

CRAZYFACE: *(Suddenly nervous)* I don't want to fly. Look what it did to you.
WORMWOOD: Oh, it was worth it, believe me, for the things I felt. My heart nearly burst.
CRAZYFACE: *(Tempted back to his side)* What was it like? Tell me.
WORMWOOD: Like being an angel.
CRAZYFACE: *(Looks behind him as if to see if a vision has appeared)* Like an angel?

*WORMWOOD NODS.*

CRAZYFACE: *(Suddenly)* Give me the wings.
WORMWOOD: Take them quickly, and hide them.

*CRAZYFACE STARTS TO SLIDE THE WINGS OFF WORM-WOOD'S ARMS. FOR THE BIRDMAN IT'S A PAINFUL PRO-CESS. BUT HE BEARS IT.*

CRAZYFACE: *(Looking closely at the wings)* They're beautiful.
WORMWOOD: Whalebone, pigskin, feathers. Works of art, they are. Now hide them, quickly, or you're dead as I am.
CRAZYFACE: Why?
WORMWOOD: I saw, up there: the land turning over in its sleep. And underneath, like under a stone, such rot.
CRAZYFACE: You saw the world turn over, you mean like in a vision?
WORMWOOD: It's all vision . . . there's nothing real at all.
CRAZYFACE: I—have visions. *(He is suddenly elated to know somebody else with the problem. He starts to unburden himself, but Wormwood, unknown to Crazyface, has died)* Nobody believes me, that's the trouble. It just upsets everybody. Last Monday I saw an angel in the market, buying a crab. Well, not buying it—stealing it. And I said, "Hey you—" *(He gets closer to Wormwood, to tell the point of the story)*

"Hey you!" I said, "You can't . . . " (*He realizes Wormwood is dead*) . . . can't . . .

*HE STANDS UP. SILENCE. FOR ONCE IN HIS LIFE HE FEELS FOOLISH. AND ALONE.*

CRAZYFACE: Stupid old man. Don't want your wings. Broken anyhow.

*HE WALKS AWAY FROM THE WINGS, THEN TURNS BACK FOR THEM, TEARS BLINDING HIM.*

CRAZYFACE: Stupid.

*HE DRAGS THE WINGS AWAY, AND HIDES THEM, JUST AS THE CROWD RETURNS, LED BY THE PRIEST. THEY ARE SILENT NOW. THEIR EARLIER ENTHUSIASM IS REPLACED BY SOLEMNITY IN THE PRESENCE OF THEIR PRIEST. HE STANDS AT WORMWOOD'S FEET.*

PRIEST: So. (*Nods his head knowingly. The crowd hangs on his every word. Between the few words he says he makes a curious selection of noises with his mouth, sucking his teeth, clicking his tongue, sighing knowingly, etc.*)
PRIEST: Well.

*THE CROWD IS ENTRANCED.*

PRIEST: You see?

*THEY ALL NOD THEIR HEADS VERY SLOWLY.*

PRIEST: We'd better . . . er . . . er . . . well . . . er . . .
JINKS: (*Prompting*) Excommunicate him?
PRIEST: No.
ZELLER: Bury him?
PRIEST: Ah!
ZELLER: In the church-yard?
PRIEST: (*Hand makes a balancing gesture*) Well . . .
CHEESBY: At the crossroads?

PRIEST: Um . . .
CHEESBY: He's a suicide.
PRIEST: Quite.
ZELLER: A deep hole. In case of earthquake.
CRAZYFACE: Or in case the world turns over.

*THE ENTIRE CROWD TURNS AT CRAZYFACE.*

CHEESBY: Who—?
IRVETTE: I think we have a volunteer. Grave-digger. You look
   like a strong boy.
CHEESBY: What happened to his wings?

*SILENCE.*

CHEESBY: We should burn the wings. We don't want anyone to
   say Loon breeds heretics.

*AT THE WORD "HERETIC" THE PRIEST SUCKS HIS TEETH
LOUDLY.*

CHEESBY: Well, do we?

*THE CROWD ALL SUCK THEIR TEETH.*

SHEBA: Maybe lions took the wings.
CHEESBY: Lions with fingers?
JINKS: Well, who's in this burial party then?
ZELLER: I'll go with the boy.
CHEESBY: (*Contemptuously*) The earth's very hard, scholar. You'll
   have to work up some sweat.
ZELLER: Somebody help me with the body.

*A COUPLE OF VOLUNTEERS STEP OUT OF THE CROWD
TO HELP CRAZYFACE AND ZELLER PICK UP THE BODY
AND CARRY IT AWAY. ANNIE WAKES ELLA, AND SHE FOL-
LOWS. SHEBA TAKES THE BAGS. PRIEST, IRVETTE AND
CHEESBY REMAIN.*

PRIEST: Way of all flesh, hmmm?

*PRIEST EXITS.*

IRVETTE: The way of all flesh?
CHEESBY: *(Seductively)* Oh . . . I can think of half a dozen other ways for the flesh to go.

*IRVETTE LAUGHS. CHEESBY FEELS HER BREASTS. SHE SIGHS, THEN REMOVES HIS HANDS.*

IRVETTE: Would you like to give me some *real* pleasure?
CHEESBY: Oh please. Just say the word.
IRVETTE: Have the idiot hanged.
CHEESBY: Your brother?
IRVETTE: —in-law.
CHEESBY: Hanged?
IRVETTE: You know. By the neck.
CHEESBY: What reason can I give?
IRVETTE: He's an idiot.
CHEESBY: That's not a crime.
IRVETTE: He stole the wings. I'm sure of it.
CHEESBY: Ah. Now that's another thing entirely.
IRVETTE: It would please me. Very much.
CHEESBY: I want to please you. *(He touches her breasts.)* Your breasts are beautiful.
IRVETTE: Please don't. Not now.
CHEESBY: But—
IRVETTE: Later. You'll find I'm much more responsive after a public execution.

*EXIT IRVETTE, FOLLOWED BY CHEESBY.*

# Scene Three

## A crossroads

*TWILIGHT. A RAUCOUS CAWING FROM THE ROOKERIES IN THE TREES ALONG THE ROAD ACCOMPANY THE EARLY PART OF THE SCENE. AS DARKNESS FALLS, THE NOISE FADES, AND NIGHT-NOISES—OWLS, INSECTS, DISTANT DOGS—REPLACE IT.*

*ENTER ALVAREZ, CALLED THE SPANISH FLY. HE CARRIES A DAGGER AND A SMALL, LOCKED BOX. HE IS NOT USED TO TREASON AND ESPIONAGE. IN TRUTH, HE'S TERRIFIED. HE LOOKS FOR A PLACE TO HIDE, AND SECRETES HIMSELF.*

ALVAREZ: *(To himself)* The flamingoes grow . . . the flamingoes . . . grow restless . . .

*ENTER CRAZYFACE, HAVING BURIED WORMWOOD. HE CARRIES A MUD-CAKED SPADE; HE HAS MUD ON HIS FACE AND CLOTHES. HE'S TIRED. ALVAREZ STEPS OUT.*

ALVAREZ: The flamingoes grow restless in Venice this year.
CRAZYFACE: What?
ALVAREZ: The flamingoes grow— *(In his nervousness, he forgets)* Shit!
CRAZYFACE: *(Prompting)* —restless?
ALVAREZ: Yes! —restless in Venice this year.
CRAZYFACE: Nice for them. *(He turns to leave)*
ALVAREZ: Wait! I'm Alvarez. The Spanish Fly? You're Allegro, the French Letter? Yes?
CRAZYFACE: No.
ALVAREZ: Alvin, then. The Englishman?
CRAZYFACE: No.
ALVAREZ: Then you're Alfonso?

CRAZYFACE: No.

ALVAREZ: Then in God's name *who are you?*

CRAZYFACE: I'm Tyl Eulenspiegel, of the family Eulenspiegel. People call me—

ALVAREZ: *(Looks at spade)* Shit?

CRAZYFACE: No it's mud. *(Puts a muddy hand under Al's nose)* See?

ALVAREZ: Where am I?

CRAZYFACE: The crossroads.

ALVAREZ: Then they're late. *(He exits, throwing Crazyface a coin)*

CRAZYFACE: *(Picks up the coin)* Spanish.

*ALVAREZ EXITS, JUST AS ALVIN, THE ENGLISHMAN, RATHER EFFETE, ENTERS.*

ALVIN: I say, couldn't trouble you? Peasant chappie?

CRAZYFACE: What?

ALVIN: One's lost one's bearings.

CRAZYFACE: It must be the cold, sir.

ALVIN: Is this the crossroads?

CRAZYFACE: Yes.

ALVIN: Obliged mightily.

*EXIT ALVIN, THROWING A COIN.*

CRAZYFACE: *(Picks up the coin)* English.

*ENTER ALFONSO, THE ITALIAN.*

ALFONSO: Ah! *(He rushes across and embraces Crazyface like a long-lost brother)* Bellisimo!

CRAZYFACE: Italian.

ALFONSO: The flamingoes, yes?

CRAZYFACE: *(Shakes his head)* No.

ALFONSO: Ah! I make the boo-boo. With all this shit on you, I take you for a Spaniard.

CRAZYFACE: He went that way.

ALFONSO: Is good. Ciao!

*THE ITALIAN EXITS AS THE FRENCH LETTER, ALLEGRO, ENTERS.*

CRAZYFACE: What's that smell?
ALLEGRO: *(Proffering his wrist)* Night of Love.
CRAZYFACE: You're the Frenchman.
ALLEGRO: You guessed.
CRAZYFACE: You want the Spaniard?
ALLEGRO: I do.
CRAZYFACE: Follow your nose.
ALLEGRO: Merci.

*EXIT FRENCHMAN.*

CRAZYFACE: *(To audience)* Must be a party.

*SUDDENLY, OUT OF THE DARK THERE COMES A TERRI-BLE SHRIEK. CRAZYFACE FALLS TO HIS KNEES AND HIDES HIS HEAD, AS THE STAGE FILLS WITH MASKED ASSASSINS, ALL CARRYING KNIVES. UNDER THE COVER OF THEIR ENTRANCE THE SPANISH FLY ENTERS. THE ASSASSINS PART. HE IS LEFT CENTER-STAGE, COVERED IN WOUNDS. A KNIFE STICKS OUT FROM THE TOP OF HIS HEAD. BLOOD POURS DOWN HIS FACE LIKE YOLK FROM A CRACKED EGG.*

ALVAREZ: *(Falling slowly to his knees)* T-R-E-A-C-H-E-R-Y.
CRAZYFACE: *(Gets up and goes to him)* Oh God! Shall I fetch a priest?
ALVAREZ: *(On his knees)* No priest will give me the Rites. I am a traitor to Spain, and to God. In my hands is the glory of the world, locked up in a box. I was going to sell it to the highest bidder. Who'd forgive me that?
CRAZYFACE: What is it?
ALVAREZ: Heaven. And I've tasted it. The saints themselves envied me. Take it, please.
CRAZYFACE: Me?
ALVAREZ: I can't go to Hell carrying my crime. Oh . . . my head hurts.

*HE DIES KNEELING UP. CRAZYFACE TOUCHES HIM. HE KNEELS OVER. NERVOUSLY, CRAZYFACE CLAIMS THE BOX FROM HIS GRIP. THEN HE BACKS AWAY INTO THE SHADOWS.*

*AS HE DOES SO, ENTER THE ENGLISHMAN, THE ITALIAN AND THE FRENCHMAN, FROM DIFFERENT CORNERS. THEY CONVERGE ON THE SPANIARD'S BODY WITHOUT SEEING EACH OTHER. A STEP OR TWO AWAY FROM ALVAREZ THEY REALIZE THAT THEY HAVE COMPANY. THEY STOP. THEY SMILE. THEY SLOWLY PUT THEIR KNIVES BEHIND THEIR BACKS. THE FOLLOWING DIALOGUE STARTS CALMLY, AND GRADUALLY GAINS PACE AND VOLUME.*

ALL THREE: Well . . .
ALVIN: I didn't know you . . .
ALLEGRO: Quelle surprise!
ALFONSO: Ah life!

*THEY ALL "SEE" THE BODY AT THE SAME TIME. MOCK SURPRISE: INNOCENT LOOKS.*

ALL THREE: Oh!
ALVIN: Isn't that the Spaniard?
ALFONSO: What Spaniard?
ALVIN: Perhaps not.
ALLEGRO: Could be.
ALFONSO: You know a Spaniard too?
ALLEGRO: Casual acquaintance.
ALVIN: And you?
ALFONSO: Yes.
ALVIN: Seems we've all been . . .
ALLEGRO: I thought it was a private arrangement.
ALFONSO: With me.
ALVIN: Damn cheat!
ALLEGRO: Well, who has the secret?
ALVIN: What secret?
ALFONSO: Oh, stop playing the silly buggers, we all know why we're here.
ALVIN: Yes.
ALLEGRO: Oui.
ALFONSO: So which of you has it? It belongs to me—to Italy. That was the arrangement. *(To Alvin)* You?
ALVIN: No. One of you fellows has it.

ALLEGRO: Always the dissembling English, the lying Italians. It's one of you. Not me.

ALVIN: It belongs to England.

ALLEGRO: England never loved Spain.

ALVIN: And France does?

ALFONSO: Neither of you could use the damn thing anyway. We're the experts.

ALVIN: Ha! Pasta and bread! Pasta and bread!

ALFONSO: Peas and cabbage!

ALLEGRO: The French must have it.

ALVIN: And smother it in sauce!

ALLEGRO: (*A warning*) There'll be reprisals.

ALVIN: It would be my pleasure. (*He slaps the Frenchman with his glove*)

ALLEGRO: Ha! (*He slaps the Englishman back*)

ALFONSO: We'll withdraw ambassadors. (*The Italian is trying to remove his gloves, but they're too tight.*)

ALVIN: I promise a systematic burning of this territory.

ALFONSO: We'll reduce every windmill to rubble until we find out where you've hidden it. Whichever of you did it (*He's succeeded with the glove. He belatedly slaps them both, and spits.*)

ALLEGRO: Rubble? I promise *dust*. Dust and ash.

ALVIN: (*Shouting at the body now*) Cheating wop!

ALFONSO: Poncing peasant!

ALLEGRO: Witless imbecile!

*THEY ALL KICK THE BODY IN THEIR FRUSTRATION AND FURY, SHOUTING INSULTS AT IT.*

ALVIN: Enough!

*THEY STOP, ALL BREATHING VERY HEAVILY. THEY ARE EMBARRASSED BY THEIR DISPLAYS. THE DIALOGUE, HAVING REACHED A CLIMAX OF SHOUTING AND KICKING, CALMS DOWN.*

ALLEGRO: Well . . .

ALFONSO: Well . . .

ALVIN: Well . . .

*A BEAT.*

ALLEGRO: Ha!

*A BEAT.*

ALFONSO: Lovely evening.
ALLEGRO: Such stars.

*A BEAT.*

ALVIN: Well, I must be running along. *(Shakes hands)*
ALLEGRO: It's been a pleasure. *(Kisses on both cheeks)* Truly.
ALFONSO: My love to your wives. *(Embraces all round)*

*THEY STEP AWAY FROM THE BODY. A BEAT. THEN, A DIF-
FERENT TONE: FATALISTIC AND GRIM. THREE MEN
CASUALLY PREORDAINING THE DEATHS OF THOUSANDS.*

ALVIN: This is it now, of course.
ALLEGRO: Of course. The Deluge.
ALFONSO: The Apocalypse.

*THEY BOW TO EACH OTHER, AND EXIT. CRAZYFACE
EMERGES FROM HIS HIDING PLACE, SHAKING WITH
FRIGHT. AS HE GETS UP, A CROWD OF ASSASSINS ENTER,
AND CROSS THE STAGE. WHEN THEY'VE GONE, SO, MAGI-
CALLY, HAS THE DEAD SPANISH FLY. CRAZYFACE STANDS UP.*

*ENTER ANNIE, RUNNING.*

ANNIE: There you are!
CRAZYFACE: No more. No more.
ANNIE: Run! Quickly!
CRAZYFACE: Lions?
ANNIE: Sisters!
CRAZYFACE: Irvette?
ANNIE: She told the priest you succored the birdman. Said you're
    a heretic. They want you taken for trial. They could hang
    you! You've got to go! *Now!*

CRAZYFACE: Where?

ANNIE: Anywhere. We'll go see the Aurora Borealis. Or China.

CRAZYFACE: We?

ANNIE: Yes, I'm coming too.

CRAZYFACE: No.

ANNIE: I've helped you, the least you can do is marry me.

CRAZYFACE: You're Lenny's wife.

ANNIE: He never married me. *(She sees the box he's nursing)* What's this?

CRAZYFACE: It's the glory of the world, locked up in a box.

ANNIE: Oh, leave the angel-talk for your mother. Where did you get it?

CRAZYFACE: There was an Englishman, a Frenchman and an Italian—

ANNIE: Is this a joke?

CRAZYFACE: No!

*OFF-STAGE, VOICES: SHEBA, IRVETTE, CHEESBY AND PRIEST.*

CHEESBY: *Boy!*

SHEBA: *Tyl! Tyl!*

CHEESBY: *(As if calling a dog)* Here boy . . . here boy . . .

IRVETTE: Crazyface! It's only us! There's nothing to be afraid of.

ANNIE: Hide!

*HE CRAWLS UNDER HER SKIRT.*

ANNIE: Not there!

*TOO LATE. HE'S DISAPPEARED UP HER DRESS. AND NOW THE PURSUERS ENTER.*

IRVETTE: Oh. Annie . . .

SHEBA: What are you doing out here?

ANNIE: . . . er . . . star-gazing.

IRVETTE: Bit cloudy for that, isn't it?

PRIEST: The boy. Where's the boy?

ANNIE: What boy?

CHEESBY: We're looking for your brother-in-law. Tyl.

IRVETTE: He's wanted for questioning.

*THEY'VE CLOSED ON ANNIE. SHE'S IN DANGER OF BEING DISCOVERED. ENTER ELLA.*

ELLA: Well, you won't find him here.
IRVETTE: *(Trying to keep up her confidence, she smiles a fake smile)* Oh Mama. Have you seen Crazyface?
ELLA: No.
CHEESBY: He was digging graves.
ELLA: Then he probably buried himself.

*THE PRIEST LAUGHS.*

ELLA: *(Humorlessly)* Like that one, do you? I've got a million.
IRVETTE: Don't protect him, Mama, he's not worth it. You know that.
ELLA: Me, protect that wretched little scumbag? He's not worth the flesh he's written on. He was a complete accident, you know. My husband was always premature. Died before his time, too. No, you find him. Hang him, burn him, break him on a wheel. He's been a complete and utter disappointment.
CHEESBY: Well, let's keep his crimes in proportion.
PRIEST: If you happen to see him . . .
ELLA: Into your loving arms he goes. On my soul.
CHEESBY: Good woman.
IRVETTE: *(Suspicious, but mystified)* Well, Mama—
ELLA: *(Face to face)* Well, Irvette?
ANNIE: Good hunting.

*THE PRIEST LAUGHS AGAIN. THE PURSUERS EXIT.*

ELLA: *(Quietly)* Burn in hell.

*CRAZYFACE EMERGES FROM UNDER THE SKIRT. HE HAS BEEN HOLDING HIS BREATH. HE LETS IT ALL OUT, AND TAKES A GULP OF FRESH AIR.*

ELLA: As for you—
CRAZYFACE: Me?
ELLA: Go on, Tyl. I'm too tired for any of your nonsense.

CRAZYFACE: But I don't want to go. You see there was this box, and an Englishman and—

*ANNIE SHAKES HER HEAD AT HIM. HE STOPS.*

ELLA: You'll survive. You're strong, you're stupid: what more do you want?

ANNIE: I've never heard you talk like this.

ELLA: I'm going to die in this town. I want to die here. I want a window, and a chair, and I want to slip away, quietly watching the world go by.

CRAZYFACE: Mama . . .

*HE'S AT HER FEET. SHE TRIES TO IGNORES HIM.*

CRAZYFACE: . . . I love you.

ELLA: Come back and tell me that when you're grown. Puppies lick anybody's hand.

*HE GETS UP, AND GOES TO KISS HER. SHE TURNS HER HEAD AWAY. HIS FACE FULL OF SORROW, HE EXITS.*

ANNIE: That was cruel.

ELLA: He's going to face beasts. Should I have sent him away with his head full of milk?

ANNIE: What beasts?

ELLA: The world, woman. Believe me, I know. I've been in its throat for years.

*EXIT ELLA. ANNIE IS LEFT TO CHOOSE BETWEEN FOL-LOWING ELLA OR CRAZYFACE.*

ANNIE: *(She throws up an imaginary coin. Watches it land. Studies it)* The beasts it is.

*SHE FOLLOWS CRAZYFACE.*

# <u>Scene Four</u>

## The Palace Gardens

*THE LIGHTS COME UP ON TWO FIGURES. ONE, A PUL-CINELLA (WHO WILL JOIN THE COOKS VERY SOON), HOLDS UP A CLOTH THAT READS "SPAIN." THE OTHER IS A SPANISH DANCING WOMAN. TO A LOUD, RESPLEN-DENT BURST OF MUSIC, SHE DANCES, STAMPING HER FEET AND CLICKING CASTANETS. THE MUSIC IS OVER-TAKEN, AS IT ENDS, BY A BURST OF THUNDER, FOL-LOWED BY THE NOISE OF TORRENTIAL RAIN. ENTER THE KING OF SPAIN. HIS ATTENDANT, A MAN WHOSE FACE IS MADE UP SO HE LOOKS LIKE A DOLL, HOLDS AN UMBRELLA OVER THE KING'S HEAD. WALKING BEHIND HIM IS MENGO, A PRIEST. HE WALKS IN THE RAIN WITH-OUT AN UMBRELLA, BUT HAS TO REPEATEDLY TAKE OFF HIS GLASSES AND WIPE THEM WITH A BRILLIANT RED SILK AND LACE HANDKERCHIEF.*

*THE THUNDER ROLLS AND THE RAIN FALLS THROUGH-OUT THE SCENE.*

KING: Must we come outside, Mengo?

MENGO: Majesty: it's not wise to raise the dead indoors.

KING: Why not?

MENGO: They may vent their fury on the furniture.

KING: Can't we at least wait until the downpour's over?

MENGO: The time is all-important. Phases of the moon, move-ments in the stars.

KING: Well, next time I want a spirit that's willing to be raised in the comfort of our own home.

*MENGO LOOKS AT THE KING, CONFUSED.*

MENGO: Next time?
KING: That's a joke, Mengo.
MENGO: Ah. *(He smiles. The attendant has hysterics)*
KING: Shut up.

*ATTENDANT'S LAUGHTER IS CUT DEAD.*

KING: Now where's your witch?
MENGO: I'll fetch her.
KING: And none of your cruelty, Mengo. If she calls the traitor from Purgatory I want you to be gentle with him.
MENGO: Majesty.

*HE WALKS BACKSTAGE TO FIND THE WITCH. WHILE HE IS DOING SO A GROUP OF COOKS ENTER. THEY ARE ALL IDENTICAL PULCINELLAS. THEY EACH CARRY A POT OF FOOD, COVERED WITH A CLOTH. THEY ARE GROTESQUELY OBSEQUIOUS.*

FIRST PULCINELLA: Sire!
KING: Oh, you again.
FIRST PULCINELLA: I have it, I think.
KING: So you keep insisting.
FIRST PULCINELLA: Will you taste it?
KING: Yes.

*FIRST PULCINELLA UNCOVERS THE POT. KING TAKES OFF ONE OF HIS GLOVES, DIPS HIS LONG FINGER INTO THE POT AND LICKS IT.*

KING: Foul! Next!

*SECOND PULCINELLA DOES THE SAME.*

KING: Tastes like dog-shit! Next!

*THIRD PULCINELLA REPEATS THE RITUAL.*

KING: Practically treasonable! Damn you, call yourselves cooks? Too much inbreeding in your family. Mushes the brain. Out of my sight.

*THEY START TO DEPART.*

KING: But don't give up, my sweet gentlemen. You're getting closer. At least I haven't vomited this time!

*THEY HURRY AWAY.*

KING: Funny lot.

*MENGO BRINGS THE WITCH FORWARD. SHE'S NOT THE STANDARD IDEA OF A WITCH AT ALL. SHE'S YOUNG, PERHAPS BEAUTIFUL.*

KING: Can she do it Mengo? Can you do it, witch? Raise the dead?
WITCH: I'll try.
KING: His name's Alvarez. He's a traitor to Spain, and I want to have words with him. If he doesn't come, you go back to the wheel. If he comes, if he speaks, we'll grant you an amnesty.
WITCH: Sweet lord. *(She kisses his hand)*
KING: Get about your preparations.

*THE WITCH LAYS A SKULL ON THE GROUND, AND DRAWS A CIRCLE, FOUR FEET ACROSS, USING THE SKULL AS THE CENTER. SHE SINGS AS SHE DOES IT. SHE SPRINKLES DEAD FLOWERS IN THE MIDDLE.*

KING: What's that? Turk's tongue? The foreskin of a crab? What is it?
WITCH: Herbs, Majesty.
KING: No Turk's tongue? *(To Mengo)* You sure she's a witch?
MENGO: Oh certainly, Majesty.

*She stands in the middle of the circle and raises her hands.*

WITCH: In the name of judgment, by the third eye of the bornless one, I summon you, Don Fernando de Alvarez, for interrogation before your masters.

*SILENCE.*

KING: Nothing . . .

*THE LIGHTS DARKEN.*

KING: I knew it. Nothing . . .
MENGO: Wait . . .

*SOMETHING APPROACHES THE CIRCLE AND STEPS IN. THE FIGURE OF ALVAREZ. HIS FACE IS ALMOST A DEATH'S HEAD, EXCEPT FOR THE MOUSTACHE.*

WITCH: Is this the man?
KING: *(To Mengo)* Is it?
MENGO: *(Very pleased)* Yes it is.
WITCH: Then speak to him. He won't stay long.

*THE KING IS PLAINLY TERRIFIED.*

MENGO: Majesty. You requested it.
KING: I did? I did. *(He approaches the circle)*
MENGO: Not too near.
KING: *(to Alvarez)* You were murdered, were you not, in the act of betraying Spain?
ALVAREZ: I was.
KING: You've squandered the birth-right of the Spanish nation. *(He spits on Alvarez, stepping closer to him)* You realize that?
ALVAREZ: Spit again, it cools me.
KING: Where's the secret now? Who has it?
MENGO: Is it with the English?
ALVAREZ: No.
MENGO: The French then?
ALVAREZ: No.
MENGO: Redeem yourself with a confession.
ALVAREZ: None of them have it.
KING: *(Jubilant)* You went to your grave with it? Is that it? Is it safe in the earth somewhere?
ALVAREZ: No. I gave it away.

*THE KING STEPS IN, FURIOUS, AND GETS HOLD OF ALVAREZ.*

KING: You did *what?*

ALVAREZ: To a fool called Tyl Eulenspiegel. A mooncalf. It meant nothing to him, Majesty.

KING: *You gave it away?* The salvation of Spain? The solution to our balance of payments, God's gift to your homeland? *Why?*

ALVAREZ: So I wouldn't go to Hell with it.

KING: Hell? Aren't you in Hell anyway?

*SUDDENLY, ALVAREZ REVERSES THE SITUATION AND GRABS HOLD OF THE KING.*

ALVAREZ: Yes I am. And you wouldn't like it.

KING: I have no intention of going there.

ALVAREZ: *(Rabidly)* It burns and burns!

KING: Oh Jesus Christ Almighty! Let go of me!

*MENGO PULLS THE KING OUT OF ALVAREZ'S GRASP.*

KING: Traitor! You'll cook forever.

ALVAREZ: Oh, speaking of cooking—

*HE POINTS. THE THREE PULCINELLAS HAVE APPEARED AGAIN.*

ALVAREZ: Bon appetit!

*STILL SHAKEN, THE KING TURNS HIS BACK ON THE SPIRIT AND CROSSES TO THE PULCINELLAS. WHILE THE NEXT SHORT DIALOGUE IS GOING ON HE IS TASTING THE THREE NEW CONCOCTIONS THEY'VE BROUGHT HIM, GETTING INCREASINGLY ANGRY.*

ALVAREZ: *(To Mengo)* May I go now? I've got pangs waiting to be suffered.

MENGO: Yes. *(Points to the witch)* And take her with you. You can burn together.

ALVAREZ: My thanks, sir.

WITCH: No! You promised! No!

*ALVAREZ PUTS HIS ARMS AROUND THE WITCH, AND DRAGS HER AWAY, SCREAMING. AS HE DOES SO, THE KING EXPLODES—*

KING: No! No! No! All filth! Take it all away!

*EXIT THE THREE PULCINELLAS, COWERING.*

KING: My bladder's fit to burst.

*HE WALKS AWAY FROM MENGO AND HIS ATTENDANT.*

KING: *(To attendant)* Follow.

*HE RETIRES TO A DISTANCE, WITH THE ATTENDANT BESIDE HIM, AND STARTS TO PISS, ON THE MAN'S LEG.*

KING: *(To Mengo)* You must find this Tyl Eulenspiegel.
MENGO: The name definitely rings a bell.
ATTENDANT: . . . sir?
KING: He must be found and silenced. It must be as though he never existed. And the secret must be returned to Spain. Then we may yet have Europe our oyster.
ATTENDANT: Excuse me, Majesty, you're wetting my foot!
MENGO: I have a fool on the wheel at the moment . . . *(An idea strikes him)*
KING: What are you thinking?

*THE KING'S FINISHED PISSING. HE WALKS BACK TO MENGO, LEAVING THE ATTENDANT SHAKING HIS SOAKED LEG.*

MENGO: That a clown knows the best working of other clowns.
KING: And the one you have in prison: Will he do the job?
MENGO: Well, he's insane. I've personally documented his descent into madness. So I think he'll do the job beautifully. You see, sire, his name is also Eulenspiegel.
KING: You mean . . . a brother?

*THE KING SMIRKS, BARELY ABLE TO CONTROL HIS EXCITEMENT. MENGO NODS.*

*THE KING WAVES AWAY THE UMBRELLA; HE'S SUDDENLY LOST HIS MELANCHOLIA.*

KING: I like the rain! *(To the attendant)* Get out from under there! Taste the rain! God is pissing on us today, because He fears we'll have Heaven again! It's a sign, Mengo, it's a sign! Horse!

*THE ATTENDANT RUNS FORWARD. THE KING JUMPS ON HIS BACK.*

KING: To the Palace!

*EXIT KING AND ATTENDANT. MENGO SMILES TO HIMSELF.*

*LIGHTS FADE.*

# Scene Five

## A wasteland

*ENTER ALVIN, ALFONSO AND ALLEGRO, FROM DIFFERENT DIRECTIONS. BEHIND THEM, A TOWN BURNS. DISTANT SCREAMS. THE SOUND OF HORSES' HOOVES. ALFONSO CRADLES A LACE-SHAWLED BABY IN HIS ARMS, WHICH HE MAKES LOVING FACES AT. THE ENGLISHMAN HAS A PIECE OF BREAD. THE FRENCHMAN A GLASS OF WINE.*

ALVIN: Well . . .

ALFONSO: Well . . .

ALLEGRO: Well . . .

ALVIN: Not much luck, eh?

ALFONSO: I wouldn't say that.

ALVIN: I've had a sniff or two.

ALLEGRO: . . . but nothing definite.

ALVIN: Not exactly.

ALFONSO: It's a matter of time. We're systematically crossing the country from South to North.

ALLEGRO: We're going East to West.

ALVIN: I'm just picking and choosing, really.

ALLEGRO: What's your modus operandi?

ALFONSO: Indiscriminate slaughter.

ALVIN: Women and children?

ALFONSO: Where appropriate. Which is almost everywhere. And you?

ALVIN: We're playing it by ear. Some places, we're razing to the ground. Others, just killing the first-born.

ALLEGRO: (Deadpan) How very original.

ALFONSO: And you?

ALLEGRO: We've been killing the livestock, burning the crops. We're going to starve them into telling us where the damned thing is.

ALVIN: Still, one gets tired.

ALFONSO: Yes.

ALLEGRO: Certainement.

ALVIN: And there just aren't the funds for a thorough-going suppression. It's so bitty; so unaesthetic.

ALFONSO: My men get closer to mutiny every few days. The only way I can placate them is to let them have a nunnery.

ALLEGRO: A nunnery?

ALFONSO: That keeps them quiet for a while.

ALVIN: Good chap.

ALLEGRO: Might try that.

ALFONSO: If you can find a nunnery left intact.

ALVIN: I have to ask . . . (He gestures towards the baby) Snatched from the conflagration?

ALFONSO: In a way.

ALLEGRO: Ah! Compassion.

ALFONSO: I couldn't help myself. I miss my bambinos.

ALVIN: Patter of tiny, etc. Mind if I . . .  (*He peers into the bundle*)
It's a tortoise!

ALLEGRO: Pardon?

ALVIN: Tort-oise.

ALLEGRO: Ah oui. (*Registers this*) A tortoise?

ALFONSO: I miss my bambinos.

ALVIN: (*To Allegro*) Italians. Always the first to break.

ALLEGRO: Ah, oui.

ALVIN: (*Practically mouthing it*) Never sign a treaty with them.

ALLEGRO: Tortoise.

ALVIN: Well . . . needs must. See you again, monsieur.

ALLEGRO: Oui.

ALVIN: Signor.

ALFONSO: (*Re: tortoise*) You like him, yes?

ALVIN: He's a delight. No. Truly. (*Shakes his head at the Frenchman*)
The end of the world's going to be like this.

ALLEGRO: Air full of smuts . . .

ALVIN: I'm going to dream that tortoise.

ALLEGRO: . . . distant horses . . .

ALVIN: We'll all be mad before this thing's over. And what for?

ALLEGRO and ALFONSO: Ssh!

ALVIN: Pandemonium. (*Formally*) Sirs.

*EXIT ALVIN.*

ALLEGRO: Bon soir.

*EXIT ALLEGRO.*

ALFONSO: (*To the tortoise*) Say "Dada."

*SUDDEN BLACKOUT.*

# Scene Six

## Another wasteland

*THE TOWN STILL BURNS, BUT MORE DIMLY. THE FULL MOON IS AMBER IN THE SKY. ALL ELSE, DARKNESS.*

*WE CAN SEE, HOWEVER, A FIGURE IN THE GLOOM. A LIGHT, VERY DIM, BEGINS TO ILLUMINATE HIM.*

*HE IS A CLOWN, THE FIRST CLEARLY RECOGNIZABLE CLOWN WE HAVE SEEN SO FAR. HE HAS ALL THE CLASSIC ATTRIBUTES. THE BALD PATE WITH TWO ERUPTIONS OF CARROT-COLORED HAIR. THE WHITE AND RED AND BLACK MAKEUP, A SLASH FOR A MOUTH, A BLOB NOSE, ETERNALLY SURPRISED EYEBROWS. HIS CLOTHES ARE VASTLY TOO BIG, HIS HANDS ARE ENTIRELY COVERED BY THE SLEEVES OF HIS JACKET. HE STARES OUT AT US, UNMOVING, MONOLITHIC, PITIFUL. THERE IS NOTHING FAINTLY FUNNY ABOUT HIM: HE'S DEFEATED AND RIDICULOUS. FROM SOMEWHERE, WHALE-SONG.*

*ENTER CRAZYFACE, RUNNING. HE HAS A RUDIMENTARY CLOWN-FACE HIMSELF: PALE SKIN, RED MOUTH. HE COLLIDES WITH THE OLD CLOWN.*

CRAZYFACE: *(Falls to his knees)* Ah! Don't kill me! I beg you, don't kill me!

*HE LOOKS UP.*

CRAZYFACE: Who are you?

*SILENCE.*

CRAZYFACE: Are you with the French, or the English or the Italians? (*He climbs his way up the Clown*) Speak to me, damn you. Are you a Spaniard? *Jesus, are you a Spaniard?*

*THE CLOWN SPITS OUT A NEAT COLUMN OF WATER.*

CRAZYFACE: You're a fountain, is that it? You want to pass for a piece of architecture? That's a good idea. Anything to keep out of their way, eh? Horsemen everywhere.

*THE THUNDER OF HOOVES.*

CRAZYFACE: Ah!

*THEY PASS.*

CRAZYFACE: My heart won't stand it, you know. It wants to stop beating, and my eyes don't want to see anymore. Too many horrors. Little babes smashed against walls.

*SILENCE.*

CRAZYFACE: I'm frightened, aren't you? I'm shitting my pants. (*Angry*) Say something, you stupid old—

*A LONG MOMENT.*

CRAZYFACE: Do . . . I . . . know you from somewhere?

*THE CLOWN MOVES AWAY.*

CRAZYFACE: I do . . . I know you . . .

*THE CLOWN EXITS. CRAZYFACE IS ABOUT TO FOLLOW WHEN ANNIE ENTERS, CHASED BY TWO SOLDIERS. WHO KNOWS WHAT SIDE THEY'RE ON?*

ANNIE: Help me!
CRAZYFACE: Annie!

*THEY CATCH HER, AND THROW HER TO THE GROUND,*

*INTENDING TO RAPE HER. SHE SCREAMS AND FIGHTS. THEY LAUGH AS THEY PIN HER DOWN.*

FIRST SOLDIER: Much easier if you don't struggle.
SECOND SOLDIER: You might even enjoy yourself.
ANNIE: God in heaven, help me!
CRAZYFACE: Stop!
FIRST SOLDIER: What's your problem?
CRAZYFACE: Leave her alone!
SECOND SOLDIER: Take your turn! Behind me, buster.
CRAZYFACE: I don't mind if I do. It's very difficult getting a woman these days.
FIRST SOLDIER: We don't do so badly.
CRAZYFACE: Ah. But you haven't got leprosy.
SECOND SOLDIER: Leprosy?
CRAZYFACE: Oh, don't worry, it's only mild . . .

*THE FIRST SOLDIER HAS FORGOTTEN ANNIE.*

CRAZYFACE: . . . no, it's the syphilis that seems to be doing most of the damage.
FIRST SOLDIER: Is it contagious?
CRAZYFACE: Only if the crabs jump. I wouldn't get too close.
SECOND SOLDIER: You can have the woman.
CRAZYFACE: Want to see the sores?
FIRST SOLDIER: Just . . . keep your distance.
SECOND SOLDIER: You heard him!
CRAZYFACE: No, I'm deaf. Must be the rabies.
SECOND SOLDIER: Oh Christ.
CRAZYFACE: Oh, now don't go and leave the lady.
FIRST SOLDIER: *(Mouthing for the deaf man)* She's all yours.
CRAZYFACE: Really? How generous.

*THE SOLDIERS EXIT, KEEPING THEIR EYES ON CRAZY-FACE EVERY STEP OF THE WAY.*

ANNIE: Oh God . . .
CRAZYFACE: Did they hurt you?
ANNIE: No. I was damn fool to follow you. Serves me right. You look sick. Have you really got syphilis?

CRAZYFACE: It's flour. I've been entertaining soldiers. Clowning. Juggling. *(He juggles)*
ANNIE: People pay for that?
CRAZYFACE: Well, no. But they pay me to go away.

*ANNIE LAUGHS.*

CRAZYFACE: *(Capitalizes on the remark)* Go on, they say, have a penny. Now go play in a battle.
ANNIE: Some career.
CRAZYFACE: What about you?
ANNIE: I've got by.
CRAZYFACE: Whoring?
ANNIE: No!! *(Pause)* Yes.
CRAZYFACE: It's less work than juggling balls.
ANNIE: Amounts to the same thing.

*THEY BOTH LAUGH.*

ANNIE: Still carrying your box around?
CRAZYFACE: I'm taking it to Rome. To the Pope. He'll know what to do with it.
ANNIE: You think the Pope'll look twice at the likes of you?
CRAZYFACE: Did you really follow me?
ANNIE: On and off.
CRAZYFACE: I'm not going to marry you, you know.
ANNIE: Don't need marrying. Never want to touch a man again.
CRAZYFACE: Not even Lenny?
ANNIE: Lenny's dead.
CRAZYFACE: You used to like him kissing you, didn't you?
ANNIE: Yes, and you liked to watch. I used to see you sometimes, peering through the window. I used to wonder if you had a thought in your head. Lenny used to say you were an imbecile.
CRAZYFACE: Well, he was wrong!
ANNIE: I didn't mean . . .
CRAZYFACE: I'm not an imbecile.
ANNIE: I know.
CRAZYFACE: Lenny wouldn't have pretended he was a leper. He'd have watched them do it to you.
ANNIE: Probably.

CRAZYFACE: Me, I . . .
ANNIE: What?

*HE KISSES HER SUDDENLY. AND PASSIONATELY.*

ANNIE: *(Impressed)* Where'd you learn to kiss like that?
CRAZYFACE: Sucking eggs. I can do what Lenny did. I just didn't
    care to.
ANNIE: Oh no, there's a lot of things Lenny did you never even
    dreamed of. Trust me.
CRAZYFACE: Like what?
ANNIE: Terrible things. And God help me, I thought he was
    beautiful. Even with blood on his hands. See, Sheba and
    Irvette were just sweet-talked by him. I knew what he really
    was, and I still liked him.
CRAZYFACE: The Angel says he's on a great wheel now. In
    Heaven.
ANNIE: I doubt that. Not the part about the wheel. The bit about
    Heaven.

*A NOISE.*

ANNIE: What was that?
CRAZYFACE: I farted.
ANNIE: Something else. There's somebody watching us.

*FOUR FIGURES EMERGE FROM THE SHADOWS. THEY ARE A
BIZARRE SIGHT: THEY ALL WEAR LONG, SHABBY COATS,
AND TROUSERS WHICH ARE VASTLY TOO BIG FOR THEM.
THEY ARE ALL WOMEN, BUT THEIR SEX IS DISGUISED
ENTIRELY BY THEIR CLOTHES. THEIR FACES ARE COVERED
WITH CRUDE LEATHER MASKS, ADORNED WITH SCRAPES
OF FUR, HUMAN HAIR AND FEATHERS. THEY CARRY STICKS.*

ANNIE: Bandits.

*THE GROUP SURROUNDS THEM. NONE OF THEM SPEAK.*

ANNIE: *(Loudly)* Well! What a coincidence.
CRAZYFACE: Eh?

ANNIE: We were just saying—weren't we—how dull things were
    getting. 'Bout time we had a flood, or a lynching, or a visit
    from some friendly bandits.

*THE RUSE FAILS. THEY RAISE THEIR STICKS TO BEAT*
*THEM.*

CRAZYFACE: Is it worth begging?
ANNIE: It's *always* worth begging.

*THEY FALL TO THEIR KNEES, AND SPEAK SIMULTANEOUSLY.*

CRAZYFACE: Don't kill me, see, because she's a lunatic and she's
    possessed of the Devil and I'm really the only one who has
    any control of her, you know when she's roused she's just
    impossible without me, she'll tear your eyes out . . .
ANNIE: Don't hurt me 'cause he's a brute if anyone hurts me. Savage
    as a beast; you know, like a dog really. If anyone so much as lays
    a finger on me he goes berserk, just tears people's arms off . . .

*THEIR APPEALS FALTER. THEY FALL SILENT. THE LEADER*
*OF THE BANDITS, MARY TOLLER, POINTS TO CRAZY-*
*FACE, AND THE OTHERS FALL ON HIM, TRYING TO PART*
*HIM FROM HIS BOX.*

CRAZYFACE: Leave it alone! Leave it alone!

*THE BOX IS TAKEN TO MARY, AND CRAZYFACE IS*
*DRAGGED AWAY.*

ANNIE: Don't kill him!

*EXIT BANDITS, DRAGGING A SCREAMING CRAZYFACE.*

ANNIE: *(Standing up)* You bastard. You scumbag. Proud of your-
    self, are you? Makes you feel like a big brave man, does it,
    hurting a half-wit like him? You haven't even got the courage
    to show your face.

*SHE RIPS THE MASK OFF, REVEALING MARY.*

ANNIE: Oh.

*OFF-STAGE A SCREAM.*

ANNIE: What are they doing to him? Are they women too.?
MARY: Yes.
ANNIE: He's not worth killing.
MARY: He's a man.
ANNIE: He's a fool.
MARY: What's this?
ANNIE: Oh, his little treasure.
MARY: (*Feeling over the surface of the box as a safe-cracker might a safe, looking for its weakness*) I've seen boxes like this before, but only in more sophisticated hands.

*THE BOX GRINDS OPEN. SHE FEELS INSIDE.*

MARY: Ah! (*Takes out small seeds*) This is his treasure? (*She crushes one and smells her hand. A revelation.*) Ha! Does he know what he's carrying?

*ANNIE SHAKES HER HEAD.*

MARY: It's best he doesn't.
ANNIE: What is it?

*MARY EXTENDS HER HAND. ANNIE SNIFFS IT. IT MEANS NOTHING TO HER.*

MARY: My husband had this once, in Spain, and he brought me a seed of it. I tried to grow it, but it died. Apparently only the Spanish possess the secret of its cultivation.

*SHE PUTS THE SEEDS BACK, AND CLOSES THE BOX.*

MARY: Would you die for it?
ANNIE: For *that*?
MARY: Men will. Believe me.
ANNIE: Some men might. But that'd only be proof of their stupidity.
MARY: What's your name?

ANNIE: Annie.

MARY: Mary.

ANNIE: Are you really bandits?

MARY: I used to be a good wife, but my husband fell in a lake. And they blamed me. They said nobody accidentally falls in a lake with a stone round their neck.

ANNIE: You murdered him?

MARY: He was the most witless creature on God's earth. And you?

ANNIE: I came from Loon.

MARY: Alone?

ANNIE: More or less.

MARY: Who's the idiot?

ANNIE: My brother-in-law.

MARY: You want to join us for a while?

ANNIE: I'm no killer.

MARY: Oh, you'd be surprised. Two of the sisters were nuns.

*ENTER CRAZYFACE, STRIPPED NAKED. THE BANDITS GIVE CHASE. HE RUNS AND PICKS UP HIS BOX.*

CRAZYFACE: Annie! They're women—

MARY: She knows.

CRAZYFACE: —they took my clothes. I'll freeze to death.

*ONE OF THE BANDITS THROWS DOWN THE BUNDLE OF HIS CLOTHES.*

SECOND BANDIT: Who's having his boots?

MARY: Fight it out amongst yourselves.

CRAZYFACE: I hate you all!

ANNIE: Now—

CRAZYFACE: And you! Let me alone.

MARY: All right, run while you can—

CRAZYFACE: Annie?

ANNIE: No . . . I'm staying . . . with the women.

CRAZYFACE: They'll hang you. They hang bandits. But I'll tell the Pope to pray for you.

ANNIE: Thank you.

CRAZYFACE: Not them. Just you. They can all burn in Hell!

*HE EXITS, RUNNING. THE BANDITS RUN AFTER HIM, WHOOPING AND CALLING NAMES.*

*THEN THEY TURN BACK.*

MARY: We'll burn your skirt. Cut your hair. It'll be as though Annie never existed.
ANNIE: Why not?
MARY: He was right, by the way. If they catch us, we'll hang for being lawless creatures.
ANNIE: I can live with that.

*THE BANDITS START TO SORT THROUGH THE CLOTHES. ANNIE STEPS FORWARD.*

ANNIE: No!

*THE BANDITS PART.*

ANNIE: The boots are mine.

*LIGHTS OUT.*

# Scene Seven

## The Torture Garden

*CANDLES FLICKER. DISTANT VOICES SING IN LATIN. ENTER MENGO. A DOOR OPENS IN THE EARTH. LIGHT AND SMOKE AND HOWLS POUR UP FROM IT. THE GROUP OF PULCINELLAS WHO WERE IN ATTENDANCE DURING THE PREVIOUS SCENE IN SPAIN ARE HERE AGAIN. BUT THEIR FUNCTION HAS CHANGED FROM*

*COOKS TO TORTURERS. THEIR APRONS ARE COVERED IN BLOOD. THEY CARRY PINCERS AND BUCKETS OF SMOKING COALS, WHICH THEY PLACE ON THE STAGE.*

MENGO: *(To one of the Pulcinellas)* Fetch up the prisoner.

*MENGO SITS DOWN.*

FIRST PULCINELLA: Yes, your worship.

*THE PULCINELLA DISAPPEARS DOWN THE HOLE. MENGO READS.*

*FROM THE BOWELS OF THE EARTH A FIGURE EMERGES. IT IS LENNY. HE HAS ONCE BEEN A SILVER-SUITED, WHITE-FACED CLOWN; IMMACULATE, ARISTOCRATIC. BUT HIS FORMER GLORY HAS LONG SINCE GONE. HIS COSTUME HANGS OFF HIM: THE BODY EXPOSED BENEATH IS PALE EXCEPT WHERE IT'S SLASHED WITH LIVID WOUNDS. HIS WHITE-FACE IS STILL IN PLACE, AS THOUGH HE PUT IT ON EVERY MORNING, DESPITE HIS SITUATION. THE DELICATE ARCH OF THE EYEBROWS, THE BUTTON LIPS. HIS HAIR IS CROPPED VERY SHORT. HIS EYES ARE SUNKEN WITH AN EXCESS OF PAIN. HIS APPEARANCE IS BOTH TERRIFYING AND PITIFUL; HIS ATTEMPTS TO KEEP HIS DIGNITY IN THE FACE OF HIS PHYSICAL HUMILIATION CURIOUSLY TOUCHING. HE IS OBVIOUSLY COMPLETELY MAD.*

MENGO: Lenny. Lenny Eulenspiegel.

*LENNY DOESN'T RESPOND.*

FIRST PULCINELLA: *(With a large pair of pincers)* Shall I snip off his thumbs?
MENGO: No. Lenny. Speak to me, won't you? Where were you on the wheel, Lenny? Ice or fire was it?
LENNY: Ice.
MENGO: Ah.
LENNY: Thank you, Mengo.
MENGO: For?

LENNY: Deliverance.

MENGO: You talked too much, I understand, and made terrible remarks about the King, and the Pope, and me. Also committed murder.

LENNY: Yes.

MENGO: Burned a baby in its cot.

LENNY: And worse.

MENGO: No boasting now. God hates a liar.

LENNY: I did it all.

MENGO: And have you suffered for your crimes?

LENNY: Yes.

MENGO: And do you repent then? Think before you answer . . .

LENNY: I . . .

MENGO: Do you repent them?

LENNY: No.

MENGO: Good. Then you're all I was promised you were. You had a brother.

LENNY: C-c-crazyface.

MENGO: He carries the heart of Spain, its most intimate secret, its rarest jewel, in his hand. Imagine that. Your own brother. Could you find him for me?

LENNY: Yes.

MENGO: Could you kill him for me?

LENNY: Yes. (*The Pulcinellas approach Lenny, and give him a coat, shoes, money*)

MENGO: What would you bring back for me?

LENNY: His heart.

MENGO: Too bloody.

LENNY: His head.

MENGO: Too ugly. (*Mengo whispers in Lenny's ear*) Maybe?

LENNY: Yes.

MENGO: Wrapped in a handkerchief.

*HE DROPS HIS HANDKERCHIEF TO THE FLOOR. LENNY STOOPS AND PICKS IT UP.*

MENGO: Gallant.

*EXIT MENGO. LENNY SMILES OUT AT US. A TERRIBLE SMILE. LIGHTS OUT.*

# Scene Eight

## A forest road

*ENTER THE REMNANTS OF A WEDDING PARTY. A MOTHER, A FATHER, A BRIDESMAID, AND A BRIDE. THE WOMEN ARE ALL CRYING. PLAIN FOLKS, ALL OF THEM. ESPECIALLY FATHER.*

FATHER: Oh for God's sake, Shirley. What's done is done.

BRIDE: What am I going to tell everybody?

MOTHER: Tell them the truth. Brian ... *(Starts to sniff again)* ... your husband to be ... was ... was ... eaten by a lion on his wedding day.

FATHER: Though it beats me how he had time to write a note.

BRIDE: *(Reads)* "I'll love you always."

BRIDESMAID: It's beautiful.

FATHER: It's bloody suspicious.

BRIDE: There's even blood on it.

FATHER: Let's have it here. *(Snatches note)* Could be blood, I suppose.

MOTHER: He was a good lad.

FATHER: He was a philanderer.

MOTHER: Don't speak ill of the dead.

FATHER: Yes, well ... it smells fishy to me. VERY fishy.

BRIDE: *(Bawling)* What about the baby?

MOTHER: Shirley, be quiet will you. Your father's thinking. Aren't you, Barty?

FATHER: I tell you, it's bloody embarrassing. Her in the family way and no husband. That I will say. They won't like it in the Pigbreeders' Guild.

MOTHER: Is that all you can think about? Us with a bastard ...

*BRIDE BAWLS.*

MOTHER: . . . unwanted child on the way, and all you can say is, "They won't like it in the Guild."

FATHER: Well, I may remark that if I bred pigs the way most people have kids, I'd be out of business tomorrow. Control! That's the thing. We've let her run wild. I blame you for a lot of this.

MOTHER: Now, don't start.

FATHER: I'm going to lose business if this gets out. You know that. People'll think I'm in favor of indiscriminate impregnation. That waters down good breeding stock.

*BRIDE AND BRIDESMAID START BAWLING AGAIN.*

MOTHER: You are a beast.

FATHER: Well, that's as may be.

MOTHER: She's only seventeen.

FATHER: Let me think will you? God Almighty!

*HE SITS DOWN. HIS WIFE SITS BESIDE HIM. SILENCE, EXCEPT FOR THE OCCASIONAL SNIFFLE. THEN, ENTER CRAZYFACE, DRESSED IN LEAVES.*

CRAZYFACE: Excuse me?

FATHER: Who the hell . . . ?

CRAZYFACE: Is this a funeral?

FATHER: What?

CRAZYFACE: It's just that I'm a grave-digger.

MOTHER: No, it's not a funeral. Well, it is, but there's no body. It was eaten.

*BRIDE BAWLS AGAIN.*

CRAZYFACE: Oh dear.

FATHER: Stick around, we'll have a christening in a couple of months.

*BRIDE BAWLS LOUDER.*

FATHER: Shut up, Shirley.

CRAZYFACE: Who's the lucky girl?

FATHER: She is.

*BRIDE BAWLS EVEN LOUDER.*

MOTHER: Who are you?

CRAZYFACE: Crazy—I mean Tyl Eulenspiegel.

MOTHER: I don't know you. Are you a local lad?

CRAZYFACE: I've been living in the woods.

MOTHER: Oh, you're a monk.

FATHER: 'Course he's not a monk. Does he look like a monk?

MOTHER: A lot of monks live in the woods. They commune with nature.

FATHER: He said he was a grave-digger. Didn't you?

CRAZYFACE: Yes.

FATHER: Plenty of work, eh?

CRAZYFACE: Yeah.

FATHER: You see, that shows enterprise, Mother. Getting yourself a trade. Going where the business is. I like that in a young man.

CRAZYFACE: You in graves too?

FATHER: No, I'm a pig-breeder, slaughterer, butcher. Pork's the trade. Pork and pig-skin. That's the glory of the pig, you can use it all. Eat it, wear it, use it on the land as fertilizer, and what you don't need, you feed back to the pigs. See, the glory of the pig is, it's a cannibal.

CRAZYFACE: Is that right?

FATHER: All taste, no waste.

CRAZYFACE: Amazing.

FATHER: Just the way God intended it. Well, you'd know that, being a grave-digger. We eat the fish that's swallowed the worm that's eaten our grandmother's eyes out. Isn't that right?

CRAZYFACE: Happens all the time.

FATHER: A man after me own heart.

CRAZYFACE: No harm in it.

FATHER: *(Has an idea)* What are you doing for the next few years?

CRAZYFACE: How do you mean?

FATHER: Married, are you?

MOTHER: Father?

FATHER: Are you?

CRAZYFACE: No.

FATHER: (*Assessing him*) Get you a decent coat. Pig-skin shoes. Maybe a shave: you'd do. Wouldn't he, Shirl? He'd do.

BRIDE: . . . um.

FATHER: Oh for Christ's sake, stop your sniffling. *Will he do*?

BRIDE: S'pose so.

FATHER: What about you, Mother?

MOTHER: He's not much.

FATHER: He's alive, which is more than can be said for his predecessor. What do you say?

MOTHER: If Shir'll have him.

FATHER: Oh, she'll have him. (*To Crazyface*) You want to marry my daughter?

CRAZYFACE: Marry her?

FATHER: Yes, you deaf or stupid? Marry her.

CRAZYFACE: Well . . .

FATHER: Oh well, if you've go to think about it.

CRAZYFACE: No . . . I'll marry her. I get a coat, is that right?

FATHER: Mother! The coat.

CRAZYFACE: I do get a coat? Only it's been chilly the last couple of months.

FATHER: It was meant for Brian. But where he's going he won't be needing a coat.

*MOTHER TAKES OUT A COAT.*

FATHER: Well, put it on.

MOTHER: It suits you. Doesn't it Shirl?

BRIDE: I s'pose so.

FATHER: Well, time's wasting. The Priest's booked 'til three o'clock. Let's get the show on the road.

MOTHER: We should leave the couple alone for a moment.

FATHER: Must we? All right. Two minutes.

*EXIT FATHER, MOTHER AND BRIDESMAID.*

CRAZYFACE: It's a good coat.

BRIDE: You any good with pigs?

CRAZYFACE: Why? You're not going to have one are you?

BRIDE: He'll want you in the business. It's all he wanted a son-in-law for. Someone to take over when he goes to the sty in the sky. I'm not good enough.

*ENTER ANGEL, WITH NEWSPAPER. IT'S DOING THE CROSSWORD. IT'S INVISIBLE TO SHIRLEY, OF COURSE. NOR CAN SHE HEAR IT. HENCE:*

ANGEL: Well, well—
CRAZYFACE: *(To Angel)* Not now.
BRIDE: What?
ANGEL: Thirteen Down. "Died on a Cross." Five letters.
CRAZYFACE: Moses.
BRIDE: Moses?
CRAZYFACE: We'll call the child Moses.
ANGEL: Moses. *(Starts to fill it in)*
BRIDE: Suppose it's a girl?
ANGEL: It doesn't fit.
CRAZYFACE: How many letters in Moses?
BRIDE: Five.
CRAZYFACE: That fits.
BRIDE: Not for a girl, it doesn't. Moses is a boy's name.
ANGEL: The third letter's got to be S.
CRAZYFACE: I give up.
BRIDE: You must know some girls' names.
CRAZYFACE: How do you spell Moses?
BRIDE: M–O–S—
CRAZYFACE: There you are then.
BRIDE: What?
CRAZYFACE: Third letter's S.
BRIDE: So?
CRAZYFACE: It must be Moses.
BRIDE: You can't call a girl Moses. Jesus!
ANGEL: Jesus. That's it. Jesus. *(Fills it in)*

*THE BRIDE'S EXITING.*

BRIDE: What am I marrying?

*SHE EXITS.*

ANGEL: Bright girl.
CRAZYFACE: From now on, stay out of my hair, okay?
ANGEL: Just paying a flying visit. Nice coat.
CRAZYFACE: Well, don't.
ANGEL: Thought you might like to know about Lenny.
CRAZYFACE: No thank you.
ANGEL: (*Still assessing the coat*) *Very* nice material.
CRAZYFACE: It's pig-skin.
ANGEL: Is it? Not selling it are you?
CRAZYFACE: No.
ANGEL: Only inquiring. Poor Lenny—
CRAZYFACE: I don't want to hear.

*CRAZYFACE EXITS.*

ANGEL: —is just down the road. He's watching a hanging, actually. He likes hangings . . .

*THE ANGEL REALIZES CRAZYFACE HAS GONE.*

ANGEL: Don't say I didn't warn you.

# Scene Nine

## The pig-breeder's house

*TABLES ARE SET UP FOR THE WEDDING MEAL, AND THE GUESTS START TO ENTER. THEY ARE ALL LIKE THE PIG-BREEDER'S FAMILY, ASPIRING MIDDLE-CLASS. THEY TALK INCESSANTLY. THE TABLE IS LAID WITH LARGE COMMUNAL PLATES OF BREAD. THE MOTHER GOES ALONG THE*

*TABLES, CHECKING THAT THEY'RE NOT TOO DIRTY, WIP-*
*ING A FEW SPOONS ETC. THE BRIDE HAS BRIGHTENED*
*UP CONSIDERABLY SINCE WE LAST SAW HER: MARRIAGE*
*SEEMS TO SUIT HER. SHE IS NOW THE CENTER OF*
*ATTENTION. CRAZYFACE HAS GOTTEN SYSTEMATICALLY*
*DRUNKER SINCE THE CEREMONY.*

*AS THE GUESTS ARE ALL SEATED BY THE MOTHER, AND*
*THE COOKS (THE THREE PULCINELLAS) ENTER WITH*
*BOWLS OF SOUP ON TRAYS, THE FATHER SPEAKS TO*
*CRAZYFACE.*

FATHER: You look after my daughter, and you'll find me a generous father-in-law. They say there's a shortage of money
around at the moment, but I'm not feeling the pinch. There's
brass in pigs.
CRAZYFACE: Thank you.
FATHER: You've done me a favor today; I won't forget that.

*HE TURNS TO THE GUESTS. THEY'RE ALL TALKING.*
*MOTHER ESCORTS CRAZYFACE TO HIS SEAT. FATHER*
*BEATS THE TABLE WITH A SPOON.*

FATHER: Hush your row! Hush your row!

*THE GUESTS ALL "SHUSH" EACH OTHER.*

FATHER: That's better. Now before we get to the meal, a few
words of welcome. It's not so long ago that Brian, God rest
his soul, said to me, "If anything were to happen to me,
Dad—" he used to call me Dad— "I want you to see my
Shirley happy." Well, of course, it did, I have, and she is.
Aren't you, Shirl?

*SHIRLEY OPENS HER MOUTH TO SPEAK. NO CHANCE.*

FATHER: We've got a feast for you today. For openers, an excel-
lent pig-brain broth, to be followed by pork sausages with
gravy, and bacon. The main course is suckling pig with
blood pudding, knuckles and trotters on the side. Enjoy it!

*THEY FALL UPON THE FOOD. HE STOPS THEM BECAUSE HIS WIFE IS STARING AT HIM.*

FATHER: I beg you also to give thanks to the Lord for this food, and for the pig, who, of all God's creatures, is most blessed. Amen.
GUESTS: Amen.

*THE GUESTS START EATING NOISILY. FATHER JOINS IN.*

BRIDE: *(To Crazyface)* There's pigs inside and out.
FIRST GUEST: What did she say?
CRAZYFACE: Pigs inside and out.
FIRST GUEST: *(Looks around the table)* Aren't they just?
SECOND GUEST: What did he say?
FIRST GUEST: He said, "There's pigs inside and out."
SECOND GUEST: It's frightful really—
THIRD GUEST: What was that?
SECOND GUEST: These guests. Pigs, most of them.
THIRD GUEST: I was just thinking that myself.

*THE PULCINELLAS HURRY BACK AND FORTH, SERVING UP FURTHER PORTIONS OF SOUP. THE CONVERSATION ABOUT PIGS CONTINUES AROUND THE TABLE. ONE OF THE GUESTS HAS A CHOKING FIT. SHE'S SLAPPED ON THE BACK, AND SOMEONE PUTS THEIR FINGERS DOWN HER THROAT.*

FIRST GUEST: The soup's superb.
FATHER: Thanks, Mother.
SECOND GUEST: It really is.
FATHER: I much prefer the meat of a mammal. Don't give me fish.
MOTHER: Oh, don't start him on fish.
FATHER: Who knows where your fish has been.
GUESTS: True.
FATHER: For all we know they may eat shit.
MOTHER: Barty!
FATHER: Isn't that right!
FIRST GUEST: Untrustworthy!

SECOND GUEST: Slippery things!
FATHER: Whereas your pig—
MOTHER: Oh do shut up.
FATHER: —is a glorious beast. Every part of the anatomy can be put to some use. Observe the silk purse of my daughter, who was so recently a sow's ear.

*LAUGHTER.*

BRIDE: You're embarrassing me.
MOTHER: He doesn't mean it, dear.
FATHER: How are you doing, son?
CRAZYFACE: Fine! Fine!
FATHER: Good soup?
CRAZYFACE: Very good soup.
FATHER: *(To the table)* My son-in-law's a grave-digger, you know. Oh yes, he's a man with a profession. Wouldn't have anything less.

*ON THE OUTSKIRTS OF THE GATHERING, A FIGURE HAS APPEARED. IT'S LENNY. HE'S STOPPED BY ONE OF THE SERVANTS.*

SERVANT: Excuse me. This is a private party.
LENNY: I'm a friend of the family.
SERVANT: Well, I'll just . . .

*THE SERVANT TRIES TO TURN AWAY, BUT LENNY HAS HIM BY THE WRIST.*

LENNY: No need.
SERVANT: The master of the house . . .

*THE SERVANT SEES THE KNIFE IN LENNY'S HAND.*

LENNY: It's a surprise.
SERVANT: Oh.
LENNY: I'd leave now if I were you.

*THE SERVANT NODS AND EXITS HURRIEDLY, TAKING*

*THE OTHER PULCINELLAS WITH HIM. LENNY TAKES A SEAT, WHERE CRAZYFACE CAN SEE HIM.*

FATHER: (*Getting drunker*) People say to me, they say, have you got pigs' trotters? I say, I say to them, no! I always walk this way.

*THE PUNCH LINE IS REPEATED AROUND THE TABLE.*

FATHER: Wonderful creature, the pig. Did you know that the male pig, the boar . . .

MOTHER: Did you say bore, sweetheart?

FATHER: That's what I said. The boar is equipped with a member that resembles a cork-screw?

MOTHER: Will you stop this lewd talk?

FATHER: Just talking about pigs.

MOTHER: Well, we don't want to hear any more about pigs. The groom's going to make a speech, aren't you?

CRAZYFACE: Am I?

MOTHER: It's traditional.

CRAZYFACE: Oh . . . I . . .

MOTHER: Stand up.

CRAZYFACE: I . . . well I . . .

FATHER: (*Applauds*) Good lad.

CRAZYFACE: Thank you all for coming.

*APPLAUSE.*

CRAZYFACE: . . . I must admit it's all come as a bit of a surprise to me.

FATHER: That's enough, boy.

CRAZYFACE: See, until this morning I'd never seen this girl in my life.

*THE TABLE ERUPTS.*

FATHER: What he means is, she's a new woman. Eh? Isn't it?

CRAZYFACE: No.

FATHER: Yes.

MOTHER: Sit down!

CRAZYFACE: I haven't . . .

MOTHER: And you.

FATHER: Stupid boy!

CRAZYFACE: I haven't finished.

FATHER: Why won't he sit down?

CRAZYFACE: Anyway, it's been a lovely wedding, and the soup's very . . . *(Sees Lenny)* Lenny!

FATHER: Eh?

*THE TABLE IS NOW COMPLETELY SILENT.*

CRAZYFACE: Lenny?

LENNY: *(Standing slowly, and raising his cup)* To the bride and groom.

*THE TABLE STANDS. ALL TOAST TOGETHER.*

GUESTS: Bride and groom!

FATHER: Who's he?

MOTHER: I don't know.

*FATHER GETS UP FROM THE TABLE. THE SERVANTS HAVE GONE.*

FATHER: Where's the cooks? The waiters? Where is everybody?

CRAZYFACE: *(To Lenny)* Go away.

BRIDE: What's wrong?

CRAZYFACE: Make him go away.

LENNY: Is he having one of his delusions?

FATHER: Who are you?

MOTHER: Delusions?

LENNY: He sees angels. Didn't you know?

*DISCOMFORT ROUND THE TABLE.*

FATHER: Angels?

MOTHER: Don't be silly.

LENNY: He'll tell you.

FATHER: What would you know?

LENNY: I'm his brother.

CRAZYFACE: He's dead.

FATHER: No, he's not.

CRAZYFACE: On a big wheel—
LENNY: How did you know?
CRAZYFACE: Please—
FATHER: Do you really see angels?
CRAZYFACE: No.
LENNY: Yes!
CRAZYFACE: Not anymore. I told it to go away.
GUESTS: He's mad. She's married a madman.
CRAZYFACE: I'm not mad!
MOTHER: I knew. She'd have been better having the child out of
    wedlock.
FATHER: Sit down, everyone. It's all part of the entertainment.

*THE GUESTS SCATTER FROM THE TABLE. LENNY IS LEFT
AT ONE END, CRAZYFACE AT THE OTHER.*

LENNY: I didn't think you were the marrying kind.
CRAZYFACE: Leave me alone.
LENNY: (*Climbs on the table*) Where's the box?
CRAZYFACE: What box?
LENNY: You know what box. Where's the box?

*HE STARTS ALONG THE TABLE TOWARDS CRAZYFACE.*

CRAZYFACE: I don't have it.

*LENNY JUMPS AT HIM, WIELDING A KNIFE.*

FATHER: All part of the entertainment. (*He goes amongst the guests,
    who are busy leaving*) Wait! Wait! Don't go.
LENNY: The box!
CRAZYFACE: Let me alone!

*LENNY STARTS TO ASSAULT CRAZYFACE, KNOCKING OFF
HIS HAT, SLAPPING HIM; A SERIES OF PETTY HUMILIA-
TIONS. CRAZYFACE DOESN'T FIGHT BACK.*

LENNY: Come on, do you want me to kill you? I will, you know.
    I've got a special dispensation to do whatever I want to you.
    Just like that.

BRIDE: Don't let him do this.

*CRAZYFACE IS UTTERLY COWED. LENNY HAS COM-
PLETE AUTHORITY OVER HIM, THE AUTHORITY OF
AN OLDER BROTHER, OF THE WHITE-FACE CLOWN
OVER THE AUGUSTE.*

LENNY: Aren't you going to tell me? Where's the box? Do I have
to tear the house apart?

*HE FLINGS THE CHAIRS OVER.*

LENNY: I will! I'll do *anything*. You ask him! *(Points at Crazyface)*
I'll do *anything*, won't I? *Won't* I?

*HE JUMPS AT CRAZYFACE, WHO RUNS.*

LENNY: Come back here, you little bastard!

*CRAZYFACE EXITS, FOLLOWED BY HIS BROTHER. A BEAT
OF SILENCE.*

FATHER: Well, that's that, then.
MOTHER. Brian was such a peaceable boy.
BRIDE: That's two husbands in one day.
MOTHER: I hope you're not going to make a habit of this.

*OUTSIDE, A TERRIBLE SQUEALING.*

FATHER: The pigs! They're in amongst the pigs!

*FATHER EXITS, AND RE-ENTERS.*

FATHER: Fetch a constable! Fetch a priest! Fetch somebody!

*THE SQUEALING GOES ON AND ON. FATHER EXITS
AGAIN, AS A GUEST ENTERS.*

GUEST: They're killing the pigs! They're killing the pigs!
MOTHER: Good for them.
GUEST: There's blood coming down like rain.

*ENTER CRAZYFACE, COVERED WITH PIGS' BLOOD.*

CRAZYFACE: Oh God, help me.
GUEST: Uh!
CRAZYFACE: Help me, somebody.
MOTHER: You get out of my house! You've caused enough trouble.
CRAZYFACE: He's taken my box! Now he wants to kill me!
MOTHER: Who are you?
CRAZYFACE: Just a fool.

*ENTER LENNY, BLOODY-HANDED. HE HAS THE BOX IN ONE HAND AND HIS KNIFE IN THE OTHER.*

LENNY: Come here, brother of mine.
MOTHER: And you can get out, too! Hear me? *Out!*

*LENNY GOES FOR HER WITH A KNIFE. SHE EXITS, SHRIEK-ING. THE BRIDE CLIMBS ON THE TABLE, WHILE LENNY CHASES CRAZYFACE. ENTER FATHER, WITH AN AXE.*

FATHER: All right, you bastards! That's quite enough!

*FATHER CHASES LENNY, WHO CHASES CRAZYFACE. THEY EXIT AGAIN, AS TWO CONSTABLES ENTER, WITH WHIS-TLES, AND GIVE FURTHER CHASE. THE BRIDE PRAYS, AND HER MOTHER ENTERS, WITH A LARGE STRING OF SAUSAGES. FATHER ENTERS, AND BEFORE HE CAN SAY ANYTHING, MOTHER HAS WRAPPED THE SAUSAGES ROUND HIS NECK AND IS TRYING TO STRANGLE HIM WITH THEM.*

BRIDE: No, Mother, no, Mother. It's Father! Father!
MOTHER: Oh my goodness. Barty! Barty! Water! Water!

*BRIDE PICKS UP THE WATER JUG AND FLINGS THE CON-TENTS AT HER FATHER, HITTING HER MOTHER.*

MOTHER: You silly bitch!
FATHER: Language!

*OFF-STAGE, A TERRIBLE SHRIEK.*

BRIDE: Tyl!
FATHER: The boar!
BRIDE: My husband!
FATHER: My pig!

*ENTER LENNY WITH SOMETHING IN MENGO'S HAND-KERCHIEF.*

LENNY: *(To Shirley)* Forgive me. I've widowed you.
BRIDE: Oh no! *(She starts to cry loudly)*
LENNY: Well . . . goodnight.

*EXIT LENNY, AS A GUEST ENTERS.*

GUEST: Someone's castrated the boar!
FATHER: No! No!
GUEST: He's hopping mad.
FATHER: Not the boar. Oh God, not the boar.

*FATHER STARTS TO CRY. THE BRIDE GOES ON CRYING.*

*ENTER CRAZYFACE, UNSEEN.*

FATHER: It was that damn fool!
MOTHER: I warned you.
FATHER: We should have never let him near us.

*FATHER GETS UP.*

MOTHER: Where are you going?
FATHER: To kick him senseless.
MOTHER: He's dead!
FATHER: I want the satisfaction.

*CRAZYFACE HIDES UNDER THE TABLE, AS THE FATHER STORMS OUT.*

MOTHER: Come on Shirl—
BRIDE: Oh, Mama . . .

*THEY EXIT. CRAZYFACE PEERS OUT FROM UNDER THE TABLECLOTH, AS A MAN ENTERS. TOP-HAT, CARNATION, GLASSES. LOOKS A BIT OF A PRAT. IT'S BRIAN. HE SEES THE WRECKAGE.*

BRIAN: Oh.

*CRAZYFACE PEERS OUT.*

BRIAN: Don't suppose you've seen a bride, have you?

*CRAZYFACE NODS.*

BRIAN: I'm Brian. I was going to elope with another woman. But she got—
CRAZYFACE: —eaten by a lion?
BRIAN: Run over by a horse. I've come to make amends.
CRAZYFACE: They went thataway.

*HE STARES AT CRAZYFACE, NOT QUITE SURE WHAT TO SAY.*

BRIAN: It looks like rain again, eh?

*SLOW FADE.*

*END OF ACT ONE.*

# Act 2

# Act 2:

# <u>Scene</u> <u>One</u>

# A wasteland

*PART TWO OPENS IN DARKNESS. WE'VE MOVED FROM THE BREATHLESS DAWN OF PART ONE INTO THE DARKER WORLD, A HAUNTED WORLD. DISTANTLY, THE SOUND OF WHALE-SONG. BUT CLOSER, HORSES GALLOPING, DISTANT INCOHERENT SHOUTS, THE CLASH OF ARMS.*

*A LIGHT COMES UP ON THE OLD CLOWN, WHO IS SITTING ASTRIDE A KNACKERED OLD PANTOMIME HORSE, PREFERABLY PIE-BALD. HE IS DRESSED RIDICULOUSLY, AS A GENERAL. HIS HAT BRISTLES WITH TATTY FEATHERS. A WOODEN SWORD HANGS FORLORN AT HIS SIDE. HE STARES OUT AT US, UNBLINKING.*

*ENTER CRAZYFACE, NOT SEEING THE HORSE AND RIDER. HE IS PANTING, HAVING RUN A LONG WAY.*

*HE REALIZES THAT HE HAS LEFT THE PIG BREEDER'S HOUSE A LONG WAY BEHIND.*

*HE'S SAFE. AND HE STILL HAS HIS COAT.*

*THE HORSE NEIGHS. CRAZYFACE TURNS AROUND.*

CRAZYFACE: You. Are you everywhere?

*THE CLOWN BLOWS OUT A LONG, SLOW COLUMN OF WATER, HIS ETERNAL GREETING.*

CRAZYFACE: What are you doing here? You'll get yourself killed. We'll *all* get killed.

*THE CLOWN SHRUGS.*

CRAZYFACE: What am I going to do? He took my box. And he tried to kill me. Ah, what do you care? I was going to go to Rome, but there isn't much use now is there? I'd go home . . . except that I keep seeing Lenny.

*THE OLD CLOWN LOOKS AT HIM, SHARPLY.*

CRAZYFACE: Oh, so you know Lenny do you?

*THE OLD CLOWN SHRUGS.*

CRAZYFACE: You do, don't you? He's my brother. Somebody once told me all the clowns in the world were related, however distantly. All parts of one great big family. Do you think that's possible?

*THE OLD CLOWN SHRUGS.*

CRAZYFACE: Nah. Neither do I.

*SILENCE. CRAZYFACE FEELS VERY LONELY.*

CRAZYFACE: I don't know where to go. Which way to go.

*THE OLD CLOWN GETS OFF HIS HORSE AND CROSSES TO CRAZYFACE.*

CRAZYFACE: Why don't you say something? Haven't you got a tongue?

*THE OLD CLOWN STICKS OUT HIS TONGUE.*

CRAZYFACE: All right, put it away.

*THE OLD CLOWN PUTS HIS TONGUE BACK IN HIS MOUTH WITH HIS FINGERS.*

CRAZYFACE: What am I going to do? (*Crazyface is near to tears*) I wish I had my fish.

*THE OLD CLOWN PRODUCES A FISH ON A PIECE OF STRING FROM INSIDE HIS COAT.*

CRAZYFACE: Oh my!

*THE OLD CLOWN SMILES.*

CRAZYFACE: For me?

*THE OLD CLOWN NODS.*

CRAZYFACE: Is it pickled? They have to be pickled, or they drown.

*CRAZYFACE SNIFFS AT THE FISH.*

CRAZYFACE: Herring.

*THE OLD CLOWN NODS.*

CRAZYFACE: They're the best.

*THE OLD CLOWN POINTS TO THE HORSE.*

CRAZYFACE: What? You want me to take the horse?

*THE OLD CLOWN NODS.*

CRAZYFACE: Are you sure?

*HE NODS AGAIN.*

CRAZYFACE: But it's your horse.

*A VOICE FROM INSIDE THE HORSE.*

VOICE: No it isn't. He stole it.
CRAZYFACE: Who said that?

*THE CLOWN SHRUGS. CRAZYFACE GOES ACROSS TO LOOK AT THE HORSE.*

CRAZYFACE: Your horse farts words.

*THE CLOWN LOOKS AT HIM DEAD-PAN.*

CRAZYFACE: I mean, don't think I'm ungrateful. I might get to Rome on this, you know. I might. Not that I want to go to Rome.

*THE CLOWN TAKES OUT HIS SWORD, STRIKES AN HEROIC STANCE, BREAKS THE STANCE, AND EXITS.*

CRAZYFACE: Thanks anyhow. Hope you win the battle! (*Assessing the animal*) Right.

*HE CLIMBS ON THE HORSE, WHICH GRUNTS AND GROANS UNDER HIM.*

CRAZYFACE: I've seen quieter horses . . . (*He's on*) Giddy-up.
FIRST VOICE: Sod off!
CRAZYFACE: I beg your pardon?
SECOND VOICE: He said sod off.
CRAZYFACE: Who said that? All right, come on, who said that?
FIRST VOICE: Him.
SECOND VOICE: Me.
CRAZYFACE: Where?
SECOND VOICE: Here!

*CRAZYFACE GETS OFF THE HORSE, AND GOES TO LOOK UP ITS BACKSIDE, RAISING THE SCRAGGY TAIL TO DO SO.*

CRAZYFACE: Who's in there? Come out, or I'll come in and get you.

SECOND VOICE: Did somebody speak?
CRAZYFACE: How did you get stuck up a horse's bum?
FIRST VOICE: *(The horse's head turns)* 'Cause he's a daft bugger.
SECOND VOICE: Who are you calling a daft bugger?
FIRST VOICE: You, you daft bugger.

*SECOND VOICE, IN THE BACK END OF THE HORSE, KICKS THE FRONT END.*

FIRST VOICE: Ow. What'd you do that for?
SECOND VOICE: Don't call me a daft bugger.
FIRST VOICE: You bruised me shin!
SECOND VOICE: *(Kicks him again)* There's one to match.

*A FIGHT STARTS IN THE HORSE, WHICH REDUCES THE "ANIMAL" TO AN INCOHERENT MESS.*

CRAZYFACE: Behave yourselves. Stop it, damn you! *(Crazyface hits the horse with a riding crop. The fight stops)* I've no time for fighting. I've got an urgent appointment. Somewhere.

*THE HORSE STARTS TO LAUGH. BOTH ENDS.*

CRAZYFACE: That's all I need: an hysterical horse.

*IT FALLS OVER, IT'S LAUGHING SO MUCH. IT'S HOLDING ITS BELLY WITH LAUGHTER.*

CRAZYFACE: Stop laughing! And stand up when I talk to you.

*IT STANDS UP. AS IT DOES SO, ENTER ALVIN, THE ENGLISHMAN. HE IS BANDAGED.*

ALVIN: I say, you, peasant chappie!
CRAZYFACE: Oh no.
ALVIN: Don't I know you from somewhere?
CRAZYFACE: You've never seen me before in all my life.
ALVIN: I'm requisitioning your horse for the troops.
CRAZYFACE: Leave it alone!

*ENTER ALLEGRO.*

ALLEGRO: Ah! Bien!
ALVIN: Oh, here come the vultures.
ALLEGRO: I am commandeering this horse.
ALVIN: I'm afraid you're too late, froggie.
CRAZYFACE: Neither of you can have it. It's mine.
ALVIN: Necessity of war, old boy. Got to feed the men.
ALLEGRO: My troops are hungry too.

*THE HORSE NEIGHS.*

CRAZYFACE: But it's my horse.
ALLEGRO: Find another.
ALVIN: I'm afraid we were here first. And my troops are hungrier than yours.
ALLEGRO: We're losing six thousand men a day.
ALVIN: Seven thousand!
ALLEGRO: Eight!
ALVIN: Oh, this is damned ridiculous. You have the front half, I'll have the back. Decent British compromise never hurt anybody.

*ENTER ALFONSO, WITH A BIGGER BABY THAN LAST TIME.*

ALFONSO: And what will I have?
ALLEGRO & ALVIN: Oh.
CRAZYFACE: And Mother makes three.
ALFONSO: We're not going to give up, you know. We'll take the horse.
CRAZYFACE: None of you can have it. It's mine!

*HE GETS ON THE HORSE.*

CRAZYFACE: Keep your distance, or I'll ride you down.
ALVIN: Now, don't be tiresome.
CRAZYFACE: Go, boy! Gallop!

*THE HORSE REMAINS STANDING.*

FIRST VOICE: You must be joking.

CRAZYFACE: Giddy-up!

SECOND VOICE: Piss off. I'm not moving 'til you get rid of this amateur up front.

FIRST VOICE: Who are you calling an amateur?

SECOND VOICE: He's the worst front-half I've ever worked with. I'm not playing the back end *ONE MORE MINUTE!*

*THE BACK END AND THE FRONT END OF THE HORSE SEPARATE.*

FIRST VOICE: (*Taking off the head*) Who are you calling amateur?

SECOND VOICE: I'm not spending another day with my nose up his bottom.

FIRST VOICE: Thought you enjoyed it.

CRAZYFACE: Come on, this is no time to argue. I need transport.

SECOND VOICE: Get yourself a bike!

*EXIT SECOND VOICE.*

FIRST VOICE: Wait! Let's not be hasty. Maybe we can do alternate days! Oh dear, now he'll sulk.

*EXIT FIRST VOICE. THE OTHERS, HAVING LOST THEIR TEMPERS, NOW FEIGN DISINTEREST.*

ALLEGRO: Well . . .

ALVIN: Well . . .

ALFONSO: Well . . .

ALVIN: How's the baby?

ALFONSO: Poorly. Can't get the milk, you see.

ALVIN: It's a damn shame. And him a growing . . . er . . . tortoise.

ALLEGRO: (*Sharpening his knife on a sharpener*) You know, there are other sources.

ALVIN: Sources?

ALLEGRO: Of sustenance.

ALFONSO: Oh God, you froggies'll cook anything. Anyway, we've eaten the dogs.

ALVIN: Even the occasional rat. Not bad, rat.

ALLEGRO: But they do say . . . human meat . . . can be . . . tasty if well prepared.

ALVIN: Human . . .

ALFONSO: . . . meat?

*CRAZYFACE HAS SAT DOWN, DISCONSOLATE. HE SLOWLY REALIZES WHAT'S BEING PROPOSED. HE RAISES HIS HEAD. THEY POUNCE ON HIM.*

CRAZYFACE: Ah! no! no!

*KNIVES ARE RAISED. SUDDENLY ANNIE ENTERS, MASKED. SHE ATTACKS THEM, AND WOUNDS THEM ALL. THEY EXIT, HOWLING. CRAZYFACE IS STILL ON THE FLOOR, A BLUBBERING MASS OF TERROR. ANNIE REMOVES HER MASK. SHE HAS CHANGED. SHE HAS LOST AN EYE, AND NOW WEARS AN EYE-PATCH. HER HAIR IS SHORT. CRAZY-FACE DOESN'T EVEN RECOGNIZE HER.*

CRAZYFACE: I suppose *you* want to eat me now.

ANNIE: Eat you? You must be joking. I don't know where you've been.

CRAZYFACE: Do I know you? *(He studies her)* Oh my Lord! Annie?

ANNIE: Tyl!

CRAZYFACE: Annie, it is you!

*THEY EMBRACE.*

ANNIE: Still on the road to Rome?

CRAZYFACE: Well, not exactly.

ANNIE: Did you lose your secret?

CRAZYFACE: Lenny took it.

ANNIE: Lenny. My God. He's alive?

CRAZYFACE: He tried to kill me.

ANNIE: For your box? *(Crazyface nods)* What does he want with that? He never had a sweet tooth.

*ENTER FRONT END OF PANTOMIME HORSE, PURSUED BY ALLEGRO, WITH A KNIFE.*

ALLEGRO: Come here! Come here!

FIRST VOICE: Bugger off, you damn heathen. I'm a horse.
ALLEGRO: We love horse-meat!

*EXIT BOTH, THE OPPOSITE SIDE OF THE STAGE.*

ANNIE: Poor fish.
CRAZYFACE: I used to say that. Poor fish. Used to feel sorry for the whole world.
ANNIE: Not now?
CRAZYFACE: Not any more. What happened to the bandits?
ANNIE: They were all hanged. Including Mary. I was very fond of Mary. I cried for a whole month.
CRAZYFACE: How did you escape?
ANNIE: I cut a few throats. Lost my eye, but I survived.
CRAZYFACE: You've changed too.
ANNIE: Maybe. I've got a few secret ambitions, and I'm not going to let a hanging get between me and—
CRAZYFACE: And?
ANNIE: And my ambitions.
CRAZYFACE: You're just a woman.
ANNIE: That's the first thing that's going to change. *(She smiles)* If you want to come with me, you can.
CRAZYFACE: Which way are you going?
ANNIE: To Rome. I've got an audience with the Pope.
CRAZYFACE: Really?
ANNIE: He doesn't know it yet.

*ENTER THE ANGEL.*

ANGEL: Ask yourself: is this wise?
CRAZYFACE: Go away.
ANNIE: What?
CRAZYFACE: Just go to Hell.
ANNIE: God, you're a funny sort. One moment—
CRAZYFACE: Not you. It.

*POINTS TO THE ANGEL.*

ANGEL: I wouldn't bother to come after you this way, except for that coat.

CRAZYFACE: Damn coat.

ANNIE: What are you pointing at?

ANGEL: Me.

CRAZYFACE: It.

ANNIE: What?

CRAZYFACE: The Angel.

ANGEL: I'm invisible to her, you dunce. Don't want you trying any more silly games like the time before last.

ANNIE: There's no angel, Tyl.

ANGEL: See? *(The Angel throws a punch at her. She doesn't flinch)*

CRAZYFACE: There is.

ANGEL: Tell her she's blind as a bat and twice as ugly.

CRAZYFACE: It's talking to me. Now.

ANNIE: What's it saying?

ANGEL: Ugly bitch.

CRAZYFACE: I can't tell you.

ANNIE: It's a delusion, Tyl.

CRAZYFACE: No.

ANNIE: Look, if you don't stop seeing angels, you're going to get yourself in a lot of trouble.

CRAZYFACE: The Pope sees angels.

ANNIE: The Pope's the master of the world. You're a flea on its backside.

ANGEL: She's right. She's absolutely right.

CRAZYFACE: Expose yourself. Please.

ANNIE: What?

ANGEL: You must be joking.

CRAZYFACE: Then leave me alone. Once and for all, leave me alone!

ANNIE: Me, or the Angel?

ANGEL: Tell her to piss off.

CRAZYFACE: *(To Angel) You* piss off.

ANNIE: You're a loony, Tyl. You're getting worse, not better.

*THE NEXT SPEECHES ARE SPOKEN SIMULTANEOUSLY.*

ANGEL: You can tell she's an unbeliever. She'll burn in Hell, that one. Look at her, dressing up like a man, strutting around like that. It's bloody shameful. She's godless, Tyl, you know that? And you know what happens to godless women. They've got special fires stoked for them.

ANNIE: You've got to stop these fantasies, Tyl. They'll burn you for them. Have you never heard of the Inquisition? They're burning people right across Europe. And there're special fires stoked for people who see angels when they're not ordained.

CRAZYFACE: Shut up, both of you!

ANGEL: Charming.

ANNIE: All right, Tyl, have it your own way. (*She goes to leave*)

CRAZYFACE: Annie.

ANNIE: I've got things to do Tyl. I can't waste time keeping you sane.

CRAZYFACE: No.

ANNIE: Besides . . . (*This is difficult for her to say*) . . . if . . . I mean I'm not saying . . . I mean . . . I suppose there's just a possibility that . . . there is an angel here. And you'll never hear me say that again, so make the most of it. See you.

*EXIT ANNIE.*

ANGEL: You want me to leave?

CRAZYFACE: Yes.

ANGEL: Give me the coat.

CRAZYFACE: Go to Hell.

ANGEL: Just the coat.

CRAZYFACE: What did I do to deserve you?

ANGEL: Believe me, the feeling's mutual. Give me the coat.

CRAZYFACE: I've given in to you too many times.

ANGEL: Tell you what, I'll play you for it. (*It takes out a pack of cards*) How's that? That fair?

CRAZYFACE: You always cheat.

ANGEL: So do you.

CRAZYFACE: (*He smiles to himself*) And if I play and win?

ANGEL: I leave you alone.

CRAZYFACE: Promise?

ANGEL: Promise.

*ENTER ALVIN.*

ALVIN: I say, peasant chappie.

CRAZYFACE: Oh no! No! (*Crazyface backs out*) You're not going to eat me!

ALVIN: No really—
CRAZYFACE: Leave me alone!

*CRAZYFACE EXITS.*

ALVIN: Just wondered if you had any salt. Caught the back end of the horse. Bit tough. Edible, but tough. A bit of salt'd improve it no end.

*THE ANGEL KNOCKS HIS HAT OFF.*

ALVIN: *(Sanguine)* Ah! Ghosts eh? Well, I can't say I'm surprised. It's been one of those days.

*HE EXITS AND ANGEL IS LEFT DOING CARD TRICKS.*

# Scene Two

## The Torture Garden

*ENTER TWO PULCINELLAS WITH A LARGE CRATE. THEY START TO POKE THROUGH THE GAPS IN THE CRATE WITH STICKS, GIGGLING TO EACH OTHER. THE CRATE CONTAINS LOBSTERS.*

*ENTER MENGO WITH THE BOX. LENNY FOLLOWS.*

MENGO: They arrived.
FIRST PULCINELLA: Yes, Mengo.
MENGO: Lobster, Lenny. The fattest and the finest.

*LENNY PEERS INTO THE CRATE.*

MENGO: Don't put your fingers in, they'll have them off. You like lobster?

LENNY: Yes.

MENGO: Well, good. We'll dine on them together. One each, with butter. I'm proud of you, Lenny. You brought back the glory of Spain: and you assassinated the thief. You brought me my trophy, I hope?

LENNY: Of course.

*LENNY PROFFERS THE BLOODY HANDKERCHIEF.*

MENGO: Later. Later. First the box. (*Mengo feels the surface of the box*) Did you open it?

LENNY: I tried.

MENGO: That's honest.

LENNY: It defeated me.

MENGO: It's a Chinese design. (*He plays with it for a moment*) There!

*HE OPENS IT. MENGO REACHES INTO THE BOX AND TAKES OUT A SEED AND A PIECE OF PAPER.*

LENNY: Rat turds?

MENGO: Of all the treasures Spain found in the New World, this is the greatest. Consider it. So small, so unprepossessing. Yet this humble seed, when ground to powder and mixed with a few spices into paste, makes chocolate.

LENNY: What's chocolate?

MENGO: It's a pleasure sought by all of Europe. Its taste is bitter-sweet, and every man who's tasted it once counts the hours 'til he next has it on his tongue. And Spain has it. Only Spain. We own the land where it grows, we own the savages who have farmed it for centuries, and until Alvarez stole it, we owned this— (*He waves the piece of paper*) —the definitive recipe, the one perfect balance of cocoa and sugar, and milk and spice.

LENNY: The Lowlands are ash. Thousands have died. For . . . chocolate?

MENGO: Priorities change. Sometimes we might go to war for a strip of land so arid you couldn't raise snakes on it; another day for a face; another for the sport of it.

*LENNY STARTS TO LAUGH.*

LENNY: All this. For chocolate . . .

MENGO: I'm glad it entertains you. It satisfies my sense of the ridiculous, too. I've woken up laughing some nights, laughing 'til I cried, thinking about this preposterous seed. You killed your own brother for it, Lenny.

LENNY: He's no loss.

MENGO: Show me the meat. *(Lenny produces the handkerchief still folded)* I wonder if he ever wormed his way into the box.

LENNY: Tyl? Never. He didn't have the wit.

MENGO: Did he die easily?

LENNY: No, he squealed like a pig.

MENGO: Show me. *(Lenny unfolds the handkerchief)* Is this a joke?

LENNY: No.

MENGO: This isn't your brother's flesh and blood? You're playing some game.

LENNY: I castrated him myself.

MENGO: This is the meat of a pig!

LENNY: No, it can't be.

MENGO: My father was a butcher. This is a pig!

LENNY: I killed him! He screamed, he struggled. Yes, it was dark, but I could have sworn . . .

MENGO: What is it about fools? *(Studying the lobsters in the crate)* The King had a jester: a dwarf he was, barely came up to the middle of my thigh. He died last winter. The King was mourning for weeks. But this fellow, he used to smile at me for no reason. Across the table; across a room. Smile meekly, with his eyes closed into little slits. I never knew why. Why he smiled sometimes: as if he . . . as if he knew my heart. *(Pause)* They say, don't they, that all fools in Europe are from one great family? You, and he, and Tyl Eulenspiegel. Common stock. Back to the beginning of the world. *(He stands up)* Suppose your fool brother opened the box by accident, and memorized the recipe. Suppose even now he has the secret in his head?

LENNY: No!

MENGO: Suppose he's going around Europe, whispering it in the ear of every cook he meets?

LENNY: No!

MENGO: Oh dear. Oh dear. Oh dear.

*THE PULCINELLAS ARE BEHIND LENNY. THEY TAKE HOLD OF HIM.*

MENGO: Goodnight, Lenny.

LENNY: Sir, it was an error. But I can correct it.

MENGO: You know, I think he's waiting for me, Lenny? Your brother. I think he's standing on a hill somewhere, looking towards Spain, and blowing kisses in my direction, saying: Come and fetch me. I dare you. Come and wipe the smile off my face.

LENNY: Please. Give me a chance.

*LENNY IS TAKEN AWAY.*

MENGO: Well, I'm coming, fool. I'm coming.

# Scene Three

## A town square

*ENTER IRVETTE AND CHEESBY. THEY'VE BEEN MARRIED FOR SEVERAL YEARS NOW, A CHILDLESS, UNHAPPY MARRIAGE.*

*AS THEY ENTER, OTHER FIGURES COME IN, TOO. CRIPPLES, BEGGARS, CHILDREN PLAYING GAMES. SO MUCH DETAIL OF ACTIVITY, ARGUMENTS, RECONCILEMENTS, SEDUCTIONS, REBUTTALS, THAT IT'S IMPOSSIBLE TO FOLLOW IT ALL.*

*ALL THIS CONFUSION BUILDS UP, HOWEVER.*

*AT FIRST, JUST IRVETTE AND CHEESBY TALKING; AT CROSS PURPOSES, OF COURSE.*

IRVETTE: What a lovely day for a pilgrimage.

CHEESBY: The profits, Irvette, imagine the profits.

IRVETTE: We can visit the shrine this afternoon. After Noon Mass.

CHEESBY: So many places in ruin.

IRVETTE: We ought to give thanks to the Lord.

CHEESBY: They'll all need bricks. Timber. Nails. The bare necessities.

IRVETTE: Maybe buy a saint.

CHEESBY: Which means business. Profit.

IRVETTE: Hallelujah.

CHEESBY: My very words. This is the right time to be selling bricks—

IRVETTE: Bricks?

CHEESBY: The profits . . . imagine.

IRVETTE: Can't you for once forget the business? We're on pilgrimage.

CHEESBY: It's a bad businessman who fails to capitalize on other people's misfortune.

IRVETTE: You're callous. You know that?

CHEESBY: I'm rich. And you get four pilgrimages a year out of it. Not to mention the lace underwear.

*ONE OF THE CRIPPLES HEARS THIS REMARK.*

FIRST CRIPPLE: You should be grateful. I'd give my good leg for some nice underwear.

IRVETTE: *(Angrily to Cheesby)* Will you keep your voice down! I don't want everybody to know what I am wearing.

CHEESBY: *(Trying to sweeten the conversation)* Think of the possibilities, Irvette. This wilderness coming to life again. New houses, new churches . . . use your imagination a bit.

IRVETTE: I don't *have* an imagination. Do you think I'd have married you if I had any imagination?

CHEESBY: Now don't start.

IRVETTE: Annie went off . . . even Tyl went off . . . saw the world.

CHEESBY: Do you want to travel more? We can afford it.

IRVETTE: No . . . I . . . Sheba's not reliable enough with Mother. I couldn't leave her.

CHEESBY: As you like. Shall we sit down, have something to drink?

IRVETTE: We should go to Mass.

CHEESBY: You're tired. We'll sit down.

IRVETTE: I'm not tired.

CHEESBY: We'll sit down, Irvette.

*IRVETTE   RESPONDS   TO   THE   BULLYING.   SHE   AND CHEESBY TAKE A SEAT.*

FIRST CRIPPLE: *(To another)* Did you hear that? She's got lace underwear.

SECOND CRIPPLE: Lace eh?

FIRST CRIPPLE: That's worth bearing in mind.

IRVETTE: Why are there so many cripples here? They surely can't all be *real*, can they?

CHEESBY: I don't know.

IRVETTE: I'm very suspicious of *so* many cripples. Maybe they're breeding somewhere.

SECOND CRIPPLE: *(To First)* She's not bad, actually.

FIRST CRIPPLE: What, lace-draws?

SECOND CRIPPLE: In the right light.

FIRST CRIPPLE: Don't fall in love again. It always ends in tears.

THIRD CRIPPLE: I'm sure she's unhappy. He probably beats her.

FIRST CRIPPLE: Beat her? Never.

*A BEGGAR APPROACHES IRVETTE AND CHEESBY.*

BEGGAR: Charity, masters, charity.

IRVETTE: On your way.

BEGGAR: I've sixteen children to support.

IRVETTE: Where are they?

BEGGAR: Well . . . I . . .

IRVETTE: Come on, show us the children! You haven't got any, have you? This man is an imposter!

BEGGAR: Shut up—

IRVETTE: *(To Cheesby)* You see?

SECOND CRIPPLE: *(Admiring)* What a woman!

*ENTER CRAZYFACE, FOLLOWED BY THE ANGEL, WHO IS READING A NEWSPAPER. SEEING A NEW POTENTIAL SOURCE OF INCOME, THE BEGGAR AND CRIPPLES APPROACH HIM.*

BEGGAR: *(To Crazyface)* Charity, mister?

CRAZYFACE: *(Taking money from the bowl)* Oh, that's very kind of you.

BEGGAR: *(Snatches it back)* I must be losing my touch.

FIRST CRIPPLE: Another new face.

SECOND CRIPPLE: Nice coat.

FIRST CRIPPLE: It is a nice coat.

SECOND CRIPPLE: Wonder who he killed for that.

FIRST CRIPPLE: *I'd* kill for that.

SECOND CRIPPLE: She'd like me in that coat . . .

FIRST CRIPPLE: Oh stop it.

SECOND CRIPPLE: *(To Crazyface)* Hey, you.

CRAZYFACE: What can I do for you?

SECOND CRIPPLE: The coat. How much do you want for it?

CRAZYFACE: It's not for sale. I'm sorry.

*THE ANGEL STEPS IN AND KICKS THE CRIPPLE OVER.*

FIRST CRIPPLE: Who did that?

SECOND CRIPPLE: He did.

FIRST CRIPPLE: Did you kick him over?

CRAZYFACE: No.

FIRST CRIPPLE: Well, if that's not the limit.

*THE CRIPPLES WITHDRAW.*

CRAZYFACE: *(To the Angel)* Do you have to behave like that?

ANGEL: It's my coat. And he had his greasy fingers on it.

CRAZYFACE: It's *not* your coat. It will never *be* your coat.

ANGEL: Give me time.

CRAZYFACE: You're an angel; you've got divine powers.

ANGEL: Thank you.

CRAZYFACE: You walk on rainbows; you juggle stars. And you can't find your own coat?

ANGEL: This is just between you and I: but we're supposed to be clothed only in the glory of our perfection, which in my case wouldn't cover my navel. But if I'm *given* something, a vest, a pair of shoes, a coat, I can wear it. It's a gift, and that's acceptable, you see. All these bits and pieces were given to me by various admirers. The coat would finish the ensemble.

CRAZYFACE: I can see that.

ANGEL: So you'll give it to me?

CRAZYFACE: No.

SECOND CRIPPLE: He's talking to himself.

FIRST CRIPPLE: Lunatic.

SECOND CRIPPLE: He kicked me over. He's probably twisted something.

FIRST CRIPPLE: He'll get his, sooner or later.

IRVETTE: *(To Cheesby)* Don't look now . . .

CHEESBY: What?

IRVETTE: That man who's talking to himself.

CHEESBY: Where?

IRVETTE: There!

CHEESBY: What about him?

IRVETTE: It's my brother-in-law, Tyl. Remember?

CHEESBY: Oh, so it is—

*HE GETS UP TO SPEAK TO CRAZYFACE, BUT IRVETTE CATCHES HOLD OF HIS ARM.*

IRVETTE: *Don't.*

CHEESBY: Why not? Excuse me—

ANGEL: *(To Crazyface)* Well, look who it is. Lenny's ex. Irvette.

CRAZYFACE: *(Hissing at the Angel)* Oh Lord. Please go away.

ANGEL: No, I'm staying to watch the sparks.

CRAZYFACE: Irvette!

IRVETTE: Well . . . isn't this a surprise?

CRAZYFACE: I didn't know I was so near to home.

IRVETTE: You're not. Mr. Cheesby and myself are on a pilgrimage.

CRAZYFACE: Is Mama with you?

IRVETTE: Mama never leaves home now. She's nearly blind.

CHEESBY: *(Cheerily)* Happy though.

CRAZYFACE: Does she ever . . . talk about me . . . at all?

CHEESBY: Yes.

IRVETTE: No. Scarcely ever.

CRAZYFACE: Well, hardly—
IRVETTE: Hardly ever.
CRAZYFACE: And Sheba?
IRVETTE: She lives in your mother's pocket most of the time. She's taken to keeping bees, of all things.
ANGEL: Bees?
CRAZYFACE: Bees?
CHEESBY: Buzz buzz, you know.
CRAZYFACE: And she had her child.
IRVETTE: Oh yes, and he's certainly Lenny's offspring.
CHEESBY: Bit of a tearaway.
IRVETTE: He won't last long.
CHEESBY: What about you? Are you—er—
IRVETTE: Sane?
CRAZYFACE: Absolutely.
ANGEL: What's it to you, you fat bitch?
CRAZYFACE: Ssh!
CHEESBY: Pardon?
IRVETTE: No more angels?
ANGEL: I wouldn't say that.
CRAZYFACE: Oh, I would.
IRVETTE: What?
CRAZYFACE: No more angels.
IRVETTE: You never grew up. That was your problem.
ANGEL: Why don't you spit in her self-satisfied face?
CRAZYFACE: Because I don't want to.
IRVETTE: Grow up?
CRAZYFACE: Spit in your face.
CHEESBY: I should think not.
CRAZYFACE: And . . . I . . . don't see angels any longer. Never. Ever.
ANGEL: Yes you do!
CRAZYFACE: I don't.
CHEESBY: Well, we're glad you don't. Very glad. (To Irvette) He's as mad as ever. (To Crazyface) Well, we must be running along. Busy day . . . lot of shrines to see.
IRVETTE: Damn fool.

*THEY TURN AWAY. THE ANGEL KICKS CHEESBY.*

CHEESBY: (Turning around furious) What are you doing?

CRAZYFACE: Nothing.
CHEESBY: Nobody kicks me, boy.
CRAZYFACE: I didn't kick you.
CHEESBY: You may think being a half-wit allows you get away
    with assaulting people. But I'm not people.
ANGEL: Damn right you're not.
CHEESBY: You want a fight?
ANGEL: Yes!
CRAZYFACE: No!

*THE ANGEL PUSHES HIM INTO CHEESBY.*

CHEESBY: Right! Right!
ANGEL: Go get him, boy!
CRAZYFACE: I'm sorry. I'm very sorry.

*CHEESBY HITS HIM.*

CRAZYFACE: Ah! My nose is bleeding.

*HE PUTS HIS HAND TO HIS NOSE. BLOOD STARTS TO FLOW.*

ANGEL: Go on, hit him back.
CRAZYFACE: No.
ANGEL: He's probably broken your nose.
CRAZYFACE: I won't hit him.
ANGEL: Just a quick one to the balls.

*CRAZYFACE BACKS AWAY. THE ANGEL IS SHADOW-BOXING.*

ANGEL: Follow it up with a quick right. One, two. Get in there.
    Three, four—
CHEESBY: Come here, boy; come and get your punishment.

*CRAZYFACE EXITS.*

CHEESBY: Come back, boy! I haven't finished with you yet. I'm
    going to kick you senseless—
IRVETTE: Not in your new shoes!

*CHEESBY GIVES CHASE. EXITS.*

IRVETTE: That man.

*THE ANGEL CROSSES TO IRVETTE.*

ANGEL: Look at her. Picture of matronly propriety.

*THE ANGEL PUTS ITS HAND ON HER FACE, WHILE MAK-ING THE NOISE OF THE FLY. SHE FLICKS IT AWAY. IT BUZZES BACK ONTO HER FACE, IRRITATING HER. THE ANGEL PASSES ITS HAND ACROSS HER BREAST, STILL IMITATING THE FLY. SHE FLICKS IT AWAY AGAIN.*

*NOW THE FIRST AND SECOND CRIPPLES HAVE STARTED TO TAKE AN INTEREST.*

SECOND CRIPPLE: Got a flea, ma'am?
IRVETTE: *(Firmly)* Go away.
SECOND CRIPPLE: Here it is.

*HE PUTS HIS HAND ON HER THIGH.*

IRVETTE: I have not got a flea. It's a wasp, or something.
SECOND CRIPPLE: Ah, you should be careful. Don't want it get-ting in your lacy underwear, do we?
IRVETTE: What?
FIRST CRIPPLE: That would be a pity.
IRVETTE: Leave me alone.

*THE FLY-GAME HAS GOTTEN WORSE. THE ANGEL HAS STARTED TO DABBLE UNDER IRVETTE'S SKIRT SO SHE'S STARTING TO DO A ST. VITUS' DANCE AS SHE SCRATCHES AND SLAPS AT IMAGINARY INSECTS.*

*THE SECOND CRIPPLE RUMMAGES UNDER HER SKIRTS.*

SECOND CRIPPLE: I've got it.
FIRST CRIPPLE: No . . . me! Me!

*IRVETTE BACKS AWAY.*

IRVETTE: Will you leave me alone?

*THE CRIPPLES FOLLOW HER, AS MENGO AND LA MOTA ENTER. LA MOTA IS MENGO'S HENCHMAN, A THUG WITH A HIGHLY ROUGED FACE.*

*THE TWO NEWCOMERS WATCH AS IRVETTE IS CHASED OFF BY THE CRIPPLES AND THE ANGEL.*

IRVETTE: Oh! Oh! Oh!
MENGO: Must be a public holiday.

*THE PEOPLE WHO ARE LEFT IN THE SPACE START TO WITHDRAW.*

MENGO: How many more gutters do we have to search, La Mota? I begin to think Tyl Eulenspiegel must be dead. If he ever lived. Maybe this is all Alvarez's revenge. Maybe he lied from the grave, just sent us out looking for a shadow. I can't go any further. Find me a seat.

*LA MOTA FINDS A CHAIR FOR MENGO.*

MENGO: And something to eat. Some fruit. Do they have any fruit in this country? Find me something.

*LA MOTA EXITS, AS CRAZYFACE RE-ENTERS. HE HAS A BLOODY NOSE.*

MENGO: You.
CRAZYFACE: Me?
MENGO: A word.
CRAZYFACE: Any one in particular?
MENGO: Clown.
CRAZYFACE: Good word.
MENGO: Seen any?
CRAZYFACE: Words?
MENGO: Clowns.
CRAZYFACE: A few.
MENGO: Locally?

CRAZYFACE: You starting a show?
MENGO: In a way.
CRAZYFACE: I'll volunteer.
MENGO: No, I'm looking for one special performer.
CRAZYFACE: (*Disappointed*) Oh.
MENGO: Maybe you've heard of the Eulenspiegel family.
CRAZYFACE: Eulenspiegel?
MENGO: They're fools.
CRAZYFACE: Yes?
MENGO: Dangerous people.
CRAZYFACE: Oh.
MENGO: Anarchists, murderers, rapists. You know them?
CRAZYFACE: Never heard the name in my life.
MENGO: I'd pay for one in particular. Tyl. Eulenspiegel.
CRAZYFACE: Tyl?
MENGO: Tyl.
CRAZYFACE: Eulenspiegel?
MENGO: Eulenspiegel. Ring a bell?
CRAZYFACE: Is he handsome?
MENGO: Face like a mule's backside.
CRAZYFACE: Who said that?
MENGO: His brother.
CRAZYFACE: Lenny?
MENGO: (*Rising*) You do know him.
CRAZYFACE: No!
MENGO: But you know his brother?
CRAZYFACE: Everyone knows Lenny. He's notorious.
MENGO: Really?
CRAZYFACE: Really!
MENGO: La Mota!
CRAZYFACE: Well, I have to go.
MENGO: *La Mota*!
CRAZYFACE: It's been nice meeting you.

*ENTER CHEESBY.*

CHEESBY: So!
CRAZYFACE: Shit!
CHEESBY: Come here!
MENGO: You know this individual?

CHEESBY: Yes.
MENGO: What's his name?
CHEESBY: Eulenspiegel.
MENGO: Hold him! Hold him! La Mota!

*MENGO EXITS, SHOUTING FOR ASSISTANCE. CHEESBY RUNS AT CRAZYFACE, WHO PUNCHES HIM. CHEESBY FALLS OVER.*

*CRAZYFACE TRIES TO EXIT, BUT RUNS STRAIGHT INTO IRVETTE, WHO GRABS HOLD OF HIS ARM.*

IRVETTE: Tyl! Tyl! I've just been attacked.
CRAZYFACE: I can't . . . talk right now.
IRVETTE: I was stripped, Tyl. By cripples.
CRAZYFACE: Cripples, eh?
IRVETTE: What's your hurry?
CHEESBY: Hold on to him!

*CRAZYFACE BITES IRVETTE'S HAND.*

CRAZYFACE: Sorry. I have to go.

*HE AGAIN TRIES TO EXIT, BUT THIS TIME THE ANGEL'S BLOCKING THE WAY. CRAZYFACE TURNS ROUND, AND THE ANGEL TRIPS HIM UP, JUST AS LA MOTA AND MENGO RE-ENTER.*

ANGEL: You should have given me the coat.
CRAZYFACE: Bastard!
MENGO: Secure him.

*LA MOTA PUTS A COLLAR AROUND CRAZYFACE'S NECK, WITH A CHAIN ON IT. CHEESBY AND IRVETTE WATCH, FASCINATED.*

MENGO: Good. *(To Cheesby)* Do you know this man?
CHEESBY: Oh no. Never seen him before in my life.
MENGO: *(To Irvette)* And you?
IRVETTE: Perish the thought.

*IRVETTE AND CHEESBY EXIT. AS CRAZYFACE IS TAKEN AWAY, THE ANGEL PLAYS THE FLY-GAME, MAKING A BUZZING SOUND AND FOLLOWING AN IMAGINARY INSECT, UNTIL IT LANDS ON HIS HAND, THEN KILLING IT WITH A SHARP SLAP.*

ANGEL: Poor fly.

*LIGHTS OUT.*

# Scene Four

## A prison

*FROM BENEATH, THE NOISE OF HOWLING PRISONERS. IT'S VERY DARK. JUST A FEW LIGHTS STAB THE GLOOM. IN ONE OF THEM SIT TWO OF THE THREE PULCINELLAS. THEY ARE ATTEMPTING TO KNOT NOOSES, BUT FAILING.*

*ENTER THIRD PULCINELLA, WITH CRAZYFACE. HE IS FLUNG DOWN, UNCONSCIOUS, OR NEAR TO IT. THE PULCINELLA SLAPS HIM ROUND.*

PULCINELLA: Wake up! Wake up!
CRAZYFACE: (*Wakes*) Don't whip me anymore. I don't know anything. I never opened the box. I carried it, but I never opened it.
PULCINELLA: We believe you! Stop whining. (*Gets out handkerchief, spits in it, cleans Crazyface's face, for all the world like a loving parent*)
CRAZYFACE: What's that noise?

PULCINELLA: Oh . . . that's Mengo's special prisoners. Either that or they're cooking lobster.

CRAZYFACE: Will they put me down there?

PULCINELLA: No. You're getting executed.

CRAZYFACE: I am?

PULCINELLA: You are.

CRAZYFACE: Hanged?

PULCINELLA: (*Laughs to other Pulcinellas*) He thinks he's getting hanged.

*THE PULCINELLAS GIGGLE.*

CRAZYFACE: Why else make nooses?

PULCINELLA: You're going to be pulled apart. By horses. By four horses. It takes hours and hours. All day sometimes. It'll turn your hair white. Sometimes the limbs don't come off: then we have to hack . . .

FIRST PULCINELLA: Hack . . .

SECOND PULCINELLA: . . . and chop . . .

PULCINELLA: . . . and chop, until we get a good tear going. 'Course, we seal up the cuts with molten lead, just so you don't bleed to death. That wouldn't do at all, now would it? Nice coat. Want to sell me the coat?

CRAZYFACE: No.

PULCINELLA: Just asking.

*THE PULCINELLA CROSSES TO HIS COMPANION, AND STARTS WORK ON ANOTHER NOOSE. ENTER THE ANGEL.*

ANGEL: Did I hear someone talking about a coat?

CRAZYFACE: How did I get into this mess?

ANGEL: You're a fool.

CRAZYFACE: I haven't done anything to deserve it, have I? How can God intend me to be torn apart by horses for a crime I haven't even committed?

ANGEL: Well, it depends on your definition of crime, of course. The first crime may have been your mother's.

CRAZYFACE: My mother's?

ANGEL: Having you out of wedlock; and then letting you live when you were clearly an idiot as well as a bastard. Might have been simpler all round if she'd taken you up a hill and left you to the hawks.

CRAZYFACE: I'm not an idiot.

ANGEL: Of course you're an idiot; your father was an idiot, and his father's father before him.

CRAZYFACE: You know my father?

ANGEL: Maybe I do. Maybe I don't.

CRAZYFACE: Is he alive?

ANGEL: That would be telling.

CRAZYFACE: Could you . . . would you . . .

ANGEL: Spit it out. I can only refuse.

CRAZYFACE: Would you get a message to my mother? Tell her where I am. Tell her that I've been tried and convicted of treason, and murder, and God knows—sorry—who knows what else.

ANGEL: Your mother's too old and too blind to help you now.

CRAZYFACE: Annie maybe. What about Annie?

ANGEL: Don't talk to me about that one.

CRAZYFACE: Why not?

ANGEL: Just don't. Interfering bitch.

CRAZYFACE: What do you know about Annie? Come on. Tell me.

ANGEL: She's flown in the face of the Church, let me tell you that. She's wheedled, she's bribed, she's connived. I don't think it's funny . . .

CRAZYFACE: What's funny?

ANGEL: Anyway, the robes don't suit her.

CRAZYFACE: What are you talking about?

*THE ANGEL IS GETTING OUT ITS PACK OF CARDS.*

ANGEL: She'll get found out, you'll see. She'll lose her head, just like you. How about playing for the coat? What have you got to lose? I can take it afterwards, but it's going to be bloody.

CRAZYFACE: You won't help me, why should I help you?

*THE ANGEL KICKS HIM.*

ANGEL: Where does it hurt?

CRAZYFACE: There!

ANGEL: (*Kicks again*) There? Pity! And there! Oh dear! You know

what I might do, Crazyface? I might take your head, when it's off, take it home to your mother. I might just do that. *(Kicks again)*
CRAZYFACE: Ah!
ANGEL: Sweet dreams.

*THE ANGEL EXITS.*

CRAZYFACE: I begin to see: angels are the problem. This world would be a fine world without angels.

*THE ANGEL RE-ENTERS.*

ANGEL: *(Kicks him)* I heard that.
CRAZYFACE: You were meant to.

*THE ANGEL EXITS.*

PULCINELLA: Do you always talk to yourself?
CRAZYFACE: What's it to you?
PULCINELLA: I'm writing a book of famous last words. What people say when they're about to die.
CRAZYFACE: Don't worry, I'll give you something memorable.

*ENTER MENGO.*

MENGO: Eulenspiegel.
CRAZYFACE: *(Cowering)* Oh no. Don't hurt me.
MENGO: The beatings are over for now. It's too late at night. *(He sits beside Crazyface)* If you told a single person about what you carried, we'll find them sooner or later. You do know that, don't you? Even if we have to raise all the dead in Christendom to point them out.
CRAZYFACE: You're not raising me. When I'm dead, I'm dead.
MENGO: Don't you believe it. A fool like you, you've got no power, alive or dead. *(A pause)* Well, I came to tell you you've been reprieved.
CRAZYFACE: Reprieved?
MENGO: You're not going to be torn apart by horses. We can't find any horses. They've apparently all been eaten. And if we

did it with dogs it would take forever. So . . . we're going to hang you. Simple as that.

CRAZYFACE: Thank you. (*Pause*) I always wondered what a reprieve was.

MENGO: Don't look so miserable. It's very quick. There are much worse ways to die . . . your brother, for instance . . .

CRAZYFACE: Lenny's here?

MENGO: Oh yes, Lenny's here. On a great wheel. You want to see?

*CRAZYFACE SHAKES HIS HEAD.*

MENGO: Of course you want to see . . . (*He goes to a hole in the ground, out of which smoke drifts. Howls greet the appearance of Mengo's face*) Come on.

*CRAZYFACE CRAWLS TO THE EDGE OF THE HOLE. FROM BELOW, LENNY'S VOICE SCREECHING.*

LENNY: (*From below*) I see you!

*CRAZYFACE LOOKS AWAY, COVERING HIS EARS.*

MENGO: What did I tell you? There are worse ways to die. Oh . . . (*He reaches into his pocket, and takes out some chocolate*) . . . for you.

CRAZYFACE: Poison?

MENGO: Chocolate. You may as well know what you're dying for. (*Crazyface tastes it*) It's good, eh?

CRAZYFACE: (*Smiles*) Yummy.

MENGO: Don't smile at me.

CRAZYFACE: Why not?

MENGO: Just don't. (*Mengo crosses to Pulcinellas*) Find a bag and put it over his head when you hang him, hear? I don't want him smiling at me.

FIRST PULCINELLA: Yes sir.

*MENGO EXITS. THE PULCINELLAS RUSH ACROSS AND STEAL THE CHOCOLATE FROM CRAZYFACE BEFORE HE CAN EAT THE REST OF IT. HE TRIES TO PUT UP A FIGHT, BUT HE'S OUTNUMBERED.*

CRAZYFACE: That was mine.

PULCINELLA: Just lie down and go to sleep.

CRAZYFACE: Don't wake me too early.

FIRST PULCINELLA: We're hanging you at dawn. That's another hour.

CRAZYFACE: I can't do much in an hour.

SECOND PULCINELLA: You could make love three or four times.

THIRD PULCINELLA: Five or six if she's ugly.

CRAZYFACE: I wouldn't know. I never did it.

FIRST PULCINELLA: Really? Oh, he's going to die a virgin. That doesn't seem fair . . .

*GIGGLING, THEY EXIT. FROM UNDER THE GROUND, LENNY'S VOICE.*

LENNY: Crazyface?

CRAZYFACE: *(Wakes)* Um?

LENNY: Your hear me, brother?

CRAZYFACE: Yes . . . yes . . .

LENNY: You see me?

CRAZYFACE: I see you.

LENNY: I'm never going to let you go. I'll find your grave and dig it up and throw your bones to the dogs. Do you hear me?

CRAZYFACE: Why?

LENNY: Because I hate you. I always hated you.

CRAZYFACE: What did I ever do—

LENNY: I hate you to the ends of the earth! You and all your *angels!*

CRAZYFACE: Hm. So there's a thing.

*CRAZYFACE GOES BACK TO SLEEP. SUDDENLY, THE PUL-CINELLAS COME BACK WITH THE OLD CLOWN, IN DRAG.*

FIRST PULCINELLA: A woman!

SECOND PULCINELLA: You must have a woman at least once.

*CRAZYFACE SITS UP.*

CRAZYFACE: This isn't a woman.

FIRST PULCINELLA: It's the best we could get you at this short notice.

SECOND PULCINELLA: Go on, give her a kiss.

*THE OLD CLOWN SITS ON THE BENCH THE PULCINEL-LAS WERE ON, AND A STAGE PARODY OF A COURTSHIP TAKES PLACE. CRAZYFACE SITS BESIDE HIM, AND THE PULCINELLAS TIPTOE AWAY LIKE GROTESQUE CUPIDS.*

*THE OLD CLOWN GIVES A BIG SIGH. CRAZYFACE GRINS AT HIM. THE OLD CLOWN GETS UP AND DOES A PIROU-ETTE AND A SOFT-SHOE SHUFFLE. CRAZYFACE LAUGHS. THE OLD CLOWN JUGGLES, AND THROWS THE BALLS TO CRAZYFACE, WHO ALSO JUGGLES, LAUGHING AS HE DOES SO. SUDDENLY THE OLD CLOWN IS DRAGGED AWAY BY THE PULCINELLAS, QUIETLY BEHIND CRAZY-FACE'S BACK. CRAZYFACE IS LEFT JUGGLING, AND SMIL-ING, AND THINKING.*

*SOMEWHERE A BELL TOLLS. THERE IS UTTER SILENCE EXCEPT FOR THE BELL. CRAZYFACE JUGGLES. THE PUL-CINELLAS COME TO HIM.*

PULCINELLA: How was that?

CRAZYFACE: Wonderful.

PULCINELLA: Didn't take too long, did it?

CRAZYFACE: No . . .

PULCINELLA: Now it's time for us to dress. Say your prayers. I think I hear the dawn chorus . . .

*THE PULCINELLAS EXIT. CRAZYFACE STILL JUGGLES.*

CRAZYFACE: Oh well. I like life, but not that much. It's all right really, not to be. Don't you think, Angel? Angel? (*Silence*) Don't tell me you've deserted me, just when I was about to give you a little token of my esteem.

*ANGEL APPEARS.*

ANGEL: Token . . . of esteem?

CRAZYFACE: For your many favors.

ANGEL: The coat?

CRAZYFACE: Don't you want it anymore?

ANGEL: I've followed you across Europe for that coat: of course I want it.

CRAZYFACE: You won't misuse it? You won't get it dirty?

ANGEL: I promise.

CRAZYFACE: You won't throw it in a puddle so some woman doesn't get her feet wet?

ANGEL: Perish the thought.

*A HAMMERING OFF-STAGE.*

CRAZYFACE: What's that?

ANGEL: Final adjustments to the gallows.

CRAZYFACE: How long?

ANGEL: A minute. Maybe a little more. The sun's just beginning to peep over the hills. It's going to be a glorious day.

CRAZYFACE: Yes it is. Are you visible at the moment, to the world at large?

ANGEL: Why?

CRAZYFACE: To show off the coat.

ANGEL: Oh yes, the world can see me.

CRAZYFACE: Good. (*He takes it off. The hammering multiplies. It becomes the noise of Crazyface's heart, a double beat*) Isn't that my heart beating?

ANGEL: (*Putting on the coat*) Not for much longer. Oh, it's so fine.

CRAZYFACE: Face the sun, it catches the light better.

*THE ANGEL STANDS WITH HIS BACK TO THE ENTRANCE TO THE CELL. CRAZYFACE BACKS AWAY. THE ANGEL IS IN A REVERIE. HE DOESN'T HEAR THE HAMMERING TAKE ON YET A MORE COMPLEX RHYTHM, AS THE THREE PULCINELLAS, ONE AS A PRIEST, WITH OPEN BIBLE, SAYING A PRAYER IN LATIN, ONE WITH A ROPE FOR THE HANDS OF THE PRISONER, ONE WITH A BLACK DRAW-STRING BAG FOR HIS HEAD, ENTER FROM BEHIND. CRAZYFACE IS OUT OF SIGHT UNDER THE BENCH. THE BAG GOES OVER THE ANGEL'S HEAD.*

ANGEL: What's going on? (*The Angel's hands are wrenched behind its back, and it is hauled away.*) No! No! There's been a mistake! No! No!

*THE DRUMMING IS A DEEPENING TATTOO. UNDER THE BENCH, CRAZYFACE IS SHAKING WITH TERROR. IT REACHES A CLIMAX. SUDDEN SILENCE. THE SOUND OF A ROPE CREAKING.*

CRAZYFACE: I just killed an angel.

*ENTER MENGO WITH THE THREE PULCINELLAS.*

FIRST PULCINELLA: Not a very good death.
SECOND PULCINELLA: A whole lot of complaining.
THIRD PULCINELLA: And kicking.

*MENGO LOOKS DOWN INTO THE DEPTHS.*

MENGO: Your brother's dead Lenny, hear me? Hanged by the neck. And it's a beautiful day. Not that you'll see it. But beautiful. A breath of spring in the air. Here . . . (*He drops chocolate down*) Chocolate for you.

*THE PULCINELLAS PEER GREEDILY THROUGH THE GRATING AFTER THE CHOCOLATE. MENGO GOES TO SIT ON THE BENCH UNDER WHICH CRAZYFACE IS HIDING.*

MENGO: Who else is to be executed today?
FIRST PULCINELLA: One or two clowns.
MENGO: Well, you'd better get on with it. Cut Eulenspiegel's corpse down. The King may want to see the body, and if we leave it up there the birds'll get at it.

*THE PULCINELLAS HURRY OFF.*

MENGO: Shall we hang you too, Lenny?
LENNY: Yes please.
MENGO: You'd like to die?
LENNY: Yes! Yes!

MENGO: Maybe we will. Just to make you happy. Shall we pray?

*MENGO FALLS TO HIS KNEES AND PUTS HIS HANDS TOGETHER TO PRAY.*

MENGO: I used to pray a great deal. Little things. A new mistress, a favor from the King. They usually came, too. And chocolate, I thanked God in Heaven for chocolate. It must be God-given, surely. So little a seed, so great a power. That sort of paradox takes genius. Either that or insanity. Maybe we worship a mad God, Lenny, have you thought of that? Our lunatic, who art in heaven—

*ENTER THE THREE PULCINELLAS. THEY ARE TERRIFIED. NONE OF THEM WANTS TO BE THE ONE TO CARRY THE BAD NEWS. THEY PUSH EACH OTHER FORWARD.*

MENGO: Why am I interrupted at my prayers?
FIRST PULCINELLA: I . . . we . . . that is . . .
MENGO: What?
THIRD PULCINELLA: . . . the body . . . we took . . . we took . . .
MENGO: Took down.
SECOND PULCINELLA: The body of . . .
FIRST PULCINELLA: Of . . .
THIRD PULCINELLA: Of . . .
MENGO: Tyl Eulenspiegel.

*THEY SHAKE THEIR HEADS.*

MENGO: Not Tyl Eulenspiegel?

*THEY SHAKE THEIR HEADS AGAIN.*

MENGO: It must be him.

*THEY SHAKE THEIR HEADS.*

MENGO: Let me see! Let me see!

*EXIT MENGO, FOLLOWED BY PULCINELLAS. CRAZYFACE*

*CRAWLS OUT FROM UNDER THE BENCH. HE CROSSES TO THE GRATING, AND OPENS IT, THEN EXITS AS MENGO YELLS OFF-STAGE.*

MENGO: *Find him!*

*THE PULCINELLAS ENTER, BUT THEY HAVE MULTIPLIED. THERE ARE TEN NOW, OR MORE, ALL IDENTICAL. THEY SWARM OVER THE STAGE, ARMED WITH ABSURD AND DISTURBING WEAPONS. ENTER MENGO.*

MENGO: Find him! Find him!

*THE PULCINELLAS DISPERSE.*

MENGO: *(Alone)* He's gone, hasn't he? *(Looks up at heaven, and yells)* HASN'T HE? Run then, Eulenspiegel, run as fast as you can. You're alive and I'm dead. You're the genius, I'm the fool. I concede the point. Bastard. *(Mengo is aware of something behind him. Lenny is out)* Ah.
LENNY: Somebody set me free.
MENGO: More fool them.
LENNY: I think it was my brother. He was always sentimental. Are you afraid?
MENGO: No. You won't harm me. You recognize the wisdom of punishment. I did what any master would do to his dog. Beat it for its errors.

*LENNY DRAGS MENGO TO THE BOWL OF CHOCOLATE. HE PUTS HIS HAND IN AND TAKES OUT A HANDFUL OF PASTE.*

LENNY: Eat.
MENGO: Thank you, no.

*LENNY FORCES THE CHOCOLATE INTO MENGO'S MOUTH.*

LENNY: Eat!

*HE FORCES ANOTHER HANDFUL. MENGO TRIES TO RESIST, BUT LENNY IS STRONGER.*

LENNY: Eat! Eat! Eat! *(Mengo chokes)* Eat! Eat! Eat!

*MORE CHOCOLATE. AND MORE. AND MORE. MENGO COLLAPSES, CHOKING. HE DIES. LENNY STANDS OVER HIM, BREATHING HARD. IT'S BEEN AN EXHILARATING EXPERIENCE FOR HIM. HIS EYES GLITTER.*

*HE LICKS HIS HAND, AS THE PULCINELLAS COME IN AND CLEAN UP, TAKING THE MESS AWAY.*

LENNY: Beautiful. *(To the deceased Mengo)* Will you excuse me? I hear my brother calling.

*HE EXITS.*

# Scene Five

## The road to Rome

*AN EMPTY ROAD, THE WIND WHISTLES. THE STARS SHINE. ENTER CRAZYFACE. HE LOOKS UP AT THE STARS.*

CRAZYFACE: Orion . . . the Pole Star . . . the Great Bear, Ursa Major . . .

*ENTER ALVIN, WITH A MAP. IT HAS HOLES SHOT IN IT, AND IT'S BLOOD-STAINED.*

ALVIN: I say . . . peasant chappie.
CRAZYFACE: Ssh! I'm star-watching. You'll scare them away.

ALVIN: Huh?

CRAZYFACE: The stars.

ALVIN: Oh. *(Whisper)* I wonder, any idea where we are?

CRAZYFACE: The road to Rome.

ALVIN: Rome? Oh hell, I'm way off the mark. I want to get back
to the coast. Don't I know you from somewhere?

CRAZYFACE: Maybe.

ALVIN: Italian, are you?

CRAZYFACE: No.

ALVIN: Why are you going to Rome then?

CRAZYFACE: I murdered an angel.

ALVIN: You had a horse. Am I right?

CRAZYFACE: That's right. You tried to eat it.

ALVIN: Damned uncivilized. Apologies.

CRAZYFACE: Accepted.

ALVIN: Nothing personal. Well, there's nothing more to be done
here. We should have mounted a full-scale suppression . . .
that would have sweated out our little secret.

CRAZYFACE: Oh, you mean this . . .

*CRAZYFACE PRODUCES A BOX FROM HIS BAG. HE GOES
BACK TO STAR-GAZING.*

ALVIN: My God!

CRAZYFACE: Signor Alvarez asked me to give it to you. Said it
contained something of interest.

ALVIN: Why didn't you pass it over earlier?

CRAZYFACE: Forgot.

ALVIN: You'll want paying.

CRAZYFACE: I wouldn't think of it.

ALVIN: Damned decent of you. *(Pumps Crazyface's hand)*

CRAZYFACE: My pleasure.

*ALVIN EXITS.*

CRAZYFACE: Lovely night.

*ENTER ALLEGRO.*

ALLEGRO: Ah, you are a fellow romantic.

CRAZYFACE: Are there holes in heaven, do you think? Is that where the rain comes through?

ALLEGRO: *(Looking up)* My Mama used to say one star burned for every dead soul.

CRAZYFACE: Oh yes; I heard that. I suppose you've come for the box? Signor Alvarez asked me to give it to you—said it contained something of interest. *(He gets an identical box out of his bag)*

ALLEGRO: *Mon Dieu!*

CRAZYFACE: For you.

ALLEGRO: *Mon brave. (Kisses him on both cheeks)* A hero! A hero!

CRAZYFACE: Just trying to be useful.

*EXIT ALLEGRO. ALFONSO ENTERS. NO BABY.*

ALFONSO: Who was that?

CRAZYFACE: The Frenchman.

ALFONSO: I wanted to say Ciao.

CRAZYFACE: Going home?

ALFONSO: Si.

CRAZYFACE: And the tortoise?

ALFONSO: Ate it.

CRAZYFACE: Don't go empty-handed.

*HE PRODUCES THE BOX.*

CRAZYFACE: For the bambinos, from Alvarez!

ALFONSO: Do you know what you're giving away?

CRAZYFACE: It's nothing. Really.

ALFONSO: Italy thanks you—

*ALFONSO EMBRACES CRAZYFACE.*

ALFONSO: —A thousand times.

CRAZYFACE: Once is fine.

*ALFONSO EXITS.*

CRAZYFACE: I made the boxes myself. As a joke. They contain rat turds.

*HE BACKS INTO THE DARKNESS AND THE TRIO RE-ENTER FROM DIFFERENT DIRECTIONS, ALL JUBILANT.*

ALLEGRO: Well!
ALVIN: Well!
ALFONSO: Well!
ALVIN: Nice to see you—
ALFONSO: Before I go—
ALLEGRO: A fond farewell—
ALVIN: I had to say—
ALFONSO: Bad luck.
ALLEGRO: Commiserations.
ALVIN: Better luck next time.
ALLEGRO: Wait! Wait! We can't all be winners.
ALVIN: Well, it's good to take it so well.
ALFONSO: No, the pleasure's mine.
ALLEGRO: Mine, I think.
ALVIN: Wrong!
ALFONSO: Wrong!
ALLEGRO: Wrong!

*THEY ALL PRODUCE THEIR BOXES AT THE SAME TIME. THEY FREEZE; STARING AT THE OTHERS. THEN, SLOW, LIZARD-LIKE HAND MOVEMENTS, AS THEY SILENTLY ACCUSE EACH OTHER. THEY DROP THEIR BOXES, AND TAKE OUT THEIR KNIVES.*

ALVIN: Nobody makes a fool of me.
ALFONSO: Thought you'd send me home with an empty box.
ALLEGRO: Put that worm of a peasant up to it, did you!

*ALL THREE CLOSE IN AT ONCE, STABBING EACH OTHER FURIOUSLY.*

ALL THREE: Ah!

*THEY STAGGER OUT OF A KNOT, SCRABBLING AT THEIR WOUNDS. DROPPING THEIR KNIVES, THEY FALL TO THEIR KNEES. THE LIGHTS DARKEN. SOMEWHERE, A DOG HOWLS. A BEAT.*

ALVIN: Well . . .
ALFONSO: Well . . .
ALLEGRO: Well . . .

*ANOTHER BEAT.*

ALVIN: Are we . . . are we dead, do you suppose?
ALLEGRO: I think so. I took a wound to the heart, one to the liver.
ALVIN: I got it in the lung. Quite deflated me.
ALFONSO: Ah! My bambinos.
ALVIN: You won't be seeing them again, chum.
ALLEGRO: I didn't say my confession.
ALVIN: Wouldn't have made much difference.
ALLEGRO: *(Getting up)* We'd better . . . *(Helping Alfonso up)* We'd better get going.
ALFONSO: Home?
ALLEGRO: Hell.

*THEY HAVE ALL STOOD UP.*

ALVIN: Isn't somebody going to come and usher us along?
ALFONSO: Maybe they've missed the turning.
ALLEGRO: Well, we can't stay here all night. Waiting.
ALVIN: Oh, this is a bit of a poor do. I mean here we are in the middle of nowhere . . . dead, and nobody says a dickey-bird.
ALFONSO: Maybe this *is* Hell.
ALVIN: Oh, don't be ridiculous.

*A BEAT. IT'S ALMOST COMPLETELY BLACK.*

ALLEGRO: Well, someone should lead.
ALVIN: Don't ask me.
ALFONSO: Maybe if we get hold of each other's sleeve. That way we won't get lost.
ALVIN: We're already lost.
ALFONSO: But at least we're all lost together.
ALVIN: That's small comfort.
ALLEGRO: All right . . . I'm going. Are you hanging on?
ALVIN: Rather.

ALLEGRO: If anyone sees a signpost, holler.
ALFONSO: Ah, my bambinos.
ALVIN: Oh, don't start that again . . .

*THEY STUMBLE OFF.*

*CRAZYFACE STEPS OUT OF HIDING. HE WATCHES THEM GO . . .*

*THEN LOOKS UP. THE STARS HAVE GONE OUT.*

CRAZYFACE: There are no stars in Hell.

# Scene Six

## The Vatican

*CANDLES GLOW IN THE DARKNESS. THE SOUND OF A DISTANT CHOIR. AN ATMOSPHERE OF REVERENCE, SUB-DUED AND SLIGHTLY EERIE.*

*ENTER TWO CARDINALS, FROM OPPOSITE SIDES. THE SEC-OND CARDINAL TRIES TO AVOID THE FIRST CARDINAL.*

FIRST CARDINAL: Pius?
SECOND CARDINAL: *(Mock surprise)* Oh!
FIRST CARDINAL: A word.
SECOND CARDINAL: I'm in a real rush.
FIRST CARDINAL: Won't keep you more than a moment. It's just that there's delegations downstairs, they've been waiting days for an audience with His Holiness.
SECOND CARDINAL: He knows. He knows.

FIRST CARDINAL: This is no way to make friends. Is he even awake yet?

SECOND CARDINAL: He's shaving.

FIRST CARDINAL: He takes so long to get dressed. Half the day's gone.

THIRD CARDINAL: He refuses help.

FIRST CARDINAL: I'd heard he had catamites.

SECOND CARDINAL: Ssh!

FIRST CARDINAL: Couple of real pretty boys.

SECOND CARDINAL: I couldn't say, I'm sure. *(Tries to break away)* I really must dash. I've a dozen things to do.

FIRST CARDINAL: Do you smell something?

SECOND CARDINAL: *(Sniffs)* Incense. Sweet.

FIRST CARDINAL: Something else. Must be my nose. My nose just runs and runs. As soon as they start raising their voices downstairs, it turns on like a tap.

SECOND CARDINAL: Dear oh dear.

*OFF-STAGE, SHOUTING.*

FIRST CARDINAL: There they go again. Wild beasts!

*EXIT FIRST CARDINAL. ENTER CRAZYFACE.*

CRAZYFACE: Psst!

SECOND CARDINAL: Huh?

CRAZYFACE: *(Stepping into the Cardinal's view)* Excuse me.

SECOND CARDINAL: Who the hell are you, my son?

CRAZYFACE: I've got to see the Pope.

SECOND CARDINAL: Join the queue. By Christ, you stink!

CRAZYFACE: It's urgent. I'm in peril of my soul.

SECOND CARDINAL: What's your sin?

CRAZYFACE: Murder.

SECOND CARDINAL: Well, there's nothing unusual in that. So on your way. The Pope sees nobody.

CRAZYFACE: He has to see me. He has to.

SECOND CARDINAL: How did you get in here?

CRAZYFACE: I came in through the sewer.

SECOND CARDINAL: You're not an assassin, are you?

CRAZYFACE: Do I look like an assassin?

SECOND CARDINAL: Frankly, you look like a fool covered in shit. Which is bad news for you, because His Holiness hates fools. He has something against them. Somebody told me he had a very bad experience with a fool in his early years. Look, why don't you go home? Where is home?

CRAZYFACE: A long way off. The Lowlands.

SECOND CARDINAL: Oh, I went there. It rained solidly every day for three weeks. Brother Julian and I practically grew webbed feet.

CRAZYFACE: Anyway, I can't go home 'til I've been forgiven.

SECOND CARDINAL: Murder's an easy sin. Was it in self-defense?

CRAZYFACE: Sort of.

SECOND CARDINAL: Easier still. I can confess you myself. Come to my room. Let me give you a bath. You can have a lie-down. Then we'll do a bit of confessing together . . .

CRAZYFACE: Really? That's very good of you.

SECOND CARDINAL: It's my pleasure.

CRAZYFACE: And it doesn't make any difference if I killed an angel?

SECOND CARDINAL: An angel?

CRAZYFACE: Yes. It was all I could do, under the circumstances.

SECOND CARDINAL: What sort of angel?

CRAZYFACE: Just the common or garden variety.

SECOND CARDINAL: You're out of your mind. You haven't seen any angels.

*ENTER LENNY.*

LENNY: That's right. You tell him. He doesn't see angels!

CRAZYFACE: Lenny.

SECOND CARDINAL: Who the hell are you?

LENNY: His brother.

SECOND CARDINAL: And what sin are you here to have forgiven?

CRAZYFACE: Oh, there are too many. Murder, Treason, Rape, Adultery, Sodomy—

SECOND CARDINAL: Well, well. Who's been a busy boy?

*LENNY GRABS HOLD OF THE CARDINAL.*

SECOND CARDINAL: Joke, joke.

LENNY: Why don't you leave us loving brothers together awhile?

SECOND CARDINAL: Yes . . . please.

LENNY: You can stop by later and sweep up the pieces.

*THE CARDINAL EXITS, AT A RUN.*

LENNY: Alone at last.

CRAZYFACE: I haven't got any secrets left.

LENNY: Oh yes you have.

CRAZYFACE: You took my box.

LENNY: I thought I'd taken more than that. *(He takes out a knife)*

CRAZYFACE: Why can't we just go our ways?

LENNY: The world isn't big enough for the two of us.

CRAZYFACE: I'll go to China.

LENNY: I'd still smell you. Brother.

CRAZYFACE: I never did you any harm.

LENNY: You're stupid, you know that? You've always been stupid. The runt of the litter. But you saw angels.

CRAZYFACE: I didn't want to.

LENNY: When you were three or four, you'd point up into the air as if there were butterflies over your cot, when there was nothing. Me? I wanted to see angels. I cursed. I prayed. I even committed murder to make them come and fetch me. But I saw nothing. That wasn't fair, Tyl. I went into the world, and I talked too loudly, and I made too many enemies and they put me on a great wheel. Day and night, sometimes in ice, sometimes in fire. And still, even though I was teetering on the brink of death, nothing.

CRAZYFACE: You believe me then.

LENNY: I've always believed you. I'm the only one who ever has.

*HE ATTACKS CRAZYFACE WITH THE KNIFE. CRAZYFACE AVOIDS THE STROKE.*

CRAZYFACE: No Lenny!

LENNY: Make them come.

CRAZYFACE: It's too late!

LENNY: Make them come, Crazyface! Make them show themselves to *me*.

CRAZYFACE: The angel's dead. It was hanged.

LENNY: Angels never die! But you will!

*HE RUNS AT CRAZYFACE. THERE'S A BRIEF, CONFUSING STRUGGLE. LENNY IS IMPALED ON HIS OWN KNIFE.*

LENNY: Ah!
CRAZYFACE: No!

*LENNY COLLAPSES IN CRAZYFACE'S ARMS.*

LENNY: I'm a damned fool.

*HE DIES.*

CRAZYFACE: *(Crying out)* Lenny!

*ENTER ONE CARDINAL FROM ONE SIDE, THE OTHER CARDINAL FROM ANOTHER.*

SECOND CARDINAL: You killed him?
CRAZYFACE: No!
SECOND CARDINAL: Your own brother.
CRAZYFACE: It was an accident.
FIRST CARDINAL: Fratricide? In the Vatican? This is unforgivable!
SECOND CARDINAL: Fetch help.

*EXIT FIRST CARDINAL, SHOUTING FOR HELP.*

SECOND CARDINAL: You're dead now: you know that? To do that *here*. That's unforgiveable. This is the nearest spot to Heaven—

*ENTER TWO CATAMITES (WOMEN, IN FACT, AMBIGU-OUSLY DRESSED). BOTH HAVE DRAWN SWORDS. THE FIRST CARDINAL IS WITH THEM.*

FIRST CARDINAL: This is the assassin!

*THE CATAMITES DRAG CRAZYFACE AWAY FROM THE BODY, AND KNEEL HIM DOWN.*

FIRST CARDINAL: Do it quickly—
SECOND CARDINAL: Quickly—

FIRST CARDINAL: If His Holiness finds out—

*ONE OF THE CATAMITES PUSHES CRAZYFACE'S HEAD DOWN, AND EXPOSES HIS NECK, TO LOP OFF HIS HEAD. THE SWORD IS ABOUT TO FALL. ENTER THE POPE.*

POPE: *Stop!*

*THE POPE IS IN FACT ANNIE, BUT SHE'S UNRECOGNIZ-ABLE. HER FACE IS COVERED IN SHAVING SOAP. SHE WEARS HEAVY GLASSES (AND AN EYE-PATCH). HER HAIR IS COVERED WITH A CAP.*

SECOND CARDINAL: His Holiness.

*THEY ARE ALL ON THEIR KNEES. CRAZYFACE HAS SCARCELY NOTICED THE ENTRANCE OF THE POPE. HE HAS HIS BACK TO HIS (HER) HOLINESS.*

FIRST CARDINAL: This man broke into the Vatican . . . he's killed
     a man . . .
SECOND CARDINAL: His own brother.
FIRST CARDINAL: Shall we have him executed?
FIRST CARDINAL: Bow to His Holiness.
CRAZYFACE: What?
SECOND CARDINAL: The Pope.
CRAZYFACE: Oh.

*CRAZYFACE LOOKS UP AT HIS HOLINESS. ANNIE RECOG-NIZES HIM. A LONG SILENCE.*

ANNIE: Leave.
FIRST CARDINAL: The man's dangerous, Your Holiness.
ANNIE: *Leave! All of you!*

*THE CARDINALS EXIT. THE CATAMITES ARE ALSO DIS-MISSED. THE POPE SNAPS HER FINGERS AND BRINGS ONE OF THEM BACK, TAKING A TOWEL FROM THE CATAMITE'S SHOULDER.*

*THE POPE AND CRAZYFACE LOOK AT ONE ANOTHER, LONG AND HARD. THE POPE CROSSES TO LENNY AND KICKS OVER THE CORPSE TO SEE HIS FACE.*

*THEN SHE CLEANS THE SOAP OFF HER FACE, SLOWLY TAKES OFF THE GLASSES, AND FINALLY REMOVES THE CAP. LONG HAIR TUMBLES ONTO HER SHOULDERS.*

CRAZYFACE: Annie?

ANNIE: Annie.

CRAZYFACE: Where's the Pope?

ANNIE: I *am* the Pope.

CRAZYFACE: That's impossible.

ANNIE: Possibly.

CRAZYFACE: The Pope's a man.

ANNIE: They think I'm a man. All but a few.

CRAZYFACE: You never used to shave.

ANNIE: It's a performance. To be glimpsed, once in a while, doing something masculine is all they require to be reassured. None of them would question my sex. I am the descendant of St. Peter, I wear the shoes of the fisherman.

CRAZYFACE: How did you become Pope?

ANNIE: It's a long story. I told few lies, I arranged a few miracles. Really, getting here was not so difficult. Staying here may be another matter. And I haven't yet got the knack of pissing standing up.

CRAZYFACE: I didn't kill Lenny.

ANNIE: Then that's your mistake. You should have done it.

CRAZYFACE: I killed others. Three men on a road. An angel.

ANNIE: I don't believe in angels.

CRAZYFACE: And the men?

ANNIE: I'm sure you had good reasons.

CRAZYFACE: Will I go to the Devil?

ANNIE: How the hell should I know?

CRAZYFACE: I came to Rome for forgiveness.

ANNIE: You're forgiven.

CRAZYFACE: But you're a cheat. You shouldn't be the Pope.

ANNIE: I'm the best man for the job; really I am.

CRAZYFACE: They'll find you out.

ANNIE: Probably. But in the meanwhile—

CRAZYFACE: Does . . . does God talk to you?

ANNIE: All the time.

CRAZYFACE: Really?

ANNIE: In my bath; while I'm dressing; at the circus. All the time.

CRAZYFACE: What does he say?

ANNIE: Mostly bad jokes. She laughs a lot. And she—

CRAZYFACE: She? God's a woman too?

ANNIE: She is when She speaks to me.

*CRAZYFACE SHAKES HIS HEAD.*

ANNIE: Lenny suffered, didn't he? I heard about the wheel they put him on. He's well out of it.

CRAZYFACE: I don't understand, I don't think I've ever understood anything.

ANNIE: That's because you're a fool.

CRAZYFACE: Yes. I suppose so.

ANNIE: Well . . . back to my performance. I've got delegations from Finland and France to see me today. I sleep through a lot of the speeches.

CRAZYFACE: Do you have spies everywhere?

ANNIE: Everywhere.

CRAZYFACE: Even in Loon? Even at home?

ANNIE: Yes.

CRAZYFACE: So do you know if Mama's still alive?

ANNIE: Oh yes, she's alive. But she's very old.

CRAZYFACE: Will she last long enough for me to get home to see her?

ANNIE: If you hurry.

*CRAZYFACE NODS.*

ANNIE: This . . . *(She looks at Lenny)* . . . goes to the dogs.

CRAZYFACE: No. Please. Bury him in a field somewhere. Where there's a good view. Where people play. Will you come home?

ANNIE: No.

CRAZYFACE: Never?

ANNIE: Never. If they find me out: I'm dead. If they don't, I'll play this game 'til I die of gout. I'm enjoying myself. Say hello to Mama.

*THE POPE EXITS. THE LIGHTS BEGIN TO GO DOWN.*

CRAZYFACE: It's a long way home.

*FIGURES COME IN AND REMOVE LENNY'S BODY. AS CRAZYFACE SPEAKS THE SET FOR THE FINAL SCENE IS ESTABLISHED. A CHAIR. A BEEHIVE. THE LIGHTS FADE AROUND HIM.*

CRAZYFACE: I don't know if . . . I saw a bird yesterday, hovering over the side of a hill . . . it was standing still in the air. I thought then, all he needed was to catch the right wind . . . the right wind can take you anywhere, more or less . . . anywhere you want . . .

*A LONG PAUSE. THE SOUND OF BEES RISES; AND BIRDS. WE'RE MOVING INTO THE FINAL SCENE.*

CRAZYFACE: . . . Even home.

*HE EXITS. SCENE SEVEN BEGINS.*

# <u>Scene Seven</u>

## A garden in Loon

*SITTING IN A CHAIR, DRESSED IN BLACK, OLD AND BLIND, ELLA EULENSPIEGEL. A BEEHIVE STANDS A LITTLE WAY BEHIND THE CHAIR. WE ARE IN A GARDEN, IN LOON.*

*BIRDS SING IN THE TREES AND BUSHES. IT IS EARLY AUTUMN. ENTER SHEBA. SHE HAS GROWN OLDER GRACEFULLY, AND LOST MUCH OF THE BITTERNESS THAT MADE HER SUCH AN UNPLEASANT CHARACTER IN THE EARLIER SCENES. SHE HAS AT LAST LEARNED TO READ. SHE HAS A VEIL FOR HER FACE, AND GLOVES. SHE'S ABOUT TO SORT THROUGH THE BEES.*

SHEBA: Are you all right out here?

ELLA: I'm fine.

SHEBA: Only I'll take you in if you're chilly.

ELLA: No.

SHEBA: It's no bother.

ELLA: It's just nice. Not too hot. I'm fine.

SHEBA: Do you want me to read to you again?

ELLA: No. I can't seem to concentrate for very long.

SHEBA: Something to drink?

ELLA: I'm fine, Sheba. Stop fussing. I'm fine.

SHEBA: Well, if you're sure. I'm going to go through the hive. The swarm may get restless.

ELLA: I can survive a sting. Are you hoping for another batch of honey?

SHEBA: Well, the garden's done well this year. They should be fat enough.

ELLA: Where's the child?

SHEBA: Asleep.

ELLA: Are the windows closed?

SHEBA: Yes.

ELLA: Don't want him stung. Bee-stings can be fatal to babies.

SHEBA: He's nine, Ella. He's not a baby.

ELLA: Nine. (*A pause*) Why don't I die, I wonder?

SHEBA: I don't think you'll ever die.

ELLA: Don't say that. That would be horrible. Not to die. (*A pause*) Where's that drink then?

SHEBA: You said you didn't want anything.

ELLA: I said no such thing.

SHEBA: You said you were fine.

ELLA: I am fine, but I'm thirsty. Can't I be fine *and* thirsty?

SHEBA: You forget what you say from one moment to the next.

ELLA: Oh well, if it's too much bother . . .

SHEBA: (*Exiting*) No, of course it's not too much bother.
ELLA: (*A little grunt of satisfaction*) Humph.

*THE BIRDS SING. SHE NAMES THEM TO HERSELF.*

ELLA: Thrush . . . lark . . . starling.

*ENTER CRAZYFACE. ELLA SENSES SOMEBODY.*

ELLA: Sheba?

*CRAZYFACE IS ALMOST FRIGHTENED TO APPROACH HER. IT'S BEEN SO LONG.*

ELLA: Is that you?
CRAZYFACE: (*Approaching*) No . . .
ELLA: (*Trying to stand*) Who . . . who . . . is . . . it?
CRAZYFACE: Mama.
ELLA: Tyl?
CRAZYFACE: . . . Yes . . .
ELLA: If you're here, come close to me.
CRAZYFACE: I'm here.

*HE RUNS TO HER, AND FALLS AT HER FEET.*

CRAZYFACE: I'm here, I'm here. Mama.
ELLA: (*Stroking his hair*) I used to think you came to my bed
    sometimes. Are you dead? Are you a ghost?
CRAZYFACE: Not quite.
ELLA: Child.
CRAZYFACE: I love you, Mama. I'm not a pup anymore, I don't
    lick anyone's hand but yours, and I love you.
ELLA: Don't cry. You'll start me.
CRAZYFACE: I want to cry.

*ELLA BEGINS TO CRY, TOO. SHE HASN'T CRIED IN HALF A
CENTURY. TYL EMBRACES HER.*

ELLA: It's good crying.
CRAZYFACE: I'll never leave.

ELLA: Yes, you will.
CRAZYFACE: No.
ELLA: You came to say goodbye.
CRAZYFACE: Not if you want me to stay.
ELLA: Another journey.
CRAZYFACE: Perhaps.
ELLA: Where, Tyl? Where now? Haven't you seen enough?
CRAZYFACE: Remember the wings?
ELLA: Wings?
CRAZYFACE: There was a man fell off a church. Years ago.
ELLA: You stole the wings. Yes, I remember.
CRAZYFACE: Maybe he fell, maybe he flew.
ELLA: He fell, Tyl. He was a fool, and he fell.

*ENTER SHEBA. SHE HAS A CUP FOR ELLA. SHE STILL WEARS HER BEEKEEPER'S VEIL.*

CRAZYFACE: Oh.
ELLA: What's wrong?
CRAZYFACE: You're not alone.
ELLA: A blind woman needs some company.
SHEBA: I'm the beekeeper.
CRAZYFACE: Do I know you?
SHEBA: No.

*SILENCE.*

CRAZYFACE: I'd better go.
ELLA: Stay awhile.
CRAZYFACE: The wind's good and strong. All the birdman needed was an up-draft.
ELLA: Tyl . . .
CRAZYFACE: Am I crazy?
ELLA: Yes.
CRAZYFACE: Is that so bad?

*ELLA SHAKES HER HEAD.*

CRAZYFACE: Watch for me, Mama.

*CRAZYFACE EXITS.*

ELLA: (*Thinking he's still there*) How can I watch for you when I'm blind, you stupid boy. My eyes aren't . . . child? Are you there, child?
SHEBA: Of course.
ELLA: Wasn't there? . . . I thought I heard . . . Tyl?
SHEBA: Yes.
ELLA: He *was* here.
SHEBA: He was.
ELLA: Fine figure of a man, is he?
SHEBA: You should be proud.
ELLA: He's been round the world.
SHEBA: Well.
ELLA: A man of experience: held in high regard, I'm sure.
SHEBA: (*Gives her the cup*) Here.
ELLA: Thank you.
SHEBA: That's the last of the honey. I hope we get a few pounds more before the frost sets in.
ELLA: (*Sips a little*) Milk and honey.

*THE WIND IS WHISTLING, VERY DISTANTLY. THE SOUND OF GUSTS IN LARGE TREES.*

ELLA: Is it windy? It doesn't feel windy. But I can hear . . .
SHEBA: We're in the lee of the house. It's sheltered here. You're not cold are you?
ELLA: No. Is it windy?

*SHEBA ISN'T LISTENING. SHE'S ATTENDING TO THE HIVE. NOW COMES THE NOISE OF GULLS, VERY HIGH.*

ELLA: Is that the child crying? Sheba?
SHEBA: No, it's birds, Mama.
ELLA: Look up, would you?
SHEBA: What?
ELLA: He said *watch for me*. Look up. Please.
SHEBA: (*She looks up, shading her face with her hand*) Yes?
ELLA: Can you see anything?
SHEBA: Just gulls.

ELLA: That's all?

SHEBA: Clouds. Really sailing along. There must be quite a breeze up there.

ELLA: Keep looking.

SHEBA: *(She's startled)* Oh!

ELLA: Something else?

SHEBA: Yes . . . another bird.

*SHE BEGINS TO CRY AND SMILE AT THE SAME TIME.*

SHEBA: Mama, another bird.

ELLA: High?

SHEBA: Higher and higher. Wheeling around.

ELLA: Does he see me?

SHEBA: I don't think so. He's too high.

ELLA: Good.

SHEBA: He's almost disappeared.

ELLA: Keep looking, child. Keep looking.

*THE LIGHTS FADE ON THIS TABLEAU. SHEBA WITH HER HAND CAPPING HER EYES AGAINST THEY SKY, STILL LOOKING DIRECTLY UP. ELLA SITTING QUITE STILL, SMILING.*

*THE WIND IS BALMY.*

*IT CONTINUES TO BLOW, LONG AFTER THE DARK.*

*THE PLAY ENDS.*

# PARADISE STREET

# Production Notes

Liverpool is a great city, but a grey one, especially in winter. Leaden skies and a muddy Mersey; grimy civic buildings and rain-soaked streets bounded by row houses, built back to back with refuse-strewn alleys between: a deeply dispiriting spot. I know, I passed twenty winters there and, apart from those few snowy Christmases of my childhood, it was a wet, gloomy place through the long winter months. This play, named after a real thoroughfare, Paradise Street, imagines what it would be like if, in the depths of that season, magic were to transform the city, replacing the grey with green blossom, and lending the people trapped in its streets a new perspective and a new purpose.

Elizabeth I is the progenitor of this miracle. Time-traveling on the beatific light of her own glorious presence, she arrives in the frigid city with a few members of her court: a group of masquers prepared to perform a piece by Ben Jonson, Jonson himself, the royal lady-in-waiting, a wilful ape called Benny Butterblood and the even more wilful Earl of Essex, Robert Devereux. And with them comes a miraculous spring. Trees crack the concrete and blossom overnight, balmy winds blow; the eponymous street, which has previously been walked by a lonely Irish derelict, is suddenly buzzing with plots and counter plots.

Unlike a clown play like *Crazyface*, which may be mounted as poor theater if necessary—rough, cheap and vital—*Paradise Street* needs some modest funds in order to be fully realized. A sense of the implacable reality of the urban landscape must be strongly established if the full impact of its transformation is to be evoked for the audience. Symbolic representations will in this case significantly undercut the impact of the piece. This is a play that deals, despite its metaphysical chat, with things tangible and viable: Bonner's body in a sack, the potency of a grenade, the health of Gloriana's ovaries. The text is therefore best served by particulars. A solid wall, a solid tree bursting with solid blossom. If you can get live musicians to come and serenade Elizabeth during her scenes, all the better. I suppose a real ape's out of the question . . . ?

As to the source material for all these details, there's plenty to be had. There are fine books on Liverpool, full of photographs to inspire designers, though I urge you to find pictures of the city *before* it was tarted up by the developers (who have the misbegotten notion they can turn it into a tourist attraction if they erase all its distinguishing features). And, of course, for every volume on the history and architecture of Liverpool, there are ten on the glories of the Elizabethan age: on its ideas, its manners, its music.

A note on the accents. To play *Paradise Street* without the locals sounding like Liverpudlians would be as phony as *Streetcar* without Blanche's Southern drawl. There is a strange music in these voices, their thickness and their lilt contrasting with the voices of the court (who have been written in a pseudo-historical high English fashion, when in truth they would probably have sounded more like Cockneys). What's important is that the audience witness a clash of cultures and of visions.

Finally: any play as filled with references to shows and masques and playhouses invites a staging that toys with the audience's sense of theatrical reality. Perhaps the grey face of Liverpool should be painted on backcloth, like one of Inigo Jones' designs, then pulled aside to reveal the Queen and her court in glory? Perhaps all of *Paradise Street* might have the feel of a masque; a fiction played out for the benefit of the audience. There are no rules, only possibilities.

Clive Barker—Los Angeles, 1996

# *The Cast:*

FIRST MASQUER
SECOND MASQUER
SHAY BONNER
JACK MULROONEY: a mathematician from Belfast
JUDE COLQUHOUN
GEORGIA VAUX
CAROLINE BONNER
QUINN BONNER
ROBERT DEVEREUX: Earl of Essex
BEN JONSON: a playwright
GUNTER: a blind fish cook
ELIZABETH I: Queen of England
BENNY BUTTERBLOOD: the Queen's Ape
LUCY LOVELACE: lady-in-waiting

# Act 1

# Act 1:

## <u>Scene One</u>

*LIVERPOOL. A WASTELAND IN THE CITY CENTER, WITHIN SIGHT OF THE MERSEY. IN THE DISTANCE, A HALF-DEMOLISHED ROW OF WHAT WERE ONCE PROUD HOUSES.*

*IT IS THE MIDDLE OF THE AFTERNOON, DECEMBER 24TH. IT IS RAINING HEAVILY: GREY, ICY RAIN. THE LIGHTS COME UP SLOWLY, TO REVEAL TWO FIGURES, FIRST AND SECOND MASQUERS. THEIR FACES CANNOT BE SEEN, HIDDEN BEHIND GORGEOUS MASKS, ELABO-RATELY REPRESENTING ALLEGORICAL FIGURES.*

*IN THE DISTANCE, A MAN'S VOICE SINGS. A TRADI-TIONAL HAULING SONG.*

As I was a-walkin' down Paradise Street,
Way-hay, blow the man down,
A pretty young maiden I chanced for to meet,
Give me some time to blow the man down.
O blow the man down, bullies, blow the man down,
Way-hay, blow the man down,
O blow him away into Liverpool Town,
Give me some time to blow the man down.

*THE VOICE HAS RECEDED, AS THOUGH THE SINGER IS
WALKING AWAY FROM US, DOWN TOWARDS THE RIVER.*

*THE FIRST MASQUER SNEEZES.*

SECOND MASQUER: Bless you.

FIRST MASQUER: The subject's love.

SECOND MASQUER: Again? Damn and blast.

FIRST MASQUER: That's what she wants. And what Gloriana
wants, Gloriana gets.

SECOND MASQUER: Is it to be *The Four Foster-Children of Love*,
then? Christ's blood, I hate that simpering piece of shite.

FIRST MASQUER: No, it's to be something new.

SECOND MASQUER: New, eh? Now we have to learn something
new. I should have been a rat-catcher, like my father. It
comes to seem a dignified profession, with hindsight.

FIRST MASQUER: And she wants it played here.

SECOND MASQUER: You mean *here*, here?

FIRST MASQUER: Yes.

SECOND MASQUER: What the hell for? What's so special about
Liverpool?

FIRST MASQUER: *(Sneezes)* Don't ask me.

SECOND MASQUER: My feet are freezing.

FIRST MASQUER: Count yourself lucky. I've got the squirts. And
I'm sewn into my costume.

SECOND MASQUER: Well, I suppose we'd better fetch the chari-
ots. And round up some boys for the chorus.

FIRST MASQUER: Oh no, none of that. She's having none of that.
She wants something realistic, if you please. She specified:
nothing French or Italian. And nothing in Latin.

SECOND MASQUER: She's impossible.

FIRST MASQUER: Ssh!

SECOND MASQUER: If she wants reality, she should go live a
life, not get in the way of a good fiction. It makes me want
to spit. I'm an actor. I've no business impersonating human
beings. It's too much.

FIRST MASQUER: Smile. It's only art.

SECOND MASQUER: I'm getting too old for this lark. It's no
occupation for a grown man. Dressing up. I'm going back to
the pavilion.

*SECOND MASQUER EXITS. FIRST MASQUER CONTINUES TO STARE OUT AT THE AUDIENCE. AFTER A MOMENT, SHE SNEEZES AND EXITS AS SHAY BONNER ENTERS. HE IS DRESSED AS A LANCE CORPORAL IN THE ROYAL CORPS OF TRANSPORT. HE'S TANNED AND HEALTHY FROM A POST-ING TO HONG KONG. HE CARRIES A KIT-BAG AND A SUIT-CASE. HE PUTS BOTH DOWN AND LOOKS AROUND HIM.*

BONNER: Bastards.

*HE LIGHTS A CIGARETTE. AS HE DOES SO, JACK MUL-ROONEY ENTERS. HE IS A RUIN OF A MAN: HIS GRIZZLED BEARD CLOGGED WITH DIRT, HIS CLOTHING FILTHIER STILL. HE CARRIES SEVERAL BAGS, BULGING WITH PAPERS. WHEN HE SPEAKS, IT'S WITH A HEAVY BELFAST ACCENT.*

MULROONEY: Would you have about your person the price of a
    small brandy, sir?
BONNER: Piss off.
MULROONEY: Right you are, sir. Thank you, sir.
BONNER: Hold on. What street's this?
MULROONEY: This isn't a street, sir, it's a pile of rubble.
BONNER: What street was this, then: when it was vertical?
MULROONEY: Why, it was Paradise Street. You're at the corner of
    what was Paradise Street and Lord Street.
BONNER: When did they knock it down?
MULROONEY: Last October.
BONNER: They knocked down the house where I was born.
MULROONEY: Makes no odds.
BONNER: Bastards.
MULROONEY: It would have been laid flat by tomorrow, anyhow.
    According to my calculations.
BONNER: What?
MULROONEY: *(Consults his watch)* The mathematics of it's quite
    simple. We should expect a fall before the middle of the night.
BONNER: A fall?
MULROONEY: A landing. A descent. A visitation.
BONNER: What, you mean like a Second Coming?
MULROONEY: No, I—

BONNER: There used to be an old fellow in Whitechapel, he had a sign: "Repent ye, the end of the world is nigh."

MULROONEY: He was right, he died. Are you sure you couldn't see your way clear to loaning me the price of a brandy? It's perishing cold.

BONNER: Then go down to the hostel, there's a soup kitchen down there. Or there used to be.

MULROONEY: Oh no, I can't do that. I've got to stay out, so's I don't miss the visit.

BONNER: That's your problem then, isn't it?

MULROONEY: I've been here three months now. I swear it hasn't stopped raining once. One solid streak of grey piss for ninety days. This city is the arse-hole of the world.

BONNER: What does that make me?

MULROONEY: A tight little get.

BONNER: *(Goes to hit him)* Eh?

MULROONEY: Go on, hit me: that's all they teach you in the army, isn't it?

BONNER: You're daft. All the Irish are daft.

MULROONEY: Been to Ireland, have you?

BONNER: Six months. Nearly ended up as daft as you.

MULROONEY: That's the magic of the place: you can't be in Ireland and stay English. It's a different world. Kill anyone, did you? *(Silence)* Did you?

BONNER: Why don't you take a fucking walk?

MULROONEY: Just a profession enquiry. I mean, you ask a jockey: win any races? You ask a soldier: blow anyone's bollocks off lately? It's a conversation starter. See bodies, did you? *(Silence)* Did you?

BONNER: A few.

MULROONEY: Funny things, bodies; don't you think? Saw a lot of them during the war, lying around; looked like they was waiting for fresh orders. *(With a smile)* From above.

BONNER: How long have you been here?

MULROONEY: I told you, three months.

BONNER: Do you know a fellow called Quinn Bonner?

MULROONEY: Bonner. Bonner.

BONNER: He's my brother.

MULROONEY: Sure, the man's got a brother.

BONNER: He lived in Paradise Street. Number twenty-four.

MULROONEY: Knocked that down. It's to be hoped he wasn't in it at the time.

BONNER: Do you know him or not?

MULROONEY: Price of a brandy?

BONNER: Perhaps.

MULROONEY: What does he look like?

BONNER: Tall, dark, layabout—

MULROONEY: Does he play a trumpet?

BONNER: He always wanted to.

MULROONEY: Lives with a fine-looking woman?

BONNER: Caroline.

MULROONEY: There's a fellow lives in a house at the end of the street fits the description.

BONNER: I thought they were derelict.

MULROONEY: One of them's occupied. Still, if it is your long-lost brother, I'd tell him get to hell out of there before tonight. There's going to be such rains here. Such rains—

BONNER: It's raining already—

MULROONEY: Ah, there's more than water falls out of the sky. There's going to be rains of tiny silver fish, ball-bearings, red dust, the Lord alone knows what else. Probably ships too, the size of small moons, larger: come to visit us. All this by early tomorrow morning. *(Takes out pamphlet)* Here.

BONNER: What's this?

MULROONEY: The Book of Jubilees. My own work. It's all in there. Miracles with us within a day, or less.

BONNER: I don't want it.

MULROONEY: Of course you don't. Scares you shitless. But you've got no choice: we've none of us got a choice. In years to come, people will walk down Paradise Street, and say, this is where it happened, this is where they first fell to earth. Price of a brandy?

*BONNER GIVES HIM A FEW COINS, AND PICKS UP HIS SUITCASE BUT NOT HIS KIT-BAG.*

MULROONEY: Thank you, sir. I'll tell them when they arrive: I'll say, that man comes with us to the Great Bear, for he's a good and generous fellow—even if he is an army man.

*BONNER EXITS. MULROONEY LOOKS AT THE COINS IN HIS HAND.*

MULROONEY: Wait, sir, you've made a little mistake. These coins aren't English, sir: they're Chinese. I can't buy brandy with a yen, you cheating bugger! Sells me short; like they always sell you short. You English bastard! Your mother was the back end of a donkey, and your father liked it!

*BONNER HAS LEFT HIS BAG ON THE FLOOR. MUL-ROONEY SEES IT.*

MULROONEY: Now look at that: just lying there waiting to be rifled.

*HE OPENS THE BAGS AND PULLS OUT A GRENADE.*

MULROONEY: Sure, the man's armed to the teeth.

*HE PUTS THE GRENADE BACK.*

MULROONEY: Jesus wept, the games they let the boys play nowadays—

*ENTER JUDE COLQUHOUN.*

MULROONEY: Excuse me, but would you have the price of a brandy?
JUDE: Would I have what?
MULROONEY: It's bitter. I'd just like a brandy—
JUDE: Oh yeah. *(Gives him some money)*
MULROONEY: That's very kind of you, miss. Here— *(Gives her a pamphlet)*
JUDE: No thank you.
MULROONEY: It's my Book of Jubilees. Take it please.

*JUDE TAKES IT. MULROONEY GOES TO EXIT.*

MULROONEY: Sure, and don't touch the bag; it's his, and he's welcome to it.

*MULROONEY EXITS. JUDE DOESN'T LOOK AT THE PAM-*
*PHLET, BUT CONSULTS HER WATCH.*

JUDE: Late. As usual.

*SHE WALKS UP AND DOWN TO KEEP WARM. EVENTU-*
*ALLY, MORE OUT OF BOREDOM THAN INTEREST, SHE*
*LOOKS AT THE PAMPHLET.*

JUDE: *(Reads)* "We shall have evidence of round worlds and
   worlds shaped like wheels. Solitary worlds, and worlds in
   hordes." Worlds in hordes? God help us, one's enough.
   Come on, Georgia, you're late.

*ENTER BONNER. HE PICKS UP HIS BAG. JUDE RECOG-*
*NIZES HIM.*

JUDE: Bonner. Shay Bonner. Isn't it?
BONNER: What of it?
JUDE: You won't remember me.
BONNER: No. I won't.
JUDE: Jude Colquhoun? I was a friend of Georgia's. The uniform,
   for a moment, put me off. Are you a captain yet?
BONNER: Lance-corporal, Royal Corps of Transport.
JUDE: Oh. Engineer?
BONNER: Driver. Do you ever see Georgia?
JUDE: Not very often.
BONNER: Does she ever . . . mention me?
JUDE: She's talked about you once or twice. Practically chokes on
   your name, if you must know.
BONNER: Well she can fuck off then.

*ENTER GEORGIA, AS BONNER GOES TO EXIT.*

GEORGIA: I'm sorry I'm late—
JUDE: Oh, Georgia—
BONNER: Georgia?
GEORGIA: Bonner?
BONNER: Yeah.
GEORGIA: What the hell are you doing here?

BONNER: It's a free country. Were you waiting for her?

*JUDE NODS.*

BONNER: *(To Jude)* Why the hell didn't you tell me—?
JUDE: *(To Georgia)* Shall we go?
GEORGIA: Wait a minute. I want a word with Bonner.
JUDE: We haven't got much time.
BONNER: Working woman, are you?
JUDE: I'm a nurse.
BONNER: Oh.
JUDE: I specialize in venereal disease. Anything I can help you with?

*GEORGIA GOES TO STAND IN BONNER'S LINE OF VISION.*

GEORGIA: How can you stand there with that look of complete
    detachment on your face?
BONNER: Easy. I just look at you.
GEORGIA: You didn't even write. I didn't know where you were.
    You could have been dead—
BONNER: Oh, as if you'd have cared.
GEORGIA: —while I was here, nursing your masterpiece.
JUDE: Let's not have a row in the middle of the street.
GEORGIA: I don't care who hears. I've waited three and a half
    years to see this piece of shit.
BONNER: For God's sake, Georgia, don't make such a fucking
    drama of it. You were pregnant. People get pregnant.
GEORGIA: No, people don't get pregnant. *I* got pregnant. Me.
    Georgia.
BONNER: And I had a career to think about.
GEORGIA: Since when's the army been a career?
BONNER: I've seen the world. Where would I have been if I'd
    stayed here? They knocked down our house. They knocked
    down the whole fucking street. What's he like?
GEORGIA: Who?
BONNER: The kid.

*GEORGIA SAYS NOTHING.*

JUDE: She had it terminated.

BONNER: You said you'd never do that.

GEORGIA: I wasn't pregnant then.

BONNER: That's murder that—

GEORGIA: Oh, now you're disappointed? You fancied the idea of coming home to see another little Bonner, lying in his cot, combing his moustache. Well, I'm glad I didn't have it, I'm glad it never took a breath, it never had a face worth looking at, because I wouldn't want to be responsible for anything that even half resembled you. You're a pig.

BONNER: It's a pig's world.

GEORGIA: (*A blind fury*) Well, you deserve each other, then, don't you, you and the world. I hope you'll be very happy together!

BONNER: (*A little intimidated*) Georgia—

GEORGIA: I wish I could hurt you as much as you've hurt me. I wish I was a man for one day, and my God, I swear I'd break you in pieces.

*EXIT BONNER.*

*EXIT GEORGIA.*

JUDE: A friend of mine, she said to me: a woman needs a man like a fish needs a bicycle. I liked that. Sensible. A woman needs a man like a fish needs a bicycle. Just then, three cod rode by.

*EXIT JUDE.*

# Scene Two

*INTERIOR OF CAROLINE AND QUINN'S SQUAT, IN PARADISE STREET. A FEW MISMATCHED CHAIRS, A TABLE, A BOTTLE OF VODKA. OFF, A TRUMPET IS BEING PRACTICED. THE MELODY IS "BLOW THE MAN DOWN."*

*ENTER CAROLINE BONNER, WITH A PRODIGIOUSLY FLOWERING CACTUS.*

CAROLINE: Quinn! *(The trumpet continues)* Hey, Quinn! *(The trumpeting stops)*
QUINN: *(Off)* What?
CAROLINE: Look at this.
QUINN: *(Off)* I'm in the bath.
CAROLINE: Well, get out; I want one.
QUINN: *(Off)* A few more minutes.
CAROLINE: You should see it—
QUINN: See what?

*CAROLINE PUTS THE CACTUS DOWN AND EXITS.*

QUINN: *(Off)* See what?

*A PAUSE. ENTER QUINN BONNER, FROM THE BATH, WITH HIS TRUMPET.*

QUINN: See what? *(Sees the cactus)* My God.
CAROLINE: *(Off)* The cactus.
QUINN: Yeah. I see it.
CAROLINE: *(Entering)* I swear there wasn't a sign of life yesterday. Now look at it.
QUINN: It doesn't smell.
CAROLINE: Have you left the bath water in?
QUINN: No, it was filthy. Do you think I'm getting the hang of the old horn, then? Be honest.
CAROLINE: No.
QUINN: Don't spare me.
CAROLINE: It's terrible. It sounds like you're in pain.
QUINN: You're supposed to be in pain. It's not jazz if it doesn't hurt.
CAROLINE: You know what jazz means?
QUINN: No.
CAROLINE: Fuck. It's black slang for fuck.
QUINN: I like that. *(He kisses her)* How much do you love me? Out of ten?
CAROLINE: Six.
QUINN: Six?

CAROLINE: Seven if you sell the trumpet.

QUINN: I will not.

CAROLINE: We could have one hell of a Christmas with the money you'd get for that.

QUINN: No we wouldn't. I haven't paid for it yet.

*HE STARTS TO PLAY.*

CAROLINE: Not in here. In the street, if you must.

QUINN: You're a cruel woman.

*HE PUTS DOWN THE TRUMPET AND BEGINS TO DRY HIMSELF.*

CAROLINE: I couldn't believe it when I saw the flowers.

QUINN: It must think it's June.

CAROLINE: There's more snow tonight. That's what I heard, anyway.

QUINN: The Mersey froze once, did you know that?

CAROLINE: The whole river?

QUINN: That's what Dad told me. He said you could skate across to Birkenhead.

CAROLINE: I don't believe that.

QUINN: Would I lie?

CAROLINE: Oh. Which reminds me. You told the woman from the Social Security I'd had triplets.

QUINN: I don't think so.

CAROLINE: You told her one of them was black. *(Quinn laughs)* They can take you to court for that: giving false evidence.

QUINN: If she's daft enough to believe it—

CAROLINE: I don't know if you're telling the truth myself half the time. You want some tea?

QUINN: Yeah.

*EXIT CAROLINE.*

CAROLINE: *(Off)* We've got no milk.

QUINN: We'll have to buy a goat. Or you could get pregnant: human milk's very nourishing.

*ENTER CAROLINE.*

CAROLINE: It'll ruin my figure.

QUINN: Then I'll have it. I don't mind.

CAROLINE: Anything to be the center of attention.

QUINN: No, I fancy being pregnant. Just . . . you know . . . lying back and giving birth.

CAROLINE: You think that's what happens?

QUINN: Nature's a wonderful thing.

CAROLINE: Unfortunately, she's left you a little deficient in the ovary department. Anyway, we're not bringing a kid into this place, wherever it comes from.

QUINN: No chance. They're knocking it down come the New Year.

CAROLINE: And where does that leave us?

QUINN: On the streets. Free.

CAROLINE: And freezing.

QUINN: Did I ever promise you anything but blood, sweat and a few cheap thrills?

CAROLINE: They'd give you your job back at the bakery, if you asked really nicely.

QUINN: Fuck that. It's too much like hard work. No, don't worry, I'll think of something.

CAROLINE: Nothing illegal.

QUINN: What, me?

CAROLINE: Quinn. Listen to me. I don't want to be visiting you in Walton Gaol.

QUINN: How could you suspect a face like this? Butter wouldn't melt in my mouth. (*She kisses him*) I'm a complete innocent. I don't even know what my hands are doing half the time. (*His hands career over her body. He talks to them*) Eh, you two! Stop that! Right now!

CAROLINE: You're mad, you are.

*THEY KISS AGAIN. A KNOCK ON THE DOOR.*

QUINN: Oh bugger. If that's bloody carol-singers—

CAROLINE: You'd better get dressed.

*EXIT QUINN AND CAROLINE, IN OPPOSITE DIRECTIONS.*

CAROLINE: (*Off*) Hello.

BONNER: (*Off*) Does Quinn Bonner live here?

CAROLINE: Yeah.
BONNER: Are you Caroline?
CAROLINE: Shay?
BONNER: Yes.
CAROLINE: Come in.
QUINN: *(Off)* Who is it?
CAROLINE: *(Entering)* It's . . .

*QUINN AND BONNER ENTER AT THE SAME TIME.*

CAROLINE: . . . your brother.
QUINN: Shay?
BONNER: Quinn!
QUINN: Christ Almighty!
BONNER: Well, don't just stand there.

*QUINN EMBRACES HIM.*

QUINN: Whoo-ee!
CAROLINE: We thought you'd joined the Foreign Legion.
BONNER: I almost did.
CAROLINE: You've put on some weight.
BONNER: *(Defensively)* Muscle.
QUINN: Oh yeah?
BONNER: I'm built like a brick shit-house.
QUINN: I wondered—
QUINN AND BONNER: —where that smell was coming from.

*THEY LAUGH TOGETHER.*

CAROLINE: Sit down. Make yourself comfortable.
QUINN: Want some tea?
CAROLINE: Or something stronger?
BONNER: *(Re: vodka)* I'd take a glass of this.
QUINN: Get a glass, sweetheart.
CAROLINE: *(He never calls her this)* Sweetheart?

*EXIT CAROLINE.*

QUINN: You look good.

BONNER: I feel good.

QUINN: Still only a lance-corporal?

BONNER: I'm working on it.

QUINN: And the moustache suits you.

BONNER: Like it? I grew it in Hong Kong.

*ENTER CAROLINE WITH GLASSES. SHE POURS VODKA.*

CAROLINE: Did you say Hong Kong?

BONNER: I'm just back for a training course at Aldershot. Got a week here, then I report to barracks. They want me trained to drive heavy goods vehicles.

CAROLINE: I'll leave you to it. I'm going to take a bath. The kettle's on. Won't be long. You look well. Really you do.

*EXIT CAROLINE.*

BONNER: And what are you doing?

QUINN: Oh, this and that.

BONNER: Playing the trumpet, are you?

QUINN: How did you know?

BONNER: Some Irish sod I met at the end of the road. He directed me here.

QUINN: Oh, him: he's been hanging around for months. So what's it like in Hong Kong?

BONNER: Magic. Women like you've never seen. Thirteen years old, maybe fourteen, go for anything in a uniform. I brought you some stuff.

*HE OPENS HIS BAG AND BRINGS OUT A SELECTION OF ORIENTAL BRIC-A-BRAC.*

QUINN: For us?

BONNER: Sure. They're just knick-knacks, you know, from the local flea-market.

QUINN: Dragons—

BONNER: Yeah, dragons. They love dragons: they're everywhere. Look at this—

*HE OPENS A BOX AND TAKES OUT SOME PRINTS.*

BONNER: Don't show them to Caroline.

QUINN: What are they?

BONNER: They're called Shunga. They're Japanese. Pornographic pictures.

QUINN: They're like comics.

BONNER: Yeah. This one—look—this fella's been locked in a box by these women—

QUINN: Why's he bald?

BONNER: I don't know. He's some sort of priest.

QUINN: He's shaved all over.

BONNER: Well, they do that quite a lot. A few of the women do it.

QUINN: What for?

BONNER: It feels good. Except it itches like buggery when it grows back.

QUINN: How do you know?

BONNER: I got crabs from a prozzie. And I couldn't get rid of 'em, so I shaved off me short an' curlies, so there was nowhere for the little bleeders to hide.

QUINN: Huh. Look at this bloke; with his dick sticking out of the box. How the fuck did you get these through customs?

BONNER: Nobody says boo to a uniform.

QUINN: What else have you got in there?

BONNER: You want to see?

QUINN: Sure.

BONNER: You mustn't breathe a word. It's more than me stripe's worth.

*HE TAKES OUT TWO GRENADES.*

QUINN: Whoo-ee! Whose balls are these?

BONNER: I was driving a dozen boxes to grenade practice. One or two just happened to get lost.

QUINN: So they're real?

BONNER: Pull that pin, and we'd be on the ceiling.

QUINN: Fuck a duck.

BONNER: Thought some of the lads might like to see the real thing.

QUINN: There's nobody much left of the old mob. Pete's gone to drive cabs in London.

BONNER: Oh yeah? Pity.

QUINN: He went a year or so ago. We never heard from him again. And Mickey Flynn's in Rome.

BONNER: What the fuck's he doing there?

QUINN: He wants to be a monk.

BONNER: Are you kidding?

QUINN: Nah. He had a revelation. He saw the Virgin Mary down the Dock Road. Said she looked just like an ordinary girl, except she had this halo and she was hovering a foot off the ground. Oh, and she was suckling the Baby Jesus.

*ENTER CAROLINE.*

QUINN: That was quick.

CAROLINE: You used up all the hot water.

QUINN: Sorry, love.

CAROLINE: What's this?

BONNER: Oh. Just some bits and pieces.

CAROLINE: Pictures?

BONNER: Well—

CAROLINE: Let me see.

BONNER: Quinn?

CAROLINE: What are you looking so guilty for? What are they? *(She picks up a print and laughs)*

BONNER: They're more a man's thing.

CAROLINE: Sex is more a man's thing, is it?

BONNER: Nah . . . just . . . you know . . .

CAROLINE: Are you embarrassed?

BONNER: Jesus—

QUINN: Well, they were for me, really.

CAROLINE: *(Re: grenades)* And those? Who are those for?

BONNER: Don't touch them.

CAROLINE: Why not? *(She picks one up)*

QUINN: Hey, sweetheart, don't drop it.

CAROLINE: You're the butter fingers in the house, not me. What do you do? Pull this pin?

BONNER: Just put it down.

CAROLINE: Lethal, are they?

BONNER: Six ounces of caudite. It could blow us to Kingdom Come.

CAROLINE: *(Sourly)* Expert.

*SHE PUTS THE GRENADE DOWN.*

QUINN: Come on, love, get dressed, we'll go out for a drink.
BONNER: They haven't knocked all the pubs down, then.
CAROLINE: I don't think I want to.
QUINN: Why not?
CAROLINE: It's your celebration.
QUINN: Caroline—
CAROLINE: No, you and Shay have a night out, eh? See all your old mates; that's what you want to do, isn't it?
BONNER: We should be off, then. *(He pockets the grenades)*
QUINN: *(Gets up and fetches his jacket)* You sure you'll be all right?
CAROLINE: Quinn— *(They kiss)* How much do you love me?
QUINN: *(Embarrassed)* What?
CAROLINE: Out of ten?
QUINN: Oh come on. Give it a rest. See you later. *(Kisses her again)*
BONNER: Yeah, see you later. *(Kisses her)*

*THEY EXIT. CAROLINE STEPS FORWARD: THE ROOM DIS-APPEARS BEHIND HER. SHE SPEAKS TO THE AUDIENCE.*

CAROLINE: I had this dream. I was in my mother's kitchen. I was only small. She was cutting open a fish. I'd seen her do it a hundred times. Our family was very fond of fish. She took a sharp knife and slit it open. And my father, who was leaning on the sink with a glass of dark beer, beer froth on his moustache, my father laughed. My mother reached into the guts of the fish she'd cut open and pulled out another fish. But this one—dreams are strange, aren't they?—this one was bigger, much bigger than the first, wet and shining and alive. It smelt fresh: of the sea, of the deep sea, of the dark sea. My father throws his glass of beer into the sink, and before we can help him, the living fish has leapt out of my mother's hand and eaten him up, in our kitchen. I woke up right then. I swear I was smiling.

*CAROLINE EXITS.*

# Scene Three

*WE'RE OUT IN THE STREET AGAIN. IT'S NIGHT. A BALEFUL SODIUM LIGHT BATHES A CORRUGATED IRON WALL, ONTO WHICH POSTERS HAVE BEEN REPEATEDLY STUCK AND RIPPED AWAY. THE WORD "VIVAT" IS SPRAYED ON THE WALL, ALONG WITH OTHER GRAFFITI. ENTER MUL-ROONEY, CARRYING A PIECE OF CLOTH ON WHICH IS PAINTED A GARDEN SCENE IN THE STYLE OF INIGO JONES, WITH NAKED LOVERS, FLOWERS AND ALLEGORICAL FIG-URES. HE SPEAKS TO THE SKY.*

MULROONEY: Charlie—it's happening. I found horse-droppings steaming in the middle of the Dock Road. How about that? They're dropping horseshit on us now. And this—I found this. It's a flag or the like: all painted. And the best, the best, Charlie. I heard a noise; snuffling. I looked around. Three horses, standing at a distance, beautiful. Breath in the air like mist. Is it possible they fell out of the sky? Are there stallions on Mars?

*ENTER ROBERT DEVEREUX, EARL OF ESSEX, HIS SWORD DRAWN. A DASHINGLY HANDSOME MAN, WHO REGRET-TABLY KNOWS IT. HE IS FOLLOWED BY TWO CLOAKED FIGURES. ONE IS BEN JONSON (A BEAR OF A MAN) AND THE OTHER A COOK, GUNTER.*

ESSEX: Stand your ground.
MULROONEY: *(Turns)* What the hell?
ESSEX: Irish?
JONSON: I think so.
MULROONEY: Since when's that been a skewering crime?
JONSON: And see what he's holding?
ESSEX: We've been looking for that.
JONSON: Look around, Devereux. He may have friends.

MULROONEY: If you smell like this, you don't have friends.

ESSEX: You watch him. (*Gets out a knife and gives it to Jonson*) Ben—

JONSON: I need no knife. If he moves I'll hug him 'til his breath stops.

MULROONEY: Why is every Englishman homicidal?

GUNTER: *Was gibt es hier zu warten? Ich muss sofort anfangen fur morgen vorzubacken. So viele Kuchen und Brote; und den Fisch ausnehmen . . .* (What are we waiting here for? I've gotta get going right away if I'm to be back tomorrow. So many pastries and breads [to buy], and the fish to gut . . . )

ESSEX: Shut him up, will you?

JONSON: You speak the tongue better than I. You tell him.

ESSEX: *Wir werden schon eine Kuche fur dich finden. Nur etwas Geduld.* (We'll certainly find you a kitchen. Just be patient.)

GUNTER: *Wenn das Essen fur Ihre Majestat fur morgen fruh nicht fertig wird, ist das eure Schuld. Ich mache euch verantwortlich.* (When Her Majesty's breakfast isn't ready in the morning, it'll be your fault. I hold you responsible.)

ESSEX: What with cooks and playwrights and actors and that damn monkey, I'm going insane—

GUNTER: *Was sagst du da?* (What are you talking about [over there]?)

ESSEX: *Ich werde wahnsinnig.* (I'm going insane.)

GUNTER: *Aber du bist doch schon als Verruckter zur Welt gekommen.* (No more crazy than the woman who brought you into this world.)

ESSEX: (*Despairing*) Kraut.


*EXIT ESSEX.*


MULROONEY: Who's he? And why's he dressed like a tart?

JONSON: When did you steal the cloth?

MULROONEY: I didn't steal it. I found it in the street. I don't want a piece of tatty cloth if it's yours. I thought it came . . .

JONSON: Came whence?

MULROONEY: Well, to tell the truth, I thought it dropped out of the sky. I thought it was a little miracle.

JONSON: I wouldn't speak like that in front of Devereux—

MULROONEY: Him?

JONSON: God, no, that's Gunter: he's just a fish cook. Devereux's the hero with the sword. And my name's Jonson.

MULROONEY: You keep Devereux away from me. I don't trust heroes.

JONSON: He doesn't much like Irishmen. He's had some unsavory experiences with them. Whereas I think a man's a man even if he's Irish.

MULROONEY: Well, that's very liberal of you.

JONSON: I've even met one or two I could like. Almost. *(Re: Mulrooney's bags)* What's this you carry?

MULROONEY: My life's work.

JONSON: Are you a writer?

MULROONEY: No, no. These are my cuttings.

JONSON: Gardener?

MULROONEY: From newspapers, magazines. Reports that I've found.

JONSON: Reports of what?

MULROONEY: Miracles.

JONSON: Cloths from the clouds? Let me see.

MULROONEY: Are you trying to make a fool of me?

JONSON: No. What sane man would not want to see a promise of miracles? Show me.

GUNTER: *Ich will nach hause. Mir gefallts hier nicht. Ich will sofort nach hause.* (I'm going home. I don't like it here. I'm going home right now.)

JONSON: *Nein, Gunter, du kannst aber nicht nach hause gehen. Sitz still und warte auf Devereux.* (No, Gunter, you can't go home just yet. Sit still and wait for Devereux.) *(To Mulrooney)* Hurry, before the hero gets back.

MULROONEY: These are, you understand, random accounts of unexplained phenomena. Charlie and I . . .

JONSON: Charlie?

MULROONEY: Charlie Fort; my dear friend Charlie Fort. Dead and gone these fifty years. He was a great collector. The damned, he called them, these occurrences that defy every system and science. He spent his life collecting and collating them. Punk and silk and charcoal.

JONSON: And you've done the same?

MULROONEY: I came to it late. I was a professor of mathematics until I was thirty-eight. Belfast never had so arithmetical a son. But reason has moons, as the saying goes. Strict logic can blossom into paradox, mathematics can lead by the clearest of routes to the most unfathomable mysteries. Breaths of states which we can only grasp in numbers, whose immensity drives us to tears. Once I began to contemplate the impossible, I was lost to mere argument. I followed Charlie 'til there was no way back. I began to collect the unexplained, like a spinster collects stray dogs. (*Shows Jonson a cutting*) Here, Birmingham, 1966. A triangular yellow cloud appears above the city, from which falls an inundation of snails. In Aberdeen, early '72, a fall of fish: *Gasterosteus Levius,* the common stickleback. You want something more, perhaps? Frogspawn on Hampstead Heath? Coins, comets, pyramids the size of a man's head, seaweed, yellow dust, red dust, a wheel, another wheel, a set of sixteen wheels with landing gear attached, made of no known metal or alloy . . .

JONSON: Have you seen any of these rains yourself?

MULROONEY: I've been at the spot not long after. I've seen the evidence. Held fallen ice in my hand that took three days to melt. I've had a silver fish leap from my grip that had fallen in a shoal of thousands out of a clear sky.

JONSON: So you have no doubt?

MULROONEY: I've given up doubt for life. There's presences up there. And they see us. And they know us.

JONSON: I've seen things in the sky.

MULROONEY: Everyone has, if you question them closely. But nobody speaks out. We keep it to ourselves for fear of being mocked. Well I say, to hell with that. You've one life and you shouldn't live in fear of mockery. Follow what's under your breastbone, and if they call it faith—the Literati, or the Criterati—

JONSON: Or the Shiterati—

MULROONEY: Or the Shiterati—if they call it faith, and try to kick the legs from under you, spit in their blind eyes and tell them to go suck eggs.

*ENTER ESSEX.*

ESSEX: There's no one else about. The whole place is in ruins. What in the name of Christ did she want to come here for?

JONSON: Don't question. Just obey. Let's find a kitchen for Gunter and somewhere where I can write in peace. This fine peat-digger here's put a new scene or two in my head.

MULROONEY: Working at the moment, are you?

JONSON: There's a little masque of mine in progress; I haven't written the end for it yet.

MULROONEY: Well, make a prophet of yourself. Write in a miracle.

JONSON: I might just do that.

ESSEX: Have you interrogated him?

JONSON: (Wearily) Yes, Devereux. Very, very closely. He lives in terror of me now.

ESSEX: So? Shall I take him prisoner or dispatch him on the spot?

JONSON: He's a harmless man—

GUNTER: *Wenn du ihm den schadel einschlagen willst tues woanders. Ich kann kein Blut sehen.* (When you bash in his skull, do it somewhere else. I can't stand the sight of blood.)

ESSEX: *Dann halte dir eben die Augen zu.* (Then close your eyes.)

MULROONEY: What's he saying?

JONSON: They're talking about the spilling of your blood.

MULROONEY: Well, isn't that charming?

GUNTER: (Hiding his eyes) *Ist es schon passiert* (Has it happened yet?)

JONSON: *Nein; kein Blut wird fliessen.* (No, no blood has spilled.)

ESSEX: He's only an Irishman, let me stick him.

JONSON: You touch a hair on his head I'll rip off your ears. Starting with those pretty little pearls.

GUNTER: *Nun macht doch schon!* (So get on with it!)

JONSON: *Sei still.* (Be quiet.) (To Essex) Now, take the scenery and give it to the actors.

GUNTER: *Bringst du ihn doch nicht um?* (Haven't you killed him yet?)

JONSON: *Nein. Du gehst mit dem Earl of Essex mit.* (No. Go with the Earl of Essex.) (To Essex) Take him with you, for God's sake. And find him a kitchen before he drives us all up the wall.

ESSEX: I'm no more than a carrying-boy. And for actors! (Spits) That's what I think of actors, and Irishmen; apologies for humanity, both—(To Gunter) *Komm schon, du deutscher bloder Hund.* (Come along, my German bloodhound.)

GUNTER: *Komm mir bloss nicht so, du Affenarsch!* (How dare you speak to me that way, you monkey's ass!)

ESSEX: *Affenarsch! Ich werd dir helfen! Affenarsch!* (Monkey's ass! I'm supposed to help *you*? Monkey's ass?) (To Mulrooney) You keep out of my way, Irishman. If I see hide or hair of you again, I won't be so soft.

*ESSEX AND GUNTER EXIT, ARGUING:*

GUNTER: *Hau doch ab eingebildetes Arscholoch . . .* (I'm going to slap you, you conceited asshole.)

ESSEX: *Ich geb dir eins in die Fresse, du mickriges Ekelpaket!* (I'll punch you right in the mouth, you pathetic piece of shit!)

JONSON: To think, he wanted to be a diplomat.

MULROONEY: Vicious little poser.

JONSON: He's been indulged, that's all. Women dote on him.

MULROONEY: Where's this little masque of yours being performed? I'd like to see it.

JONSON: It's playing at the moment, actually. Somewhere in the vicinity.

MULROONEY: What's it called?

JONSON: I haven't really a title for it. I wrote a piece for Haddington's marriage, which I dubbed *The Hue and Cry After Cupid*. There were nuptial songs, dances, little scenic devices by Jones; it was quite charming.

> *"Beauties, have ye seen this toy*
> *Called Love, a little boy*
> *Almost naked, wanton, blind—"*

People wept for the prettiness of the thing. But she, in her regal perversity, wanted something less fantastical tonight. So she's getting it. I'm writing an unsavory fiction, in which I will uncover the bitter truth of the business between men and women. A business—I may add—about which she knows less than nothing.

MULROONEY: Is it salacious?

JONSON: In parts. But it can't end well.

MULROONEY: Even with a miracle?

JONSON: Even with a miracle. Well, goodnight, Ireland.

MULROONEY: Goodnight, England.

JONSON: If I chance upon an inundation of frogs, I'll send them hopping to you.

*EXIT JONSON.*

MULROONEY: Ha!

*RE-ENTER JONSON.*

JONSON: The backcloth.
MULROONEY: Oh, yes.
JONSON: Thank you. Not that we'll need it. (*He takes the cloth and exits*)

*MULROONEY PUTS HIS PAPERS AWAY.*

MULROONEY: False alarm, Charlie, but it's barely eleven-thirty. No decent miracle appears before midnight.

*HE EXITS, AS BONNER ENTERS WITH SEVERAL CANS OF BEER.*

*QUINN FOLLOWS, RUNNING A STICK ALONG THE COR-RUGATED IRON. IN HIS SEMI-INEBRIATED STATE HE'S LIKE A KID AGAIN.*

BONNER: Where is everybody?
QUINN: Gone to Timbuktu.
BONNER: Gone to hell. And fuck 'em all.
QUINN: Wait, I need a piss.

*HE PUSHES OPEN A GATE IN THE WALL, AND GOES THROUGH.*

BONNER: It's like a bloody necropolis, this.
QUINN: Is it me, or is there a smell in the air—
BONNER: (*Sniffs*) Horses.
QUINN: Eh?
BONNER: (*Belch*) Horses. I saw piles of manure on the road.
QUINN: Come off it. Horses?
BONNER: Eh—didn't show you my prize possession, did I?
QUINN: What's that?

*BONNER UNBUTTONS HIS SHIRT.*

BONNER: Cost me a packet, this. Look.

*QUINN APPEARS FROM BEHIND THE WALL, AND LOOKS AT BONNER'S BELLY. HE HAS A DRAGON TATTOO. IT DIS-APPEARS BELOW HIS BELT.*

QUINN: Whoo-ee.

BONNER: I told you. They draw dragons on everything.

QUINN: I always wanted a tattoo.

BONNER: One of the lads had a "W" tattooed on each buttock.

QUINN: What for?

BONNER: When he bends over—wow!

QUINN: Wow? Wow! Ha! You're joking.

BONNER: Wow.

QUINN: Whoo-ee!

BONNER: It's another world, Quinn. Another fucking world . . .

*SILENCE.*

QUINN: Didn't we used to play round here? You could see the sea.

BONNER: The river.

QUINN: We thought it was the sea.

BONNER: I knew it was the river.

QUINN: Thought I'd conquer the fucking world.

BONNER: *(Arm around Quinn)* The Bonner brothers.

BONNER AND QUINN: *(Quietly)* Whoo-ee.

*SILENCE.*

QUINN: When you're away—do you think about Liverpool?

BONNER: What for?

QUINN: Mum and Dad?

BONNER: Dead and gone. What's the use?

QUINN: *(After a beat)* Do you think about . . . you know who?

BONNER: Who?

QUINN: Georgia.

BONNER: Why Georgia?

QUINN: Great tits. Sweetest tits. Don't you remember?

BONNER: You can't just have her tits. You have to have the rest of her too. Her mouth, for one thing.

QUINN: Suppose you had just her tits. One in each hand.

BONNER: Now you're talking—

QUINN: Be happy then, would you?

BONNER: And her eyes: on strings, over my bed. Watching me all night—never closed.

QUINN: That's disgusting—

BONNER: No more than a tit in the hand—

QUINN: Is worth two in the bush.

BONNER: Yeah, her bush. I'd have that.

QUINN: In a box.

BONNER: Her pussy in a box. Open it up once a week.

QUINN: Take it out.

BONNER: Gently now.

QUINN: Whoo-ee.

BONNER: Love it a bit, put it back. Lock it up again, safe and sound.

QUINN: Women.

BONNER: Who needs them?

QUINN: I do.

BONNER: Didn't need them when we were kids. Didn't need a thing. I remember running out of the house when I was small, stark bollock naked, ran down the street, all the old biddies cooing like pigeons over me. All loving me, just for being there. Didn't need anything then, did we? I hate being alive sometimes, don't you?

QUINN: *(Uneasy)* No.

*SILENCE.*

BONNER: Well . . . dead soon enough.

QUINN: Jesus.

BONNER: Dead and buried.

QUINN: I'm barely thirty.

BONNER: I can feel my teeth rotting.

QUINN: You always get morbid with a drink in you.

BONNER: I know what it'll be like. I've got inside information.

QUINN: Anyone I know?

BONNER: Don't you laugh—

QUINN: I'm not laughing.

BONNER: There was an accident, on one of the practice ranges, with one of these.

*HE TAKES OUT A GRENADE.*

QUINN: Christ.

BONNER: I was first there. He was a good-looking lad: blew his chest open. He lay there, dying. He knew: I knew. I said to him: Does it hurt? He said: It's like eating a stone. They took him to hospital—he was dead on arrival. Like eating a stone, he said. I dream that now. A huge stone on me. I'm eating it, I'm chewing and swallowing it, mouthful after mouthful. My gut's full and my throat's full and I'm choked on it. Stone cold dead.

QUINN: Jesus.

BONNER: *(Turns away, nervous laugh)* And you know what? All he wanted was his mother. A grown man and he thought his mother could make it better for him.

*SILENCE.*

QUINN: Race you to the end of the street and back. Go!

*EXIT BONNER AND QUINN AT A RUN. ENTER JUDE AND GEORGIA, EATING FISH AND CHIPS FROM A NEWSPAPER.*

JUDE: You've been difficult all night.

GEORGIA: I haven't.

JUDE: Are you cross with me for some reason?

GEORGIA: No.

JUDE: Was it Bonner?

GEORGIA: I don't want to talk about it.

JUDE: If you've got something to say, say it.

GEORGIA: Well ... I don't think we should go out together again. I'm sorry.

JUDE: No. If you don't want to, that's up to you.

GEORGIA: All you talk about is venereal warts. It puts me off, Jude. I'm chatting up some bloke, and you're a foot away discussing scabs and drips. I can't look at a man's mouth without seeing germs sitting on his lips.

JUDE: Everything's infested with life of one kind or another. We've got colonies of bacteria all over us.

GEORGIA: Well, I'd prefer not to know about it. What did you think of Gordon?

JUDE: You could do better.

GEORGIA: He was the only decent-looking man at the party.

JUDE: Not decent enough to drive you home.

GEORGIA: I didn't want to spend the night with him anyway.

JUDE: You're still thinking about Bonner, aren't you?

GEORGIA: Maybe.

JUDE: Forget about him. He's not worth thinking about. He's a social leper.

GEORGIA: There you go again. I thought the uniform suited him.

JUDE: I didn't notice.

GEORGIA: He was always smart. Well groomed.

JUDE: So are racehorses.

*ENTER BONNER, RUNNING.*

BONNER: *(Yelling back at Quinn)* Me! Me! Ha! *(Sees the women)* Oh—

*ENTER QUINN.*

QUINN: You didn't touch the wall at the other end—

BONNER: Quinn—

QUINN: Fucking cheat— *(Sees the women)* Oh, I'm sorry.

JUDE: What are you apologizing for?

BONNER: His face.

QUINN: Shut up.

BONNER: Don't mind him. He's just my brother.

GEORGIA: I know.

BONNER: Georgia, this is Quinn. And this is Julie.

JUDE: Jude.

BONNER: Jude.

QUINN: Quinn. What are you doing out this late on your own?

BONNER: Want us to walk with you?

GEORGIA: No thanks.

QUINN: Caroline had some guy flash her—

JUDE: We're all right if we're together.

QUINN: She told him if he didn't put it away she'd bite it off.

GEORGIA: Good for her.

BONNER: Dream come true that, isn't it Georgia?

QUINN: Hey, come on—cool down.

BONNER: Oh, I'm cool. I'm so fucking cool I'm freezing. Want a feel?

GEORGIA: Why are you so offensive?

BONNER: Practice. I take lessons: Farting, belching and otherwise generally making a pig of myself.

QUINN: He's drunk.

BONNER: Don't apologize for the slob, he's quite capable of talking through his own arse-hole.

JUDE: Is this the man you said was well groomed?

BONNER: Oh, been talking about me, have you? What have you been telling her? Intimate details of our love life? *(To Jude)* You'd like that, wouldn't you? She's a venereal woman, Quinn, this one. Watch her. But you needn't bother with Quinny-boy, he hasn't put it about for years, he's too pussy-whipped by his lady-wife, aren't you?

QUINN: Shut up—

GEORGIA: *(To Quinn)* Has he always been like this?

BONNER: You should know.

QUINN: He's never been much good with a drink inside him.

BONNER: *(Taking hold of Quinn)* I could drink you under the table any day of the week. *(Laughs)* See my brother here, he likes you Georgia—

QUINN: Shut up, Bonner.

BONNER: Said you had great tits. Nice couple of wobblers, he said.

JUDE: Oh, the endless fascination of talking dirty. We get your type in the clinic all the time. Talking about the adventures of their little Roger, or Willie, or Jack-the-lad. Pathetic.

BONNER: Who are you calling pathetic?

JUDE: You.

GEORGIA: Jude—

JUDE: I can only take so much of men like him.

BONNER: How much? Exactly?

JUDE: All talk.

BONNER: Am I all talk, Georgia?

QUINN: *(To Bonner)* Why don't you lay off?

GEORGIA: You want me to tell them? First time, he couldn't even get it up.

BONNER: That's not true! She's lying! That's not true!

GEORGIA: It lay there like two peas and a baby's thumb.

BONNER: Take that back.

QUINN: You asked for that.

BONNER: It's not true.

QUINN: I don't care whether it's true or not.

BONNER: Well I do. *(He tries to hit Georgia)*

QUINN: *(Taking hold of him)* Eh! Eh! Let her alone.

GEORGIA: Goodnight, Bonner.

BONNER: *(Yelling after her)* Take that back!
GEORGIA: You're worse than useless.
BONNER: I got you fat fast enough.
GEORGIA: A dog could do that.
BONNER: And you'd let it, too.
JUDE: Are you coming?
GEORGIA: In a minute.
JUDE: Don't cause any more trouble, Georgia. Please. Come on.
GEORGIA: Go to hell!

*JUDE EXITS.*

BONNER: Why are you such a bitch?
GEORGIA: Cause, God help me, I still love you.
BONNER: What?

*GEORGIA EXITS.*

BONNER: What? Let me go! What did she say? Let me go!

*BONNER WRESTLES FREE OF QUINN AND TURNS TO HIM.*

BONNER: You stupid bastard! If I want to kick the shit out of someone, that's my business.
QUINN: Well, aren't you tough?
BONNER: You talking to me or chewing a brick? Either way you get your teeth busted.
QUINN: I've been listening to you boasting all night. Bonner fucked this: Bonner fucked that. Judging by her, you're not much with women.
BONNER: And you are, are you?
QUINN: I know how to treat a woman, yeah.
BONNER: You don't believe that shit?
QUINN: Why'd she lie?
BONNER: She was pregnant by me. She hates my guts for it.
QUINN: She was right. You're no better than an animal.
BONNER: Caroline didn't complain.
QUINN: What?
BONNER: She loved every minute of it. Couldn't get enough of it.
QUINN: What? *What?* You're lying.

BONNER: You're the liar in this family, Sonny Jim.

QUINN: You haven't laid a finger on her. You haven't, you hear me! You haven't.

*HE WANTS TO HIT BONNER, BUT HE HASN'T THE COURAGE.*

BONNER: Go on home. Ask her. Unless you're afraid of the answer. Go on.

QUINN: You'd better be fucking lying.

*QUINN EXITS.*

BONNER: That felt good. Sometimes the right word can be as satisfying as hitting somebody. Well, almost. I screwed your wife, brother. Wham! He's on his knees. Wham!

*ENTER MULROONEY.*

MULROONEY: What's that? Oh, it's you.

BONNER: Yeah. Going to make something of it?

MULROONEY: Sounded strange. That was all.

*MULROONEY TURNS TO GO.*

BONNER: Not so fast. Bonner wants you here.

MULROONEY: I've got business.

BONNER: At one in the morning?

MULROONEY: Let me alone.

BONNER: Fucking Irish cunt. Get on your knees.

MULROONEY: Now, don't do anything I'll regret.

BONNER: You know what we do to the likes of you? (*Grabs one of his bags*)

MULROONEY: No, please. Now, don't do that.

BONNER: Don't argue with the man. (*Hits him*)

MULROONEY: Ah!

BONNER: (*Emptying bag of its contents*) Now—

MULROONEY: Please . . .

BONNER: (*Puts it over Mulrooney's head*) This is what we do to the likes of you. Put you back in the dark, where you came from.

MULROONEY: Now, look, I've done no harm.

*BONNER KICKS HIM. MULROONEY FALLS OVER.*

BONNER: It's the harm you're planning I'm taking care of, Paddy. It's the future we've got to protect from the likes of you. *(Kicks him again)*
MULROONEY: What do you want? I've got no money. What do you want?

*BONNER DRAGS HIM TO HIS FEET.*

BONNER: I want the satisfaction of hitting you. I want the pleasure of it, that's all. You're a lucky man, Mulrooney, you can give me a few happy minutes, just letting me beat the shit out of you.

*MULROONEY TRIES TO RUN. BONNER CATCHES HIM.*

BONNER: You want to go somewhere private, is that it? Somewhere dark?
MULROONEY: For God's sake—
BONNER: Come on, sweetheart: Bonner wants you.

*HE DRAGS MULROONEY OUT OF SIGHT BEHIND THE WALL.*

# Scene Four

*SQUAT INTERIOR. A SINGLE LIGHT BULB. ENTER CAROLINE AND QUINN.*

CAROLINE: And you believed him?

QUINN: Shouldn't I?

CAROLINE: Bloody fool.

QUINN: Who?

CAROLINE: You.

QUINN: Me?

CAROLINE: I've never slept with Bonner.

QUINN: Why would he lie?

CAROLINE: Because he's jealous of you. Of us.

QUINN: Oh yeah. He's got the world there— *(Touches his palm)*

CAROLINE: Has he?

QUINN: Anything he wants.

CAROLINE: He twists you round his little finger.

QUINN: A lot of women go for him. No reason why you
    shouldn't.

CAROLINE: That's true. I've a taste for good-looking imbeciles.

QUINN: Meaning me?

CAROLINE: He's showing off, like a little boy.

QUINN: I didn't say I believed him.

CAROLINE: Yes, you did.

QUINN: I was just testing you.

CAROLINE: Quinn.

QUINN: I know he's a shit. He was baiting Georgia.

CAROLINE: Did she bite?

QUINN: She bit.

CAROLINE: I'd like to meet Georgia. We've got a lot in common.

QUINN: But you can't get one over on Shay—he doesn't care
    what he says or does—

CAROLINE: We'll see.

QUINN: What do you mean?

CAROLINE: I mean I'm going to make him sorry he was born.

QUINN: Don't mess with him.

CAROLINE: Oh, so now you want to protect me?

QUINN: Why do I let him wind me up like that?

CAROLINE: Maybe you want to be out shooting people, like him.
    Is that what you want?

QUINN: Nah. Not shooting people. But out somewhere.

CAROLINE: Where?

QUINN: Anywhere. Away from this dump. All the names I heard
    when I was a kid. Nova Scotia, Singapore, Newfoundland.
    New. Found. Land.

CAROLINE: And that's what makes you mad? That he's gone off, and you've stayed here?

QUINN: Yeah.

CAROLINE: And if he'd slept with me, he would have had his cake and eaten it—

QUINN: I wanted to kill him tonight.

CAROLINE: Why didn't you?

QUINN: He's stronger than I am. Always has been. I didn't know what I was saying, love: about you and him. I'm sorry.

CAROLINE: Oh, if he'd asked me very politely—which he never has—and I'd been in the right mood for an assault course—which I have been known to be—he might just—I say might, just—have made it between the sheets. Are you coming to bed? I don't think Santa's coming tonight.

*EXIT CAROLINE.*

QUINN: Before they knocked it down, there used to be alleys and little yards all round the back of Paradise Street. Tiny places with high walls, pigeons flapping up as you looked in. The smell of something strange. Black corners; bright sun. And on one of these walls, someone had painted a woman: crudely, with a thick paint brush. Glops of paint dripping off it. Ugly, really. But I couldn't resist that yard. Hot days, on my own, I'd go there. There she was, beautiful. I waited for the day I'd find her, real, standing in the sun, breathing. She still wouldn't speak, of course, because the tongue would be made of brick—but I'd go in there, and I'd—you know, I didn't know what I'd do to her. I knew I wanted her to be there, naked, alive, but what the hell was she for? I was only eight. When I found out what men and women do together, I was disappointed. I've always thought she would have asked for something different altogether.

*QUINN EXITS.*

# <u>Scene Five</u>

EXTERIOR. THE WALL. NIGHT. A SOFT WIND IS BLOW-ING UP FROM THE RIVER. BELLS TINKLE; SNATCHES OF SONG CAN BE HEARD FROM SOMEWHERE FAR OFF.

*ENTER JUDE. A GROAN.*

JUDE: Who's there?
MULROONEY: *(Off)* Help me.

*JUDE CAUTIOUSLY INVESTIGATES BEHIND THE WALL.*

JUDE: Oh my God.
MULROONEY: *(Off)* Ah. Careful.
JUDE: I'm sorry.

*JUDE AND MULROONEY EMERGE FROM BEHIND THE WALL. MULROONEY HAS A BLOODY NOSE, HIS CLOTHES TORN.*

MULROONEY: *(Looking at the blood on his hands)* Where am I bleeding from?
JUDE: *(Gives him a handkerchief)* Your nose. Here. Where does it hurt?
MULROONEY: Where doesn't it?
JUDE: What did you do? Fall off the wall?
MULROONEY: Damn fool question. What do I want climbing on a wall? Where are my papers?

*HE GOES ROUND THE WALL AGAIN.*

MULROONEY: They're gone.
JUDE: The wind must have caught them.
MULROONEY: Impatient to be off and away from me.
JUDE: Were they important?

MULROONEY: Only my life's work.

JUDE: It's a hospital for you—

MULROONEY: It is not.

JUDE: You may have broken bones.

MULROONEY: I can roll with a blow. I'm not moving from here. What time is it?

JUDE: I don't know, my watch has stopped. About four in the morning.

MULROONEY: What's a woman like you doing out here?

JUDE: It's so hot.

MULROONEY: It is hot.

JUDE: I had the window open. I heard voices, and music. I looked out, and you know what? Somebody was performing a play in the middle of the street. I went down to find out what they were doing, and they'd gone. Have you noticed the smell?

MULROONEY: My nose is in no fit state to smell.

JUDE: There's a scent, scents, in the air, like flowers; no, not like flowers; like the day before flowers. Some March morning, waking up. There's a green smell in the air.

MULROONEY: Four o'clock, you say? Oh fuck.

JUDE: What's wrong?

MULROONEY: All my life, I've been waiting for one particular train: collecting the time-tables, the ticket stubs, the signs of it. And when it comes, where am I? Dead to the world. The visit's over. It must be. I have to join the queue of people who just missed the miracles. The man who had diarrhea, and missed the Last Supper. The fellow who was blowing his nose when Lazarus took his first breath. Oh God—I think I've wet my pants.

JUDE: You can't stay here.

MULROONEY: I'll walk down to the river.

JUDE: What for?

MULROONEY: To throw myself in.

JUDE: Mulrooney.

MULROONEY: What do I care if the land sinks, if the whole world's only fit for fishes? (*Yelling, to the sleeping city*) Drown, you blind ignorant bastards! Starved of fancy, aren't you? Grey with truth. Wandering the world up and down. Well, I tried to tell them. Did my best. They took no notice. There's visions over Dogger Bank, Viking, Forties, lights on the Irish Sea and all the promise of Jerusalem rolling away to meet the Pole, and do they care?

JUDE: They dream.

MULROONEY: (*Reluctantly conceding the point*) Sure, they do that.

JUDE: Isn't that something?

MULROONEY: I don't distrust the internal vision. I don't say what the mind sees is less than what the eye sees. I say there's a threshold, where one becomes the other. Where the fruit of the mind becomes edible, where the waters of the imagination become available to wash in. The rest is politics, the rest is sociology, the rest is commerce with dissolution and I want none of it.

*APPLAUSE FROM BEHIND THE WALL.*

MULROONEY: Listen to yourself, Mulrooney.

*THE WALL OPENS. A GLORIOUS LIGHT SPILLS OUT ONTO THE FILTHY STREET. MULROONEY HASN'T NOTICED YET. JUDE HAS. SHE'S IN AWE.*

MULROONEY: Piss soaking in your socks and you're talking like a madman. How long does it take to drown?

*IN THE ROSY HEART OF THE LIGHT STANDS GLORIANA HERSELF, ELIZABETH I, WITH HER MANDRILL, BENNY, ON A SILVER CHAIN. BEHIND HER STAND ROBERT DEV-EREUX, EARL OF ESSEX, AND LUCY LOVELACE, HER LADY-IN-WAITING.*

ELIZABETH: We applaud your sentiments.

MULROONEY: They're not sentiments: they're accusations.

JUDE: Mulrooney. I don't think you missed the miracle after all.

MULROONEY: What? (*Turns*)

ESSEX: Bow your head, you heathen. You stand before Her Majesty Queen Elizabeth of England, Scotland and Ireland.

LUCY: (*To Jude*) Curtsy.

JUDE: (*Curtsies*) What am I doing?

MULROONEY: Do you know you're the spitting image of somebody?

ELIZABETH: We are Gloriana.

MULROONEY: Been to a party have you? Fancy dress, is it? (*To*

*Jude)* Or are these maybe the actors you saw in the street? The monkey's very fine, by the way.

ELIZABETH: *(To Essex)* It's a pretty irony when the entertainment presumes the patron to be on show.

MULROONEY: I'm no entertainment.

ELIZABETH: It was certainly a well-written speech you just delivered.

MULROONEY: I'm suicidal is what I am. It's the right of every man within an ace of dying to say his piece.

ELIZABETH: Your name's Mulrooney?

MULROONEY: Yes.

ESSEX: Acknowledge Her Majesty.

ELIZABETH: Hush, Robin—

ESSEX: Ma'am, he has not so much as bowed his head.

MULROONEY: Breed pimps with a bit of bite these days, don't they?

ELIZABETH: *(To Jude)* You?

JUDE: What?

ELIZABETH: Who are you?

JUDE: Jude Colquhoun.

ELIZABETH: Scottish name.

JUDE: Is this a joke?

ELIZABETH: Of course, you don't expect us.

MULROONEY: The woman's drunk.

ESSEX: *(Unsheathing his sword)* What?

ELIZABETH: Robin—

MULROONEY: Oh Lord, where's Jonson? He swore he'd keep you off my back.

JUDE: Who are you?

ELIZABETH: We are Elizabeth. Queen of—

MULROONEY: Drunk. Every one of them.

JUDE: She's been dead four hundred years.

ELIZABETH: We were dead before we were born, yet we were born.

ESSEX: This is Her Infinite Majesty.

ELIZABETH: Absolute Majesty.

ESSEX: In flesh and blood.

JUDE: And you?

ESSEX: I am Robert Devereux, Earl of Essex. You may touch me if you doubt it—

JUDE: No thank you. Why have you no shoes on?

ELIZABETH: It is our punishment. We are displeased with him in the matter of Ireland.

MULROONEY: Ireland is it?

ELIZABETH: He has mislaid several thousand good Englishmen in that country.

ESSEX: No man could have done better, ma'am.

ELIZABETH: That's not our opinion. Our opinion is that you were both arbitrary and vicious. Until he solves the Irish question he will go barefoot.

MULROONEY: Then his cobbler will get no more business from him.

ESSEX: I bristle, ma'am. Allow me to cut this Irish clod in two.

MULROONEY: *(Re: Essex's sword)* Have you got a license for that, by the way?

ESSEX: Every Irishman is half phlegm and half mud.

MULROONEY: And what are you, her bum-boy?

ESSEX: No more!

*ESSEX STEPS FORWARD AND SWIFTLY BRINGS MUL-ROONEY TO THE FLOOR, HIS SWORD-POINT TO MUL-ROONEY'S NECK.*

ESSEX: This is where you belong.

MULROONEY: You bloody coward! I'm unarmed!

JUDE: Leave him alone!

ESSEX: May I dispatch him?

ELIZABETH: You may not.

ESSEX: Ma'am, he as good as called me a catamite.

ELIZABETH: If you harm him, Robin, we'll have you beheaded again. And this time we won't be so quick to resurrect you.

JUDE: This isn't funny anymore. Stop it.

ELIZABETH: You still think this is a pretense?

JUDE: Of course.

ELIZABETH: Touch us, Jude. Come on. Close to us. Touch our skin. Are we warm?

JUDE: That doesn't prove anything.

ELIZABETH: *Touch us.*

*JUDE IS INTIMIDATED. BUT SHE TOUCHES ELIZABETH.*

JUDE: Lord, you smell. Powder and sweat a year old.

ELIZABETH: We don't like to bathe. It is our opinion it takes the youthful vigor out of us.

JUDE: Mulrooney.

MULROONEY: Yes?

JUDE: Suppose it is her. Just . . . suppose.

MULROONEY: Then you're welcome to her.

JUDE: Suppose this is your miracle. Not out of the sky, but out of the past. Why are you here?

ELIZABETH: We've come to look at England. And if it suits us, to unmake it. We do not like what we see. Not remotely. This was a glorious country in our age. It could have been Paradise on earth.

JUDE: And how do you intend to change it?

ELIZABETH: With daughters. A country's like a body. A system of physical states, a geography of entrails, limbs and bones. A head: us. A trunk: the people. A hand to fight: the army. A hand to trade with: the merchants. A leg to hop to heaven on: the Church. Another to skip to hell on: government. Now, look at this England. It is a body at war with itself. It bites its own tongue, so its voice is half sores, it tears out its hair, it weeps, it bleeds, it bleeds and weeps again. Now ask yourself, what sex is this body, England? Male. The army, male. The Church, male. Philosophy, commerce, government, male, male, all male. So, I say, if the male body cannot live without mutilating itself, setting its parts in war against each other, dividing head from heart from lung from stomach, then let us unsex it. Tear off its manhood and fling it into France, dig a hole where our men built towers; no longer aspire to being steel, but make a glory of love's body, where we shall be pocketed in peace, where the rule of Venus is law, and every breath is pleasure.

MULROONEY: I thought she was the Virgin Queen.

*ESSEX UNSHEATHES HIS SWORD.*

ESSEX: One more word—

ELIZABETH: You apologize for that.

MULROONEY: If you're Elizabeth the First, I'm Mickey Mouse.

ELIZABETH: That's your fucking problem. Now apologize. Or your neck will wonder where your head went.

JUDE: A very male display, ma'am, if I may say so.

ELIZABETH: What?

JUDE: You were saying something about being pocketed in peace.

ELIZABETH: We must have them in their place, or they'll tread on us. (*To Mulrooney*) Apologize!

JUDE: (*To Mulrooney*) She means it.

MULROONEY: I won't do it.

JUDE: I'm squeamish. Do it. For me.

MULROONEY: (*Reluctantly*) Oh Christ. All right. Yes.

ELIZABETH: Yes what?

MULROONEY: I apologize.

ELIZABETH: Very nice. That was much to our pleasure. You may kiss us, and leave.

JUDE: (*Reluctantly*) Go on.

*MULROONEY KISSES HER HAND. ELIZABETH DOESN'T LET GO OF IT.*

MULROONEY: Can I have my hand back?

ELIZABETH: What age are you?

MULROONEY: Forty-one.

ELIZABETH: I'm sick of boys, Jack Mulrooney. My appetite is for wisdom without platitudes, and a bed without lust. Your hand is shaking. *"Cras amet qui numquam amavit quique amavit cras amet."*

MULROONEY: My Latin's shite. What did she say?

ESSEX: Tomorrow . . . er . . .

ELIZABETH: "Tomorrow may he love who has never loved before, and may he who has loved love too."

*SHE LETS MULROONEY GO. HE LOOKS AT HER AS HE BACKS AWAY.*

ELIZABETH: Go to bed. Dream of us.

MULROONEY: Not if I can help it.

*MULROONEY EXITS.*

ELIZABETH: (*To Jude*) Your business is the pox?

JUDE: Yes.

ELIZABETH: Tomorrow, we will debate syphilis.

JUDE: We will?

ELIZABETH: We will. We've learned much already, being here.

This age is America's, as the age before was ours, as the age before that was Bethlehem's. We shan't be great as we were; but greatness is defined by men, who mean a metaphor for how full they find their codpieces. I say, we shall not be great, but deep, as our cunts, and moist and mighty. You will attend on us tomorrow. 'Til then, goodnight.

*EXIT ELIZABETH, HAVING PETTED HER APE, AND PASSED IT TO ESSEX.*

JUDE: What am I smiling for?

*ESSEX PRODUCES A TINY NOSEGAY FROM HIS JACKET. JUDE TAKES THE FLOWERS.*

JUDE: For me?
ESSEX: For you. Goodnight.
JUDE: Goodnight . . .

*EXIT JUDE. AS SOON AS SHE HAS GONE, LUCY AND ESSEX ARE IN EACH OTHER'S ARMS, KISSING, AND ESSEX IS UNBUTTONING LUCY.*

ESSEX: I thought she'd talk all night.
LUCY: My little Cock-Robin.
ESSEX: Lucy: I'm burning for you—
LUCY: Your poem—
ESSEX: Yes. Yes . . .
LUCY: What did it mean?
ESSEX: I'll explain it later.
LUCY: It vexed me a little.
ESSEX: No . . .
LUCY: *(She has it, she reads)* "O bloom for me, thou flower of life—"

*ESSEX KISSES HER.*

LUCY: *"And take me into thy sweet garden*
    *Where my joy in thee may harden—"*
ESSEX: *(Kisses her breasts and reaches up under her skirts)* Harden.
    Yes . . .

LUCY: *"Into love, and as a knife—"*
I'm not sure I like this bit.
*"—as a knife*
*May serve to claim the pardoned*
*blossom, I may harvest thee to wife."*
ESSEX: It's beautiful. Brings tears to my eyes.
LUCY: Oh, do that again . . . again . . . *(Over her shoulder)* Benny
is watching us—
ESSEX: Forget the ape. It doesn't understand what it sees.
LUCY: I think it does. Can't you blindfold it or something?
ESSEX: Lucy.
LUCY: *(Pouts)* For me.
ESSEX: Oh, very well. *(He approaches the ape with a handkerchief to*
*blindfold it)* Come here, Benny—

*THE APE BACKS OFF.*

ESSEX: Damned thing!

*HE BEATS THE APE. AND FINALLY BLINDFOLDS IT,*
*THOUGH THE EFFORT LEAVES HIM GASPING.*

ESSEX: Better?
LUCY: Much better. You're so brave.
ESSEX: Lift up your skirts. Let me see your cherry—
LUCY: Do you love me?
ESSEX: Would I write poetry for you if I didn't love you?
LUCY: There's a bit I don't understand.
ESSEX: *(Back to kissing her)* What's that?
LUCY: *"The pardoned blossom."*
ESSEX: Beautiful.
LUCY: What does that mean?
ESSEX: Later.
LUCY: No, now. What's a pardoned blossom? Is it something to
do with me?
ESSEX: Lucy, my dear Lucy. Flattering though it is, this is not the
time, *please*, to discuss my poetry.
LUCY: Or is it because you had "garden" and "harden" and you
couldn't find a rhyme—
ESSEX: *(Insulted)* No!

LUCY: Well, why then?
> "—*as a knife*
> *Is used to claim the pardoned*
> *blossom, I may harvest thee to wife.*"
> That doesn't make any sense.

ESSEX: Lucy. Forget it. It's art. You wouldn't understand.

LUCY: Oh I wouldn't, wouldn't I? Well. You can have your poem back then. It's not worth much to me if I'm too stupid to appreciate it.

*LUCY EXITS.*

ESSEX: Oh Lord.

*THE APE HAS PULLED OFF HIS BLINDFOLD.*

ESSEX: Don't you look at me that way! Wretched monkey.

*THE APE STARTS TO MOVE AWAY.*

ESSEX: (*Moderating his tone*) No, no. Don't you dare. If I lose you she'll have my balls.

*THE APE TEASES HIM. STANDS STILL. MOVES. STANDS STILL. MOVES. NEVER LETTING HIM GET CLOSE ENOUGH TO POUNCE.*

ESSEX: Come here . . . come on . . . I've got fruit. I've got tobacco.

*HE PROFFERS THE TOBACCO. THE APE SNATCHES IT AND RUNS.*

ESSEX: Come back here, you flea-bitten animal!

*THE APE EXITS, WITH ESSEX IN PURSUIT.*

*END OF ACT ONE.*

# Act 2

# Act 2:

## Scene One

*EXTERIOR. THE FOLLOWING MORNING. THE LAND-
SCAPE HAS BLOSSOMED. THE AIR IS FULL OF BIRDSONG.
JUDE SITS ON A CHAIR. UNDER A SMALL TREE STANDS
ESSEX WITH THE APE, WRITING IN A BOOK, WHILE A
VOICE SINGS.*

*I saw three ships come sailing in, On Christmas Day,
on Christmas Day, I saw three ships come sailing in,
On Christmas Day in the morning. And what was in those ships
all three?
On Christmas Day, on Christmas Day, And what was in those
ships all three
On Christmas Day in the morning.
Oh, Joseph and his wife Mary, On Christmas Day,
on Christmas Day, Oh, Joseph and his wife Mary,
On Christmas Day in the morning.*

ESSEX: It's all so simple. Ireland's not large, is it? I mean, it's a
speck in the sea. I propose to sink it! I shall take three
thousand strong men over to Ireland, and we'll make our
way, under cover, to somewhere south of Fermanagh. We'll
pass ourselves off as ditch-diggers. They won't realize what

we're about. Then, by night, we'll dig a hole, a deep hole, 'til we get through to the sea. The waters will rise, the country will flood, and disappear forever. Every Englishman will carry his own boat, the size of a cot, no more, and using our shovels as oars, paddle back to England, having solved the Irish question once and for all. Is that good, or is it brilliant?

JUDE: It won't work.

ESSEX: Why not, Miss Mighty?

JUDE: Ireland does not float. If you dig forever you won't reach the sea, unless you dig right through the earth and meet the South Pacific.

ESSEX: Shite. Are you sure?

JUDE: Besides, isn't Ireland one of her Protectorates? Would she be very pleased if you left it to sink?

ESSEX: I have to solve the problem somehow. A man loses dignity walking around without his shoes on.

JUDE: How long is she going to keep me waiting?

ESSEX: Oh, she's been known to leave people days. Weeks. Her favorite trick's to simply stand, and as no one may sit while she is standing, we all stand with her. And stand. And stand. And stand. She has the constitution of a—

JUDE: Horse?

ESSEX: You said that, not me.

JUDE: Have you traveled with her long?

ESSEX: Oh yes. I don't exactly know *how* long. It's hard to keep track when you're in one century for a day, and another for a week, and—well, I just go with the flow of her will.

JUDE: How's it possible?

ESSEX: She gets it from her father.

JUDE: Not the will. The time-travel. Do you have a machine?

ESSEX: Don't be ridiculous. What kind of machine could ever . . . No, it's Gloriana. She is the light, and we travel in the light. Faster than the light sometimes. I don't understand the details. I just want to go home. Back to live the old life.

JUDE: Was it so good?

ESSEX: Oh yes, it was good.

JUDE: She seems to think it was golden.

ESSEX: For her, maybe it was. She's Gloriana. Adored like a goddess. The heart of allegory: Gloriana. The proof for metaphor: Gloriana. No woman had ever been so loved, and no woman will be so loved again.

JUDE: And the ape?

ESSEX: Benny Butterblood, she calls him. He was a gift from an admirer. I forget who. She has so many.

JUDE: Why does she keep it?

ESSEX: Oh, she loves it, more than me, she loves it. I would gladly dispatch the thing, but she'd only have me beheaded again.

*ENTER GEORGIA.*

GEORGIA: Jude?

JUDE: Hello—

GEORGIA: What's going on? The weather.

JUDE: Incredible, isn't it?

GEORGIA: *(Sees the ape)* Oh God—

ESSEX: It won't hurt you. It smells you, that's all.

*THE APE APPROACHES GEORGIA.*

ESSEX: It's quite tame.

JUDE: Stand still, Georgia. Essex, call it away.

GEORGIA: I don't want it near me.

ESSEX: There must be something under your skirt that smells good.

GEORGIA: *(Panicked now)* Jude!

JUDE: Essex! Make it behave itself.

ESSEX: Here boy! Come here—

*THE APE HAS HOLD OF GEORGIA.*

GEORGIA: *(Screams)* Ah! Help me!

ESSEX: *(Hauling the ape off)* Hey, Benny. Bad monkey! Bad, bad, monkey!

*ESSEX FLOGS THE APE.*

JUDE: Don't do that. It couldn't help itself. Are you all right?

GEORGIA: Who's that?

ESSEX: *(Still hitting Benny)* Robert Devereux, Earl of Essex.

JUDE: Tie it to a tree. But don't beat it.
GEORGIA: You know him?
JUDE: As of last night.
ESSEX: Please introduce us.
JUDE: Robert Devereux, Earl of Essex. Georgia Vaux.
ESSEX: Georgia . . .
GEORGIA: What's gone wrong with the weather? It's Christmas Day, and it's like the first day of spring. And where did all the trees come from? And the flowers.
ESSEX: A new reign brings new growth. There's a poem there.
JUDE: Just ignore him.
ESSEX: Will you excuse me? I feel inspired.

*HE EXITS.*

GEORGIA: This is so weird. It's like I was dreaming.
JUDE: It is. And you're not.
GEORGIA: Oh, by the way. What I said last night, I'm sorry. I shouldn't have said all that, about you and your warts.
JUDE: They're not my warts.
GEORGIA: You know what I mean.
JUDE: No harm done.
GEORGIA: I couldn't sleep properly. I was thinking about Bonner. He's very beautiful, isn't he? Don't you think so? I know, you're not supposed to talk about men like that, but he is. I kept thinking about him all last night, laid out on clean sheets, all tanned.
JUDE: Each to their own.
GEORGIA: Who did plant these trees?
JUDE: They just grew.
GEORGIA: Not overnight. That's impossible.

*ENTER ESSEX.*

ESSEX: Jude? Her Majesty awaits you. She's at the end of Paradise Street, watching one of Jonson's stupid scenes. But she's bored with it now. She asks you attend upon her pleasure.
JUDE: I'll see you later.
GEORGIA: Oh. Yes.

JUDE: Enjoy the weather.

*EXIT JUDE.*

ESSEX: *(Calling after her)* Don't forget to curtsy. And don't sit down unless—Ah! Never mind.

GEORGIA: What's your real name?

ESSEX: Robert Devereux; but I'm called Robin by those who know me well. And what do you like to be called? By your intimates.

GEORGIA: I leave that for my intimates. Do you own a zoo?

ESSEX: G.

GEORGIA: G?

ESSEX: I'll call you by your initial; the little hook of your name, G. It's already in my throat, through my lip. I'm caught like a fish. Just haul me in.

GEORGIA: Did you know you've got no shoes on?

ESSEX: Don't you like simile? I thought that was quite clever.

GEORGIA: Don't your feet hurt?

ESSEX: She makes me go barefoot—

GEORGIA: Who?

ESSEX: Gloriana.

GEORGIA: Your wife?

ESSEX: I wish. But of course she hates me.

GEORGIA: Why?

ESSEX: She claims it's the matter of Ireland. She says it's all political, this deliberate humiliation of me. She gives me favors, then takes them away again. Elevates me to high office, then makes me keeper of the ape. I'll tell you something, I've been privy to affairs of government, to affairs of war, and there's not a thing in the halls of power that's not done for private reasons. Acts of moment are made from a paucity of love, or laxatives, and the man who tells you other's a liar.

GEORGIA: Maybe it's true the other way about?

ESSEX: What do you mean?

GEORGIA: That private arguments are kinds of war. Like the war between men and women?

ESSEX: Oh no, no—

GEORGIA: It's war. That's what it's always been. I'm at war with Bonner.

ESSEX: Who?

GEORGIA: Whatever I think of him, whether I love him or hate him, I'm at war. Look out! The ape's getting away!

ESSEX: No, you don't!

*HE FLOGS THE APE.*

GEORGIA: It wants to be off.

ESSEX: Don't we all.

GEORGIA: Liverpool doesn't suit you?

ESSEX: It's a wilderness.

GEORGIA: You should let the monkey go. It probably feels at home here.

ESSEX: It would be so easy. And she'd be distraught.

GEORGIA: And you'd like that.

ESSEX: To discomfort her? Yes.

GEORGIA: Do it then.

ESSEX: Would you think better of me if I did? If I braved her displeasure for revenge?

GEORGIA: Maybe.

ESSEX: Then I will. I will. I'll let him go.

*HE LOOSES THE APE. IT RUNS OFF.*

ESSEX: I've done it.

GEORGIA: Good.

ESSEX: Revenge is a kind of wild justice: Bacon told me that. She may even have me flogged. (*His face falls*) I hate being flogged. Oh shite.

GEORGIA: It's done now.

ESSEX: You shouldn't have persuaded me. She'll have the skin off my back. What was I thinking of?

*HE GIVES HER A POEM.*

ESSEX: Here. I think I love you.

*EXIT ESSEX.*

ESSEX: (*Off*) Come back, you fucking monkey!

GEORGIA: (*Reads*) *"O bloom for me, thou flower of life*
*And take me into thy sweet garden,*
*Where my joy in thee may harden—"*
This is obscene.

*SHE SCREWS UP THE PAPER.*

*ENTER CAROLINE.*

CAROLINE: Where is he?
GEORGIA: Essex?
CAROLINE: Bonner.
GEORGIA: Bonner—how the hell should I know?
CAROLINE: You're Georgia, aren't you?
GEORGIA: Yes.
CAROLINE: I just assumed he'd be with you. He didn't come back to the house last night. He left all his bags. I'm Caroline. I'm his—
GEORGIA: Sister-in-law. I know. I haven't seen him since last night.
CAROLINE: So he was with you?
GEORGIA: Not exactly. We had a fight in the middle of the street.
CAROLINE: But you were together once, right?
GEORGIA: All that's in the past.
CAROLINE: Good for you. Who's been planting all the trees?
GEORGIA: I don't know. What do you want him for?
CAROLINE: I just want a word with him. He's spreading some lies about me.
GEORGIA: The only way to get him to listen's to get hold of his—
CAROLINE: Balls?
GEORGIA: Balls.
CAROLINE and GEORGIA: You know what he did—

*THEY LAUGH.*

CAROLINE: He's a lying bastard.
GEORGIA: He's a mad dog. He should be put in a sack and thrown in the river. Except I'd miss him.
CAROLINE: There are plenty of attractive men in the world, Georgia.

GEORGIA: I'd just like him to feel, once, what it's like to be help-
less—

CAROLINE: On his knees—

GEORGIA: On his back—

CAROLINE: Quinn says he hates the dark—

GEORGIA: Oh, that's true. He breaks out into a sweat if he
doesn't know where he is—

CAROLINE: So . . . maybe . . . I should do as you say. Put him in
a sack.

GEORGIA: Are you kidding?

CAROLINE: I suppose it's too dangerous.

GEORGIA: It is. If you did it single-handed. But if you had
help . . . (*She smiles*)

CAROLINE: You'd help me?

GEORGIA: Oh yes. He always goes out drinking at lunchtime, so
he won't be sober. We could knock him unconscious.

CAROLINE: How?

GEORGIA: Half a brick'd do it.

CAROLINE: We might brain him.

GEORGIA: So what? Then we strip him.

CAROLINE: Why?

GEORGIA: What's the use of taking the risk if we don't have some
fun? We strip him and into the sack he goes. Then he's ours.
To do whatever we want with.

CAROLINE: This is crazy. (*A beat*) There'll be some sacks behind
the market. Fruit sacks. Meat sacks.

GEORGIA: Revenge is a kind of mad justice.

CAROLINE: If it does go wrong somehow . . . he wouldn't hurt
us, would he?

GEORGIA: I'll take the risk. Smile. It's only war.

*EXIT GEORGIA AND CAROLINE.*

# Scene Two

*INTERIOR. THE CACTUS SITS ON THE TABLE, IN EVEN MORE ELABORATE FLOWER. ENTER QUINN, WITH TRUMPET. HE STARTS TO PLAY "AS I WAS A-WALKIN' DOWN PARADISE STREET." HE STOPS.*

QUINN: Who's there?
MULROONEY: *(Off)* No one.
QUINN: Come out.
MULROONEY: *(Off)* No need for violence.

*ENTER MULROONEY.*

MULROONEY: You must be Quinn.
QUINN: Yes.
MULROONEY: I'm Jack Mulrooney.
QUINN: How did you get in here?
MULROONEY: Up the fire-escape and through the window. All the windows are open.
QUINN: It's so bloody hot.
MULROONEY: Have you been out in the street this morning?
QUINN: No. It's too bright out there.
MULROONEY: It's like the middle of April on Christmas Day. All we need's the bloody baa-lambs. I love a trumpet myself— I've been an admirer of your playing awhile. Is Bonner here?
QUINN: Bonner? You know Bonner?
MULROONEY: Intimately.
QUINN: He isn't here—
MULROONEY: I'll wait then. You don't mind do you?

*HE SITS. STUDIES THE PLATE OF PARTIALLY EATEN FOOD ON THE TABLE.*

QUINN: . . . no . . .

MULROONEY: Last night, I wanted to drown myself. This morning, I don't care. Why should I carry the responsibilities of
the world? Would this be the congealed remains of a
spaghetti bolognese?

QUINN: Yeah.

MULROONEY: Will you be wanting it?

QUINN: It's all yours.

MULROONEY: You're a decent man. Would you have a shot of
brandy about to wash it down with?

QUINN: I think we've got some vodka.

MULROONEY: I'm not fussy.

*QUINN EXITS.*

MULROONEY: (*Calls*) I saw your lady-wife this morning.

QUINN: Caroline.

MULROONEY: Caroline. Lovely woman. You're a lucky man. I
gave up love at an early age myself. I was something of an
addict in my adolescence. But I didn't have the stomach
for it.

QUINN: (*Entering with glasses and vodka*) Where was she?

MULROONEY: Oh, back in Cork: a lovely girl name of Molly.

QUINN: I meant Caroline. Where did you see her?

MULROONEY: I don't remember. Somewhere up behind the market was it? With another woman. Thrown her out, have you?

QUINN: *No.*

MULROONEY: Thrown you out then, did she?

QUINN: I wouldn't blame her.

MULROONEY: Bit of a shit, are you?

*SILENCE.*

MULROONEY: Are you?

QUINN: Yes.

MULROONEY: And you can't play the trumpet either, while we're
telling the truth.

QUINN: I know.

MULROONEY: They're going to knock this place down. And
right and proper. It stinks of damp.

QUINN: I was happy here once.
MULROONEY: When was this?
QUINN: Yesterday.
MULROONEY: And what happened?
QUINN: Bonner.
MULROONEY: Oh.
QUINN: He said he slept with my wife.
MULROONEY: And did he?
QUINN: Nah. He was just making trouble—
MULROONEY: Somebody should have done the decent thing, and strangled him at birth. I was thinking of having words with him myself. That's why I came here. Thinking of thanking him for his many kindnesses.
QUINN: Such as?
MULROONEY: Oh, relieving me of my responsibilities. Destroying my life's work in a single night. Kissing me all over with those pouting little fists of his.
QUINN: He hit you?
MULROONEY: He certainly did.
QUINN: I think it's time we stood up to him.
MULROONEY: Why don't we both wait here 'til he comes back, and you can take his head and I'll take his feet—
QUINN: No. I want him now.
MULROONEY: Well, then I'll stay here and keep your vodka company, how's that?
QUINN: Fair enough.
MULROONEY: And if you get to him first—
QUINN: Yes.
MULROONEY: Break his nose for me.
QUINN: Consider it done.

*QUINN IS ABOUT TO EXIT.*

MULROONEY: You're a better man than I took you for. I should know not to judge a man by his musical abilities, eh?
QUINN: Did you know you've got a note pinned to your back?
MULROONEY: No.
QUINN: Hold still. *(Unpins it)* There.
MULROONEY: The postal service's not what it was, is it?
QUINN: I'll see you later.

*EXIT QUINN.*

MULROONEY: *(Opens the note. Reads.)* "Mulrooney. You are ordered to attend upon the pleasure of Her Serene Majesty Elizabeth." Serene Majesty, my arse. What kind of trick are they trying to pull? Bloody English sense of humor. Where's the wit in that? *(He screws up the note. But there's a seed of doubt in him.)* Besides . . . the woman's been dust for Lord knows how long. I won't believe it, Charlie. Not this. Frogspawn from an empty heaven: that I can believe. But this? This is madness.

*EXIT MULROONEY.*

# Scene Three

*EXTERIOR. MIDDAY. IN THE SHADE OF THE WALL, A DINNER TABLE IS BEING SET UP BY LUCY LOVELACE. THERE ARE THREE CHAIRS AROUND THE TABLE, ONE BIGGER AND MORE SUMPTIOUSLY CUSHIONED THAN THE OTHER TWO.*

*ENTER QUEEN ELIZABETH AND JUDE. GLORIANA IS IN FULL FLOW.*

ELIZABETH: . . . so there was a farmer and his daughter, you see, and they were returning from market one day, and they were set upon by thieves. Before they knew it, the thieves had stolen their horse and cart. Well, the farmer was distraught, and he sits down in the middle of the road and curses everything, until his daughter says: "Don't worry, father," and lifts her skirts, opens her legs and pulls the day's takings, a sack of gold, out of her cunny-hole. "Oh Jesus," says the farmer, "if only your mother had been here, we could have saved the horse and cart as well."

*ELIZABETH LAUGHS. JUDE JOINS IN.*

ELIZABETH: . . . horse and cart as well! Eh? Is that a good story? Robin told it to us. Heard it before?

JUDE: No.

ELIZABETH: Are you hungry? Of course you are. We hate women who pick at their food like birds. Let's eat. We can't wait for Mulrooney: he can have the bones. We always thought appetite would diminish with age, but no. If anything, it demands more. More food, more young men—

JUDE: May I ask a question?

ELIZABETH: Ask it.

JUDE: Is Essex your lover?

ELIZABETH: Oh Lord, no.

JUDE: So the history books are right? You're a virgin?

ELIZABETH: Yes.

JUDE: Why then this fascination with men?

ELIZABETH: We are Gloriana. Beauty reflects upon us. And there are no men as fine as those raised from English stock. The French are sugar mice, the Italians fart all the time and the Spanish wash in olive oil and garlic.

JUDE: But—

ELIZABETH: Don't argue. Just eat and listen. Lucy, you may serve us.

LUCY: Yes, ma'am.

ELIZABETH: Where's my little monkey, by the way? Bring him here.

LUCY: He's escaped, ma'am.

ELIZABETH: Escaped?

LUCY: Robin is in pursuit of him—

ELIZABETH: Oh, so we call him Robin now, do we? Robin, is it, little Miss Muff? Everyone, everyone deserts us! Cheats us! Lies to us! Compromises us! Even an ape! An ape! (*She turns on Jude*) We know what it is: it's this God-forsaken age of yours—this twentieth century: it breeds indifference to nobility—

JUDE: Why'd you bother to come here, then?

ELIZABETH: It's our dominion.

JUDE: No, it isn't. You're dead and gone—

ELIZABETH: You're as simple-minded as the others. Get out of our sight! Go!

JUDE: I will not!

ELIZABETH: What?

JUDE: You're pompous and hypocritical, you're worse than the men you want to subvert. You're full of half-formed notions—we'll change the world, we'll make the cunt mightier than the sword. It's nonsense: you're living in a fairy tale.

ELIZABETH: Hm. *(She ponders a moment)* Maybe . . . we should talk more. Sit.

JUDE: No.

ELIZABETH: Please . . . sit. Eat.

JUDE: I don't want to eat.

ELIZABETH: Don't be sour, now.

JUDE: I'm a vegetarian. I don't eat meat.

ELIZABETH: Sit and talk then. Lucy, we'll have beers. You're a doctor, aren't you? A venereal doctor.

JUDE: What of it?

ELIZABETH: My papa died of the pox, you know, amongst other things.

JUDE: Syphilis.

ELIZABETH: *(Starts to eat)* He'd had it for years. Oh, this capon's good. Try a little of the sauce, at least.

JUDE: *(Dipping bread in the sauce)* Go on—

ELIZABETH: Pox gets into the blood of children, doesn't it?

JUDE: It can, in some cases.

ELIZABETH: Isn't that tasty?

JUDE: It's very good.

ELIZABETH: And the children can be deformed?

JUDE: Congenital deafness, yes, and brain deformation. But you're obviously healthy.

ELIZABETH: And our children?

JUDE: The chances are remote. But I suppose they could suffer.

ELIZABETH: And is there a way you could discover if we carry the pox?

JUDE: We could do blood tests.

ELIZABETH: Then that's what you'll do. Today.

JUDE: It's Christmas Day.

ELIZABETH: Will we be more poxy tomorrow? You'll do this, Jude, for England. Have some more sauce.

JUDE: Thank you, no.

ELIZABETH: Beer, Lucy?

LUCY: Ma'am. (*She pours out more beer*)

ELIZABETH: Where's Mulrooney, by the way? He was invited?

LUCY: I think so, ma'am.

ELIZABETH: By your Robin?

LUCY: Not mine, ma'am.

ELIZABETH: We like Mulrooney, even though he's Irish.

JUDE: Aren't you a mixture of bloods yourself?

ELIZABETH: Sssh! (*A beat*) What I need is daughters. I must have daughters: I must have daughters. If I'm poxless, I'll go back to my last life with Mulrooney and conceive—

JUDE: Why Mulrooney?

ELIZABETH: We like him. We'll put a Queen on the throne to follow when we're gone, a daughter in every position of power. One by one, we'll destroy every belief Englishmen are trapped by. Show them death is no end: love is no weakness—

JUDE: It's impossible.

ELIZABETH: According to men's rules: I'm impossible. Dead is dead, isn't that the fashion of the day? But here we are.

JUDE: Maybe I'm going mad.

ELIZABETH: Men make these distinctions, Jude: it's their territorial instincts misplaced. They divide existence as they do land. Life here, death there, and a border between. They guard it with the Church, with science . . . only poets defy the divide, and even they can be sentimental about it. It's taken us four hundred years to realize that if the Golden World is to be won, and kept, it must be won with ambiguities. There is no certain thing on earth worth knowing. Now, men are not subtle enough to grasp this simple idea. They have a fear of ambiguity. They think it's weakness, they think it's senility, a sign of death. They box it up and bury it; they tell us we should be certain or be slaves. Well, they are about to witness revolution; and we would rather it be brought to them out of love for life, from us, who like their beauties and admire their wit, than from the earth, despairing of its sons, and burning them all away. Don't aspire to be like them—

JUDE: You have.

ELIZABETH: I was wrong, and I'm unlearning myself. Help me make daughters, Jude. It will be difficult for me. De Silva, I remember, he said I'd never loved anyone, but I expected everyone to love me. I had him expelled from the country for saying that: but it's true. I've never wanted union. When I was both King and Queen of England, why should I relinquish half my state? I'll have to change. It'll hurt me. But to have the gold again, and not lose it to a wilderness . . . that's worth the ache. Well?

JUDE: Majesty.

ELIZABETH: My darling Jude. *(Kisses her)* Lead us. Take our royal blood. I'm ready.

*THEY EXIT. LUCY STARTS TO CLEAR THE TABLE. SHE SITS DOWN TO EAT A PIECE OF CHICKEN.*

*ENTER ESSEX.*

ESSEX: Has she gone?

LUCY: Yes.

ESSEX: Was she very cross?

LUCY: Furious.

ESSEX: Am I exiled?

LUCY: No.

ESSEX: The monkey's disappeared.

LUCY: She'll never forgive you.

ESSEX: Oh God, I can't bear another execution. How about a little sympathy?

LUCY: My poem—

ESSEX: Yes?

LUCY: The one you wrote specially for me.

ESSEX: Yes?

LUCY: Why is it written out fifty-four times in this little book of yours?

ESSEX: Where did you find that?

LUCY: And why is there a space for the name of the woman you're giving it to at the top of each page?

ESSEX: I can explain.

LUCY: No wonder you've got no energy left. No wonder you look like a sick man!

ESSEX: Lucy, I adore you—

LUCY: Rearrange these words to make a well-known phrase or saying: Off. Fuck.

*EXIT LUCY.*

ESSEX: Damn! Damn! Damn! Damn!

*ENTER BONNER.*

BONNER: I thought I smelt food.

ESSEX: Don't move.

BONNER: Is there a circus in the city?

ESSEX: Not that I know of.

BONNER: It's just that a woman in Wood Street says she saw a monkey in her back yard trying on her knickers.

ESSEX: Which way?

BONNER: This is an hour ago.

ESSEX: Damn!

BONNER: Lost an ape, have you?

ESSEX: What do you find so funny?

BONNER: You, a lost ape, trees from nowhere—

ESSEX: The Queen demanded entertainment.

BONNER: And you're it.

ESSEX: *(Unsheathes sword)* One more word like that.

BONNER: Ha!

ESSEX: Maybe you'd please the Queen: trussed up—

BONNER: What?

ESSEX: —orange in your mouth—

BONNER: Keep your distance.

ESSEX: —prisoner of war—

BONNER: *(Gets out grenades)* I'm warning you—I'll blow you apart.

ESSEX: Weapons?

BONNER: Grenades.

ESSEX: You're a soldier.

BONNER: Yes.

ESSEX: Name?

BONNER: You tell me yours.

ESSEX: I asked first.

BONNER: I've got the grenades.

ESSEX: They look harmless enough—

BONNER: They could blow you up—

ESSEX: They inflate flesh?

BONNER: Explode! Bang! Get it, idiot? What's your name?

ESSEX: Essex. Yours?

BONNER: Lance-Corporal Bonner, S. 24255998.

ESSEX: *Earl* of Essex. For what it's worth.

BONNER: Earl?

ESSEX: Are we going to stand here forever: or shall I prick you with this, and you blow me up with those and be done with it?

BONNER: Feeling suicidal?

ESSEX: Yes.

BONNER: I wouldn't mind joining you.

ESSEX: Death pact—

BONNER: Something like that.

ESSEX: What's your problem?

BONNER: What's yours?

ESSEX: I asked first, and I answered first last time.

BONNER: It's personal.

ESSEX: Oh . . .

BONNER: Yours?

*SILENCE.*

ESSEX: Ireland. That's what broke me. I wish I'd never seen the God-forsaken country.

BONNER: I've been in Ireland.

ESSEX: What's a man if he can't subdue a few savages? They should be flattered we take the interest. But the Queen—

BONNER: The Queen sent you to Ireland? When was this?

ESSEX: 1599.

BONNER: Is this some sort of joke?

ESSEX: I wish it were. I wish all of Ireland was another of her entertainments: and they'd pull down the curtain over it. We'd applaud and all go home.

BONNER: You could withdraw—

ESSEX: And lose face?

BONNER: Negotiate?

ESSEX: And concede that there's justice in their resistance?

BONNER: You're quite serious, aren't you?

ESSEX: Seems to me you're showing undue sympathy for them.

BONNER: Me?

ESSEX: Spy, perhaps.

BONNER: Hey, whoa-up.

ESSEX: Brown eyes: always suspicious in an Englishman. Maybe I should simply run you through and take your carcass to the Queen. Put those . . . grenades of yours on the ground. Down! Put them down! *(Bonner does so)* Good. Now, tell me: what do they do, precisely?

BONNER: I told you. They explode.

ESSEX: How?

BONNER: By pulling out that pin—

ESSEX: Bang?

BONNER: Yes.

ESSEX: In your hand: what's the use of that?

BONNER: There's a delay. You pull, and throw it—

ESSEX: Pull and throw. Bang!

BONNER: Bang!

ESSEX: That'd be a new trick, eh?

BONNER: Not really—

ESSEX: Not here, perhaps, but in 1599. How much damage do they cause?

BONNER: In a confined space? A great deal.

ESSEX: I want them.

BONNER: No.

ESSEX: Give them to me: for England.

BONNER: England sucks.

ESSEX: What does that mean?

BONNER: It's an insult: England sucks. On its knees. Between the legs of the world. Get it?

ESSEX: Clever. I'm going to slit your throat for that remark.

*ESSEX ADVANCES ON BONNER, WHO DEFENDS HIMSELF WITH A KNIFE FROM THE DINNER TABLE. THEY FIGHT. BONNER IS OVERCOME.*

ESSEX: Say your prayers, Bonner.

BONNER: Take the grenades. If you like them, come back, I'll get some more for you—

ESSEX: Shall I take off your balls? I think perhaps I should. One at least.

BONNER: Essex . . . please . . .

ESSEX: That foot—

BONNER: Yes?

ESSEX: Would you care to tell that foot how very thankful you are for my many mercies to you? Tell it very closely. With your lips?

BONNER: Kiss . . . your . . . foot?

ESSEX: Kiss my foot.

BONNER: If you insist.

ESSEX: A gentleman never insists, Bonner, not with virgins. He asks politely first, as I have, and, if he encounters resistance, then, and only then, he pricks them 'til they bleed.

BONNER: (Kisses Essex's bare foot) Satisfied?

ESSEX: Suck the toe a little. Affectionately now. No teeth.

BONNER: Fuck off!

ESSEX: At last: a little courage. You *are* an Englishman, Bonner, brown eyes or blue. I'll leave you intact.

BONNER: You bastard.

ESSEX: I'll be back.

BONNER: Hey. If I'd consented—

ESSEX: Yes?

BONNER: If I'd sucked your toes. What would you have done?

ESSEX: Killed you on the spot.

*EXIT ESSEX WITH GRENADES. BONNER BREATHES A SIGH OF RELIEF. HE SITS AT THE TABLE AND SIPS SOME OF THE BEER, WHICH HE SPITS OUT IN DISGUST. HE STANDS UP AS GEORGIA APPEARS BEHIND HIM AND SLIPS THE SACK OVER HIS HEAD.*

BONNER: What the fuck!?

GEORGIA: (Hisses) Hurry!

*CAROLINE APPEARS, WITH HALF A BRICK.*

GEORGIA: (Hisses) Now!

BONNER: What's going on?

*CAROLINE HITS BONNER.*

BONNER: Ow! (*He falls to his knees.*)
GEORGIA: Again!

*CAROLINE HITS HIM A SECOND TIME. HE COLLAPSES.*

GEORGIA: Good. Quickly now—

*THEY STRIP HIM.*

GEORGIA: Oh, this is fun.
CAROLINE: He stinks of sweat.
GEORGIA: I like it. Oh, look at him. Like a baby.
CAROLINE: He'd kill us if he was awake.
GEORGIA: He might huff and puff a bit, but he's all talk.
CAROLINE: Can we stop admiring him now and get him into the
    sack?

*THEY PUSH HIM INTO THE SACK.*

GEORGIA: (*Scarcely believing*) We've done it, Caroline.
CAROLINE: Efficient, aren't we?
GEORGIA: The little shit.
CAROLINE: Now what?
GEORGIA: Tie up the sack.
CAROLINE: He's not going to suffocate . . .
GEORGIA: Maybe he will. Maybe he won't.
CAROLINE: Georgia—
GEORGIA: (*As to a nervous child*) No. He's not going to suffocate.
CAROLINE: Perhaps we ought to make a hole in the sack. Just a
    small one. He's very still.
GEORGIA: You hit him hard.
CAROLINE: Oh Christ. Suppose I've done some serious damage?
GEORGIA: Don't get cold feet now. It's done.
CAROLINE: We've descended to his level, haven't we?
GEORGIA: Listen, love, I know his level. We're nowhere near.
CAROLINE: This isn't as much fun as I thought it'd be. He's just a
    lump of meat. What have we done to him worth doing?
    Nothing. He'll come round, rub his stupid head and behave
    the way he's always behaved.
GEORGIA: But we'll know.

CAROLINE: That we tied him up in a sack for half a day? So what?

GEORGIA: Keep your voice down. Maybe we should throw his clothes away. Then at least he'll be embarrassed.

CAROLINE: Half of me wants him never to find out who was responsible.

GEORGIA: Yes, I know, and the other half wants him to see us . . .

CAROLINE: Yes.

GEORGIA: Know who's put him down . . .

CAROLINE: Quinn would never forgive me.

GEORGIA: I didn't think they were that close.

CAROLINE: They're not. But if he thought I'd had the pants off his brother—

GEORGIA: Monogamous, are you?

CAROLINE: Why do you ask?

GEORGIA: Just . . . wondering.

CAROLINE: No. Not always.

GEORGIA: Does Quinn get jealous?

CAROLINE: He doesn't know. He thought I'd been with Bonner—

GEORGIA: And have you?

CAROLINE: No.

GEORGIA: Ever wanted to?

CAROLINE: No.

GEORGIA: Um.

CAROLINE: What do you mean: um?

GEORGIA: We could do it. With Bonner.

CAROLINE: I knew you were thinking that.

GEORGIA: Lying in the dark: he won't know whether he's alive or dead.

CAROLINE: I keep thinking of what he said—

GEORGIA: That's right: think why we've done this. And then think one step further.

CAROLINE: We make a hole in the sack—

GEORGIA: Yes.

CAROLINE: He never sees us.

GEORGIA: And it isn't adultery if you can't see his face.

CAROLINE: He's my brother-in-law. (*A beat*) What do we do if he comes round?

GEORGIA: There's two of us to one of him. He's lying down, we're on top of him.

CAROLINE: Maybe we should tie his hands together.

GEORGIA: Good.
CAROLINE: With his bootlaces.

*SHE STARTS TO TAKE THE LACES FROM THE BOOTS.*

GEORGIA: Let's take him behind the wall. It's a bit open here.

*GEORGIA STARTS TO TEAR UP BONNER'S UNIFORM.*

GEORGIA: Nice belt.

*THEY BOTH HAVE THEIR BACK TO BONNER'S HEAD. AS THEY WORK, HE SITS UP, UNSEEN. HE HAS HIS EYES CLOSED, STILL PLAINLY DAZED.*

BONNER: . . . what . . . ?
GEORGIA: Jesus!

*GEORGIA FORCES BONNER'S HEAD DOWN, AND SITS ON HIM. BONNER STRUGGLES, WHILE CAROLINE FINDS THE HALF BRICK. BONNER THROWS GEORGIA OFF, AS CAROLINE HITS HIM AGAIN. HE COLLAPSES.*

GEORGIA: Jesus! That was a near thing.
CAROLINE: Behind the wall before we go any further.

*THEY DRAG BONNER OFF, WITH GREAT EFFORT.*

CAROLINE: Hell's teeth, he's heavy.
GEORGIA: It's all that muscle—
CAROLINE: Which of us is going to go first?
GEORGIA: We'll toss for it.
CAROLINE: I haven't got any money on me.
GEORGIA: We'll toss him. Heads, it's me. Tails, it's you.

*THEY DRAG HIM OFF, LEAVING ONE BOOT ON STAGE. ENTER JONSON, WITH A TEXT, SMILING.*

*ENTER QUINN.*

QUINN: Where the fuck did he go? Bonner . . .

JONSON: Good afternoon.

*QUINN WALKS ACROSS THE STAGE.*

JONSON: Which way is it to the Dock Road?

QUINN: That way.

JONSON: I'm sick of this infernal place.

QUINN: I don't blame you.

JONSON: Doesn't this age care about art? Elizabeth ignores us, and none of the locals seem to give a damn!

QUINN: They don't want art here. Art's for somewhere nice. Try Manchester.

JONSON: It's not the city. It's the age. Nobody understands: art's like bread—

QUINN: I used to work in a bakery.

JONSON: Then you know bread—

QUINN: Up to my eyes in the fucking stuff.

JONSON: Art's hot bread.

QUINN: Eh?

JONSON: It's necessary. It's not like religion. Religion's a plum: it stops mouths. And it's not truth, that's meat—

QUINN: What do you mean, meat?

JONSON: It's for cannibals. But art's bread. Warm, fresh. Made with our hands. See?

QUINN: Not really.

JONSON: Everywhere I go: incomprehension. I've met one man who understood. Mulrooney.

QUINN: I wouldn't be too proud of that.

JONSON: I'm going to find the actors and go home. Gloriana can have her little promenade through your grubby little lives, I hope she's enjoying it.

QUINN: Who?

JONSON: Don't you hear the applause? She likes you better than art, better than poetry—that's why we've no audience. She's too engrossed in your domestic comedy—if you see any actors, tell them Jonson's gone home, will you?

QUINN: Jonson's gone home.

JONSON: Forgive the outburst. I don't resent you. You can't help being on show—

QUINN: I don't know what you're talking about.
JONSON: Why should you care?
QUINN: The actors—how will I recognize them?
JONSON: They strut around like geese: you can't miss them.
QUINN: Geese?

*EXIT JONSON.*

QUINN: What's a geese look like?

*EXIT QUINN—*

*—AS GEORGIA AND CAROLINE ENTER.*

GEORGIA: Well?
CAROLINE: Well. It's amazing what you can persuade people to do in their sleep.
GEORGIA: If he only knew.
CAROLINE: Oh, he knew.
GEORGIA: Do you think so?
CAROLINE: He wasn't dead to the world. He felt it all. Why are you so glum? It's only sex.
GEORGIA: You've changed your tune.
CAROLINE: Spilt milk. Want a cup of coffee?
GEORGIA: Yes.
CAROLINE: Can we go to your flat? I need a wash.
GEORGIA: Coffee—
CAROLINE: We left his boot out— *(She throws it over the wall)*

*THE WOMEN EXIT TOGETHER AS QUINN ENTERS.*

QUINN: *(Yelling)* Bonner! Where are you? Come on out of the woodwork, you creep!
BONNER: *(Off)* Who's that?
QUINN: Bonner?
BONNER: *(Off)* Quinn?

*ENTER BONNER, STUMBLING, WITH ONE LEG AND HIS ARMS OUT OF THE SACK.*

BONNER: Where am I? Quinn? Is that Quinn?
QUINN: Jesus! Bonner!
BONNER: For God's sake, speak to me—
QUINN: What are you doing in there?
BONNER: In where?
QUINN: You're in a fucking sack!
BONNER: A sack? Oh fuck! That's it: I'm in a sack, aren't I? Where are you?
QUINN: Here.
BONNER: (*Grabs Quinn*) I'm not dead, am I?
QUINN: No.
BONNER: Did you put me in here?
QUINN: No.
BONNER: Then help me get the fuck out of it!
QUINN: Stand still—

*WITH QUINN'S HELP, BONNER EMERGES FROM THE SACK. HE IS NAKED. HE COVERS HIMSELF WITH THE SACK.*

QUINN: What the hell were you doing in there?
BONNER: I went to heaven.
QUINN: In a sack?
BONNER: It was like nothing on earth, Quinn. I was lying there: weight on me, soft, moving gently up and down. It felt like—I was fucking God.
QUINN: You're off your rocker.

*BONNER TOUCHES HIS HEAD. IT'S TENDER.*

BONNER: Somebody hit me. Look. Blood.
QUINN: Why did you lie to me?
BONNER: Is it bad? Eh, Quinn, take a look. Is it bad?
QUINN: It's just a cut. You said you slept with Caroline.
BONNER: Maybe I should get it looked at.
QUINN: She's never touched you, has she?
BONNER: No.
QUINN: I fucking knew it!

*QUINN HITS HIM.*

BONNER: That hurt.

QUINN: Come on, you've wanted a chance to fight. So here I am, ready and waiting.

BONNER: That really hurt.

QUINN: Are you listening to me?

BONNER: Look at this. There's holes in the sack—

QUINN: Fight, damn you!

BONNER: I'm not going to fight.

QUINN: Why not?

BONNER: . . . I think . . . I've been . . . raped . . .

QUINN: That shouldn't be much to a man of the world like you.

BONNER: Ha! You can take the world and stuff it.

QUINN: What are you talking about?

BONNER: It stinks, Quinn: stinks worse than I do, stinks all over. Hong Kong, Hamburg, all stink. There's nothing out there, Quinny, there's not a damn thing.

QUINN: I don't like you, Bonner.

BONNER: Well, I don't like you. So what? Just because we're brothers, doesn't mean we have to like each other.

QUINN: You're a shithead, Bonner.

BONNER: You're a useless little wanker.

QUINN: Thanks.

BONNER: You're welcome. That it?

QUINN: Suppose it is.

BONNER: Go our separate ways.

QUINN: I was ready to skin you alive.

BONNER: Too late.


*AN EXPLOSION.*


QUINN: Jesus Christ! What was that?

BONNER: It sounded like . . . a grenade. Oh Christ Almighty. He did it.

QUINN: Who? Did what?

BONNER: Those grenades I had: I gave them away.

QUINN: Who to?

BONNER: A bloke called Essex.

QUINN: Why?

BONNER: He wanted to blow up a house.

QUINN: A house?

BONNER: Yes.

QUINN: Any house?

BONNER: Yes.

QUINN: There's only one house left in Paradise Street worth destroying, you arse-hole. Mine! Caroline! Caroline!

*EXIT QUINN.*

# Scene Four

*THE RUINS OF CAROLINE AND QUINN'S HOUSE. CLOTHES, BROKEN FURNITURE, BRICKS AND BELONGINGS LITTER THE STAGE. SMOKE HANGS IN THE AIR. POKING FROM UNDER A PILE OF RUBBLE, A HAND, CLASPING QUINN'S TRUMPET. IT IS DARKER NOW, AND THE LIGHT OF THE DAY FADES THROUGH THE SCENE, AS THE MAGIC OF THE DAY FADES.*

*ENTER CAROLINE AND GEORGIA, PICKING THEIR WAY THROUGH THE RUBBLE.*

CAROLINE: Quinn . . . Quinn . . .

GEORGIA: He's not here, love.

CAROLINE: What happened? What in God's name happened?

GEORGIA: We can't do anything until the police arrive.

CAROLINE: *(Sees the hand)* Ah! Jesus! Quinn! Quinn! *(She starts to dig at the rubble)*

GEORGIA: Stay back, love—

CAROLINE: Quinn? Quinn? *(To Georgia)* Help me, damn you! *Somebody* help me. Oh Christ, Christ, Christ—somebody help me.

*ENTER QUINN.*

QUINN: What do you want?
CAROLINE: Help me, Quinn's under there.
QUINN: I am?
CAROLINE: Quinn? Quinn! Oh— *(They embrace)*
QUINN: I thought you were dead. I love you. I love you.
CAROLINE: I thought you— *(She turns)* Who's that, then?
QUINN: Help me clear the bricks—
GEORGIA: He must be dead—
QUINN: *(Clearing enough rubble to see the face)* It's Mulrooney.
GEORGIA: Who?
QUINN: The Irishman.

*ENTER JUDE.*

JUDE: Has somebody called the police?
GEORGIA: They're coming.
CAROLINE: Was it a gas leak?

*JUDE EXAMINES MULROONEY.*

QUINN: He's dead, right?
JUDE: He's dead.
QUINN: He won't have known what hit him.
GEORGIA: Does anybody know who he was? I mean, I saw him
    wandering around sometimes, but—
JUDE: His name was Jack Mulrooney. He was a professor of
    mathematics.
QUINN: Can we get something to cover him up? A piece of cur-
    tain, anything.
GEORGIA: I've never seen a body before.
JUDE: She liked Jack. She's going to be very pissed off about this.
GEORGIA: Who will?
JUDE: The Queen. Gloriana.

*CAROLINE COVERS MULROONEY'S BODY.*

QUINN: Well, it wasn't Bonner did it.
JUDE: Would you swear to that?

CAROLINE: Quinn . . . he had those grenades.

QUINN: He was with me. I was talking to him when we heard the bang.

GEORGIA: This is murder, isn't it?

JUDE: Manslaughter, at least. Bonner had grenades?

CAROLINE: He didn't do this. He wasn't here.

QUINN: How do you know?

CAROLINE: I . . . saw him.

QUINN: Oh?

CAROLINE: Didn't we, Georgia?

GEORGIA: Yeah, we saw him. From a distance.

JUDE: So if it wasn't him, who was it?

QUINN: He said he gave the grenades to a man called Essex.

JUDE: Essex?

QUINN: That's what he said.

JUDE: She'll have him flayed alive.

GEORGIA: Are we back to the Queen again?

JUDE: Queen Elizabeth the First. She came out of the past to see England. And to have a medical examination.

GEORGIA: Are you drunk?

JUDE: No. I X-rayed her. Took a blood sample.

GEORGIA: Blue, was it?

JUDE: She's . . . just like the rest of us. Only wiser.

*ENTER BONNER, WRAPPED IN THE SACK.*

BONNER: Jesus Christ, he did a good job on this place, didn't he?

CAROLINE: Enter the hero.

BONNER: He must have blown one wall and the rest caved in.

JUDE: Where's Essex now?

BONNER: How should I know?

QUINN: We've got a dead man here.

BONNER: Shit. Who?

QUINN: The Irishman.

BONNER: He said this place was coming down. He should have taken his own advice. Where's my stuff?

CAROLINE: Buried.

BONNER: I need it. I'm due in Aldershot. I haven't got a uniform.

CAROLINE: We've got nothing left at all.

BONNER: You'll get compensation.

QUINN: We're not even insured.

BONNER: That's a bit of a fuck up.

CAROLINE: This was your fault! We've got nothing. Not even a bed.

BONNER: No way you pin it on me.

CAROLINE: It was your grenade.

BONNER: It was that queer with the pearl in his ear. You can't blame me.

CAROLINE: We'll just let the police sort it out.

BONNER: I want my stuff! And I want it now!

CAROLINE: Well, you'd better start digging then.

QUINN: I'm going to fetch the boys in blue.

BONNER: Hey, Quinn-boy, whoa there. Let's not be hasty. Some old fellow has a wall fall on him: it's not the end of the world. They'll court-martial me, stealing army property. Think on, eh? Give us a break.

QUINN: This was my house. Tough. I'm getting the police.

*EXIT QUINN.*

BONNER: *(Yelling after Quinn)* And a happy fucking Christmas to you, an' all. When I get my hands on that Essex. Frigging psychotic.

JUDE: Did you see Elizabeth too?

BONNER: Who?

GEORGIA: Don't start again, Jude.

JUDE: I saw the Queen. I touched her. I'm not crazy. Am I?

BONNER: You asking me?

CAROLINE: There's snow in the wind. That was a quick spring, wasn't it?

JUDE: It was her spring. That's the proof. How do you think the trees appeared? Up out of the pavement, for God's sake—

CAROLINE: Someone planted them.

JUDE: In full blossom?

GEORGIA: Give it up, Jude.

JUDE: She can't have gone. She can't.

GEORGIA: I'm going back to my place. Are you coming, Caroline?

CAROLINE: I'm waiting for the police.

GEORGIA: Jude?

JUDE: She'll come, with Essex, with Lucy—

BONNER: Could be he went up with the blast: forgot to let go. Anyone standing on a bit of Essex?

GEORGIA: Don't be foul.

BONNER: You've got your fantasies, I've got mine.

GEORGIA: Didn't take you long, did it?

BONNER: What?

GEORGIA: To get back where you started.

BONNER: I never went anywhere.

GEORGIA: That's not what I heard. I heard you were alive this afternoon.

BONNER: Daft bitch.

GEORGIA: I heard you weren't Bonner at all.

BONNER: You don't know what the hell you're talking about, as usual. I was beaten up. There was five of them.

GEORGIA: You don't look that bruised to me.

BONNER: Oh, I can look after myself. No problem.

GEORGIA: Do you know how ridiculous you sound?

BONNER: Fuck off.

GEORGIA: The tough guy act doesn't work without the costume.

BONNER: I was nearly killed by these bastards, I'll have you know. They smothered me, assaulted me. Indecently.

GEORGIA: It's terrible, isn't it? The things people do to each other. Never mind, Bonner, you'll get over it. Back on duty, pistol in your pocket. Nobody need ever know.

*SHE IS ABOUT TO GO.*

BONNER: Did you ever love me?

GEORGIA: Oh, Bonner . . . *(A beat)* Oh, by the way: I like the dragon. It must have hurt. Especially the tail.

*EXIT GEORGIA.*

BONNER: How did she know?

*TRUMPET, OFF.*

JUDE: That's her.

CAROLINE: Jude, give it a rest.

JUDE: She's coming. Listen.

CAROLINE: She's dead. She's been dead for hundreds of years.

JUDE: So?

CAROLINE: You know, you do sound a little crazy.

JUDE: I won't let you take her away from me. It's hard enough accepting in the first place. I've always hidden those hopes away. I didn't want to be called weak or silly. But there's miracles here, Caroline. Right here. It's not a pig's world. It's not.

BONNER: Was that for my benefit?

CAROLINE: Shut up.

BONNER: She's a lunatic. You said it first.

CAROLINE: I wonder how long they'll put you away for?

BONNER: No one's locking me up.

CAROLINE: You're already locked up, in that sad little head of yours. Why did you tell Quinn we'd slept together?

BONNER: Bit of a laugh.

CAROLINE: Fancy yourself as a dangerous man, do you?

BONNER: Depends.

CAROLINE: So what did they do to you: once they had you in this sack?

BONNER: None of your business.

CAROLINE: Was it painful?

BONNER: There was six of them. The size of tanks. I did my best. Put two of them out, maybe three—

CAROLINE: What did the rest do?

BONNER: I told you, it's—

CAROLINE: I heard you liked it.

BONNER: What?

CAROLINE: I heard you lay back like a baby and let them do whatever they wanted. At one point, I heard, you said "thank you."

BONNER: I never . . .

CAROLINE: No?

BONNER: No! (*The truth dawns*) Oh Jesus. Oh. Jesus. It wasn't you.

CAROLINE: None of your busines.

BONNER: And Georgia. It was you and Georgia.

CAROLINE: Talk sense, Bonner.

BONNER: Was it you? It was you, wasn't it?

*ENTER ESSEX.*

ESSEX: Hide me.

BONNER: *(To Caroline)* Answer me!

CAROLINE: Well, all the boys are here now, aren't they?

BONNER: I've been waiting for you.

ESSEX: I'm glad to see you too, Bonner. You see, the fact is, I've got myself in a jam. For England.

CAROLINE: You blew up this house?

ESSEX: It wasn't intentional.

CAROLINE: This was my house.

ESSEX: I know. She's been watching the whole thing here: I thought, a little drama . . . And of course, the matter of Ireland—

CAROLINE: I don't understand.

JUDE: You killed Mulrooney.

ESSEX: I know. I heard him scream. She won't be pleased, will she? She'll have me beheaded—

CAROLINE: Are you one of those poor sods who thinks he's Napoleon, or Florence Nightingale—

ESSEX: I wish I were a nightingale. I wish I were a bee, a flower, a cloud, anything just so she wouldn't notice me a while. Bonner, S. My friend. Find me a little nook, eh, where I can put my head?

BONNER: You've got my boots on.

ESSEX: I found them.

BONNER: Give me them back.

ESSEX: I've got every right to footwear. I've solved the Irish question! The grenades: we bury them amongst the potato crop: they dig them up, boil them, eat them—bang! Brilliant!

BONNER: I want my boots—

ESSEX: Finders, keepers—

*BONNER DIVES FOR THE BOOTS.*

ESSEX: Hands off, you peasant—

BONNER: Peasant?

ESSEX: Everyone in this dung-heap is a peasant, except Jude. She loves me, don't you?

JUDE: Where's Elizabeth?

ESSEX: Don't you care what happens to me?

BONNER: Don't whine. You'll get used to it.

ESSEX: None of you seems to appreciate my situation. I'm the Earl of Essex. See that scar? Axe-cut. Spring 1601.

BONNER: See that scar? Fell off my bike. Summer 1962.

ESSEX: This is a matter of life and—

*ENTER ELIZABETH.*

ELIZABETH: Death.

ESSEX: *(Quietly)* Shite. Shite. Shite.

JUDE: Thank God you've come.

ELIZABETH: Why wouldn't I come?

JUDE: I thought . . . maybe I'd dreamed it all.

ELIZABETH: No. Whatever fictions Jonson wrote for us today, this part is real. *We are real.* But where is my Paradise Street?

ESSEX: Still here, ma'am.

ELIZABETH: I liked it better when the walls were standing.

CAROLINE: *(Re: Essex)* Are you in charge of this idiot? Do you know what he's done?

ELIZABETH: I have eyes.

ESSEX: *(Re: Bonner)* He did it. I was in Manchester.

ELIZABETH: You never lied well, Robin. I always liked that about you.

CAROLINE: Listen to me. This is my house.

ELIZABETH: It was ours too. Our playhouse.

CAROLINE: What do you mean—playhouse?

ESSEX: She's been watching you.

CAROLINE: How?

ELIZABETH: Through the walls.

CAROLINE: Watching?

ELIZABETH: I tired of Jonson's interminable masques: poncy little dancers, prettified little speeches. The world isn't like that—

CAROLINE: So you spied on us?

ELIZABETH: Your dramas have the sour ring of truth. The betrayals, the lies. You're well out of it. Better forget these men, or use them, like you used him—

BONNER: It *was* you.

ELIZABETH: A witty little device—the sack. He looked so comical with that fat little dragon-tail of his sticking up in the air. I find sexual intercourse very amusing.

CAROLINE: This isn't a zoo.

ELIZABETH: What's a zoo?

CAROLINE: You've got no right spying on us! I love Quinn. And I love having a life with him. A private life.

ELIZABETH: There's no such thing—

CAROLINE: You're just a dirty old woman is all you are!

ELIZABETH: Ah! You've got no sense of humor. Where's Mulrooney! Bring me my Irishman—

*SILENCE.*

ELIZABETH: Where is he?

ESSEX: He's not well, ma'am.

ELIZABETH: Sick?

ESSEX: To death, ma'am.

ELIZABETH: Not dead? Oh Jesu. I'll have you strung up over a
slow fire, both of you, 'til your blood boils out—

JUDE: Hasn't there been enough violence?

*SILENCE.*

ELIZABETH: Where is he?

JUDE: Here, ma'am.

ELIZABETH: Did he suffer?

JUDE: I hope not.

ELIZABETH: (*Looking at the corpse*) It's a good face. There's faith in
it. I like that. Oh, to hell with forgiveness!

*SHE TURNS ON ESSEX AND BEATS HIM, THEN LAYS INTO
BONNER.*

ELIZABETH: Bastards! Bastards! (*At length, she stops, panting*)
That's better.

ESSEX: I didn't mean anything to happen to him.

ELIZABETH: Oh, do shut up.

ESSEX: If I haven't loved you enough, it's because my heart can't
contain you.

ELIZABETH: Why can't you just apologize?

ESSEX: I'm sorry. I'm sorry. I'm—

ELIZABETH: Once is enough.

ESSEX: I did it for England.

ELIZABETH: England's a pitiable place if we kill for it. Well . . .
we've been deserted by our ape, our gentle Irishman is dead,

our stage has been blown to tinder, and we shall not, it
seems, see the end of the romance. Jude, please tell us you're
the bearer of good news.

JUDE: I am.

ELIZABETH: You're sure?

JUDE: You've got no pox.

ELIZABETH: Then we shall have daughters; flocks of them, fit to take
the world in harness. I'm in heat at last! After four hundred
years Gloriana's in season! Come here, Robin. Fertilize me.

ESSEX: I . . . think not, ma'am.

ELIZABETH: I won't strike you: bring your dart, the wound's
ripe—

ESSEX: Here?

ELIZABETH: Why not? We'll lie us down in this ash, and we'll
make daughters—

ESSEX: I'm afraid I've lost the knack.

ELIZABETH: What? You've waited centuries for this cherry of
mine. Take the thing!

ESSEX: I don't have the wherewithal.

ELIZABETH: Left you waiting too long, did I? Ah well. There's
plenty more men, prettier than you. (*To Bonner*) What about
you?

BONNER: Me?

ELIZABETH: Come on . . .

BONNER: I'm not touching you.

ELIZABETH: Little dragon—

BONNER: No.

ELIZABETH: Am I too old?

BONNER: You smell.

ELIZABETH: You want a doll, not a woman! Get out of my sight.
Both of you.

ESSEX: Bess?

ELIZABETH: You heard me! You're fit for nothing!

ESSEX: I can't go back to the past without you—

ELIZABETH: I don't want you back there! This age deserves you.
Sterile—

ESSEX: Ma'am, I appeal to you.

ELIZABETH: No you don't. Go away. Enjoy this New World for as
long as it's yours. Because I'm going to loose a tide of daughters that will wash you out of power forever.

ESSEX: I'm lonely already.

ELIZABETH: Robin. They say the men who first sailed north found a green country, which they called Iceland, to dissuade other adventurers from following. Sailing further, they were lonely, and so they called the next country Greenland, though it was icier than the first, because they wanted others to come after them, and save them from themselves. A lesson to adventurers, Robin.

ESSEX: Ma'am.

ELIZABETH: Kiss us goodbye, Robin.

*HE KISSES HER HAND.*

ELIZABETH: On the lips. Just once.

*HE KISSES HER ON THE MOUTH, AND EXITS. SHE WATCHES HIM GO.*

BONNER: You enjoy yourself this afternoon?

CAROLINE: Not particularly.

BONNER: You're a hypocrite.

CAROLINE: Probably.

BONNER: He wanted to bust my head because he thought I'd had you. Now I have, and I didn't even know it.

CAROLINE: You lay there like a baby, Bonner. Well, almost a baby. I even began to see what she loved you for.

BONNER: Georgia. She never loved me.

CAROLINE: It'd kill you to admit it, wouldn't it. You could never believe there was love in the world: you'd have to start thinking there was something worth living for.

BONNER: Tell Quinn I'm sorry, will you?

CAROLINE: I'll tell him.

BONNER: I am, you know.

*EXIT BONNER. ELIZABETH APPLAUDS APPRECIATIVELY.*

ELIZABETH: Ah, nothing Jonson wrote equals this—

CAROLINE: Satisfied, are you?

ELIZABETH: We admire your way of handling these men.

CAROLINE: I'm glad I'm an education.

ELIZABETH: But now you should forget them. Think instead about the way the world will be when we have power—

CAROLINE: I don't care.

ELIZABETH: There'll be daughters of mine in the Church, in the universities—

JUDE: What if you have sons?

ELIZABETH: Then I'll bring them up as daughters. My milk is for women: I don't want killers at my tit.

CAROLINE: You had Essex beheaded—

ELIZABETH: That was for private reasons.

CAROLINE: There's no such thing: you said that yourself.

ELIZABETH: Don't tie me in knots.

CAROLINE: Men are children. We should help them grow up.

ELIZABETH: Bonner, a child? Essex, a child?

CAROLINE: Yes. They're not certain of anything.

ELIZABETH: And what are you certain of?

CAROLINE: Love, perhaps. Myself, even.

JUDE: It's not a pig's world.

ELIZABETH: I'm not convinced.

CAROLINE: Well I'm not convinced of you. Jude believes in you, but I don't.

ELIZABETH: Then I'll show you—

JUDE: Show her what?

ELIZABETH: What we are. Our miraculous self. Uncover our sweet Jack.

JUDE: What for?

ELIZABETH: Just do it. He's coming with me. Aren't you, Jack?

*THE SAME GOLDEN LIGHT THAT APPEARED AT ELIZA-BETH'S FIRST ENTRANCE SPILLS OVER MULROONEY'S CORPSE.*

JUDE: He's dead, Bess.

ELIZABETH: The dead talk to the dead. Mulrooney?

*MULROONEY SITS UP.*

MULROONEY: Price of a brandy?

JUDE: My God.

ELIZABETH: *(To Caroline)* Do you believe in us now?

MULROONEY: There was a blast. A terrible din, it was. And the walls falling in.

ELIZABETH: It's all over: get up.

MULROONEY: Is this heaven?

CAROLINE: This is Paradise Street.

MULROONEY: But was I . . . ?

JUDE: Dead? Yes. You were dead.

ELIZABETH: We called you back from limbo, Jack. We need a husband.

MULROONEY: I don't think I'm fit for that.

ELIZABETH: Why not? We could travel a little; a honeymoon: America.

MULROONEY: Damn America! It's full of the Irish.

ELIZABETH: We'll make children. Produce them in torrents.

MULROONEY: I haven't had an erection in twenty years.

ELIZABETH: We'll change that. Essex will stay here. You'll come with me.

MULROONEY: I don't want the past—

ELIZABETH: Why not? The future's very like the present once you get there.

JUDE: I wish I were dead. I'd come with you.

ELIZABETH: We'll see each other again, in time. Or out of it. Embrace me, my sweet. Keep your children well, Caroline. (*To Mulrooney*) Come or stay, but make up your mind quickly.

*EXIT ELIZABETH.*

MULROONEY: This is a lot to handle when you've just decided you were dead. I have to think it through.

*EXIT MULROONEY.*

JUDE: She's gone. I can't bear it.

CAROLINE: I was wrong, Jude. She was real.

JUDE: How can I keep remembering? How can I hold on to what I know right now? It'll slip away.

CAROLINE: It's getting very cold.

JUDE: It's already slipping away.

*ENTER QUINN, WITH FLOWERS.*

QUINN: I'm sorry I was so long. I lost my way. It's strange out there. Where is everyone?

CAROLINE: Gone.

QUINN: You look miserable.

CAROLINE: No, I'm fine.

QUINN: I can't find a single police car. Found these though—

CAROLINE: Lovely.

QUINN: We'll creep up into them, eh? Lie there tonight: make love. Who needs a house—

CAROLINE: We do.

QUINN: I wish it was the same as it was.

CAROLINE: You and Bonner?

QUINN: You and me.

CAROLINE: I love you.

QUINN: I love you.

CAROLINE: So that's a start.

*THEY KISS.*

CAROLINE: Goodnight, Jude.

QUINN: 'Night.

JUDE: Goodnight.

*EXIT QUINN AND CAROLINE.*

JUDE: We'll have evidence of round worlds and solitary worlds—

*ENTER MULROONEY.*

MULROONEY: Is that Venus?

JUDE: I wouldn't know.

MULROONEY: I think it is. *(A beat)* Are you absolutely certain I was dead?

JUDE: Absolutely.

MULROONEY: You're a nurse: you should know.

JUDE: It was a miracle, Jack.

MULROONEY: So I have to concede it?

JUDE: Oh, for certain. It's what you were waiting for.

MULROONEY: I'd better go with her then.

JUDE: Somebody should.

MULROONEY: But I'm not riding a horse. Them beasts bite. Goodnight then.

JUDE: Goodnight.

*EXIT MULROONEY. JUDE IS LEFT ALONE. AND THEN, AFTER A MOMENT, THE SECOND MASQUER ENTERS, WITH A SPEECH IN HIS HAND.*

SECOND MASQUER: Have you seen a fellow in a fancy mask?

JUDE: No.

SECOND MASQUER: Damn. He's gone on without me. Well, you'll have to help me. Here. (*He proffers the paper*)

JUDE: What's this?

SECOND MASQUER: Just read the part that isn't underlined. It's Jonson's work, and frankly it's overwrought, but—

JUDE: Why are we bothering? There's nobody watching.

SECOND MASQUER: There's God.

JUDE: I don't believe in God.

SECOND MASQUER: Well, I can't help that. Read.

JUDE: (*Reads*) "*Dream; forget yourself and rise
        Out of your mind and into others.*"

SECOND MASQUER: "*Men, be women—*

JUDE: "*—Fish, be flies.*"

SECOND MASQUER: "*Girls, take beards—*"

JUDE: "*—Sons, be your mothers.*"

SECOND MASQUER: "*The future of the world now lies . . .* " (*He stops. Nudges Jude.*) It's you. You've got the last line.

JUDE: Oh . . . er . . .

SECOND MASQUER: Let's try again. "*The future of the world now lies—*"

JUDE: "*In coral wombs behind our eyes.*"

SECOND MASQUER: (*Reclaiming the paper*) Good. That's it then. That's the last of it.

JUDE: I want the words back.

SECOND MASQUER: Oh no, I couldn't possibly. This is my copy, and—

JUDE: Just give it to me. I did you a favor, you do me one.

SECOND MASQUER: Suppose somebody asks for it?

JUDE: Tell them to come and get it.

*SHE TAKES THE PAPER.*

*THE SECOND MASQUER EXITS.*

JUDE: I'll be waiting.

*SHE LOOKS UP AT THE SKY. DISTANTLY, SOMEBODY IS SINGING.*

*As I was a-walkin' down Paradise Street, Way-hay, blow the man down . . .*

*AND THEY SING ON, AS THE LIGHTS FADE TO DARKNESS.*

*THE PLAY ENDS.*

# SUBTLE BODIES

# Production Notes

This is a dream play; a comedy of altered states in which images that have been shaped by the private rages, frustrations and desires of the characters take public, or at least semi-public, form. On occasion, these dream-images seep almost unnoticed into the "real world" of the play, like the sand that is constantly blowing in under the doors of the Atlantic Hotel, where the story is laid. At other times, they supplant that world entirely, the most spectacular example of which occurs in the Third Act, when the hotel becomes a ship, and sails off into the night on what is to be its final voyage.

Plainly, such transformations make hefty demands upon the play's designer. In *Subtle Bodies'* first production these challenges were met by creating an environment that was a kind of no-man's-land between the real and the illusory, with the details of the hotel sketched in, but not completed. Walls were not solid, staircases were skeletal, windows were suspended in space. Reality was provisory here, and it seemed almost inevitable that the stuff of dreams would invade such an unfixed place.

This is by no means the only solution to the challenge however. Depending on the scale of the budget, and the sophistication of the stage machinery available, the play would certainly not be harmed by much more physical transformation. I'm a great fan of stage illusions, for instance; this might be a fine place to put the smoke and mirrors to work in a dramatic context. It would be quite something to see the hotel become a vessel in front of us, as Lear proclaims:

"*Suppose a ship . . . And the sea. The way Sean dreamed it. Foamy and vast.*"

A little too elaborate for a lot of companies, I realize. Most productions will have to rely upon more stylized transformations, to which end I introduced the Dream Technicians, who–like Bunraku puppeteers–move about the stage unseen by those they manipulate (the characters), and largely ignored by the audience. For a production of modest means, the Technicians are a useful device. They can construct and strike the scenic elements around people as scenes play out, helping to create the kind of flow of images that dreams are made of. The ship, the lifeboat and the sea can be nearly symbolic: cardboard cutouts, scrawls of light in the darkness, a patch of colored light and the sound of waves . . .

About the dialogue. Though the banter of the piece is designed to evoke the texture of ordinary conversation, it is, of course, highly stylized. There should be a whiff of artifice in even the most naturalistic scenes: in the Feydeauesque precision of the comings and goings, in the overlapping of dialogue, in the "confessional" scenes, when the characters, posing for a picture, speak their secret hearts. (These are, by the way, people who come from the North of England, their accents unmusical. At least, that's the way I've always heard them in my head.)

Finally, although the play has its farcical moments, and at its heart sits a poet dedicated to the poetry of nonsense, it is in fact a highly structured piece, providing every character with a very specific line of action. It is important that the audience be able to trace those lines of action, be able to see through the general mayhem into the nature of each of these people. We're not simply here to watch their exterior lives, after all. The glory of dreamplays is that they carry us past the superfice of behavior, into the maelstrom of motive. The passengers in Lear's doomed ship have a night in which to play out their most private dramas on the secret stage of their psyches. Little do they know there is an audience on the other side of the footlights.

Clive Barker—Los Angeles, 1996

# The Cast:

DEXTER JUFFS: the bridegroom to be
CARYS SKINNER: the bride to be
SEAN
MRS. CORCORAN: a widow, now running the Atlantic Hotel
A VIRGIN
A GORILLA
MR. FOSS: a nonsense poet and watercolorist, also known as
    EDWARD LEAR
ULYSSES
YOUNG MAN with bow and arrow
BEACH PEOPLE
MRS. MOCATTA of the Bureau
MR. TREADAWAY also of the Bureau
DREAM TECHNICIANS

   *THE WEDDING PARTY*
PHOEBE SKINNER: Carys' mother
LINDBERG SKINNER: Carys' father
DONNA-MARIE SKINNER: Carys' sister
MELBA JUFFS: Dexter's mother
FRANK JUFFS: Dexter's father
ROSE GIDDY
VINCE BURROUGHS
ROBERT KIDD: the best man

PASSENGERS on the *Bear of Amsterdam*, a cruise ship
GUESTS at Mr. Foss' Wedding

# Act 1

# Act 1:

*GULLS ON THE SOUNDTRACK. ORCHESTRAL MUSIC. SLOWLY THE LIGHTS COME UP ON ATLANTIC HOTEL, A SMALL, TATTY ESTABLISHMENT ON THE NORTH-WEST COAST OF ENGLAND.*

*THE HOTEL IS PRESENTED TO US, AS IT WERE, IN SNATCHES.*

*THERE IS A FRONT DOOR; A BALCONY; WINDOWS WITH VENETIAN BLINDS, INTERNAL DOORS PERHAPS, CERTAINLY A BACK EXIT LETTING ONTO A PATIO. ALL FRAGMENTS OF ARCHITECTURE WHICH WILL, WHEN LIT ACCORDINGLY, EVOKE A VARIETY OF SPACES.*

*SOMETIMES A BALCONY, SOMETIMES A ROOM, SOMETIMES A DREAM-SCAPE: A BEACH, A SHIP, THE SEA. THESE SPACES MAY BE ISOLATED BY A LIGHTING EFFECT, BUT OFTEN THE HOTEL CAN BE SEEN IN ITS STRANGE ENTIRETY, WITH VARIOUS EVENTS (OR NON-EVENTS) RUNNING SIMULTANEOUSLY BUT DISCREETLY. CAUSE AND EFFECT, OR SIMPLY EFFECT.*

*THE SOLID STRUCTURE OF THE BUILDING IS SCARCELY REPRESENTED. NO SOLID WALLS OR DOORS, JUST FRAMES. THE BUILDING IS ALMOST TRANSPARENT, A DREAM HOTEL, HOVERING ON THE BRINK OF EXISTENCE. THE COLORS THE HOTEL IS PAINTED PERHAPS EMPHASIZE THIS. TONES OF MILKY LILAC, OF PALEST AMBER, OF TWILIGHT BLUE. A RECEDING WORLD, ONLY HALF-TRUE.*

*THROUGH THE LATTICE OF DOOR FRAMES, WINDOWS, ETC., WE CAN SEE THE DUNES THAT ENCROACH ON THE HOTEL ON EVERY SIDE. THERE IS NO SIGN OF THE SEA: THE DUNES ROLL ON FOREVER, IT SEEMS. THE TIDE HAS WITH-DRAWN FROM THIS STRETCH OF COASTLINE, LEAVING VAST EXPANSES OF SAND WHICH SPREAD TO THE THRESH-OLD AND BEYOND, THREATENING TO INVADE THE HOTEL.*

*THERE ARE A FEW LINGERING SIGNS OF FORMER SPLEN-DOR IN THIS WASHED-OUT (OR RATHER DRIED-OUT) WORLD. LOOPS OF COLORED LIGHTS HANG AROUND THE OUTSIDE OF THE HOTEL, AND OVER THE PATIO. THERE IS ALSO A SIGN, ONCE IMPRESSIVE, NOW ERODED, WHICH READS: "WELCOME TO THE ATLANTIC."*

*THE SET IS SIMPLY FURNISHED. ON THE PATIO A SMALL WICKER TABLE AND A CANVAS CHAIR (NOT A DECKCHAIR, THE UPRIGHT VARIETY); INSIDE, SUCH FUR-NITURE AS THE ACTION REQUIRES. NOT MUCH, PROBA-BLY, SO THAT EASE OF TRANSFORMATION FROM PLACE TO PLACE, FROM SCENE TO SCENE, CAN BE PRESERVED.*

*THE FLOOR, I IMAGINE, IS TILED; THE SAME WORN PAS-TEL TONES HERE AS ELSEWHERE. THERE SHOULD BE SOME CACTI IN POTS, FAIRLY LARGE—THIS DESERT HOTEL'S EQUIVALENT OF POTTED PALMS.*

*BEYOND THESE FEW DETAILS, THE SHAPE OF THE SPACE AND THE EPHEMERA THAT DECORATE IT ARE DISCRE-TIONARY. IN TRUTH, ALL OF THESE ARE DETAILS ARE. IF YOU HAVE A DIFFERENT DREAM OF THIS PLACE, BY ALL MEANS DREAM IT, AND GOOD LUCK TO YOU.*

*IT IS THE MIDDLE OF THE AFTERNOON OF FRIDAY, SEPTEMBER 22ND. A LIGHT WIND IS BLOWING OFF THE SEA. THE STRINGS OF LIGHTS ROCK GENTLY.*

*MAYBE THE SOUNDTRACK CARRIES, AT THE EDGE OF AUDIBILITY, THE LISP OF THE SEA.*
*STANDING AT THE FRONT DOOR OF THE HOTEL ARE DEX-*

*TER JUFFS AND CARYS SKINNER. THEY ARE IN THEIR EARLY
TWENTIES; WELL-DRESSED; A GOOD-LOOKING COUPLE.
DEXTER CARRIES A SUITCASE, CARYS A SMALL BAG. THERE
IS AN UNMISTAKABLY FUGITIVE AIR ABOUT THEM.*

DEXTER: You're not crying?
CARYS: I've got something in my eye.
DEXTER: Let me—
CARYS: *(Coldly)* I can do it, Dexter.
DEXTER: Sorry. *(He watches her nervously)* Shall we go in?

*SHE LOOKS AT HIM, RELUCTANCE ON HER FACE.*

DEXTER: *(Sighs)* Carys. We're not going back. Not 'til we've had
    time to sit down and be honest with each other.
CARYS: *(Plainly)* I don't want to be honest. I want to get married.
DEXTER: Listen to yourself.
CARYS: All right. I agreed to talk. But we're not fugitives. Are we?

*DEXTER STEPS INTO THE HOTEL.*

CARYS: *(To his back)* Is that what you think we are, Dexter? Run-
    away lovers? Will you speak to me?
DEXTER: Are you coming in or not?
CARYS: *(Quietly)* I hate you.

*THE LIGHTS COME UP MORE STRONGLY ON THE REST
OF THE HOTEL, AND WE ARE AWARE OF TWO OTHER
FIGURES. ONE, MR. FOSS, IS ASLEEP IN THE CANVAS
CHAIR ON THE PATIO. MORE OF HIM LATER. THE OTHER,
SEAN, A YOUNG MAN IN A T-SHIRT AND JEANS, IS
BRUSHING UP SAND AT THE FAR END OF THE HALL, HIS
BACK TO THE FRONT DOOR. THIS RITUAL (SAND-
BRUSHING) SHOULD GO ON THROUGHOUT THE PLAY.*

*DEXTER COUGHS. SEAN TURNS.*

SEAN: Yeah?
DEXTER: I'm Dexter Juffs.
SEAN: You'll get over it.

*SEAN GOES BACK TO HIS BRUSHING.*

DEXTER: My—er—my wife and I have a reservation here.
SEAN: *(Disinterested)* Oh?
DEXTER: Juffs. We have booked.
SEAN: All right. Hold your horses. I'll tell herself.

*HE EXITS. CARYS STEPS INTO THE HOTEL.*

DEXTER: It's been a long time. It's smaller than I remember.
CARYS: It's falling apart.
DEXTER: Mind you, I was five. Worm's-eye view.
CARYS: It's still early. We can go back—
DEXTER: *(Without looking at her)* No.
CARYS: Tell them we took a long drive, just to chat things over.
    They'd understand.
DEXTER: You make it sound like a clash of taste in carpets.

*CARYS IS SILENT.*

CARYS: *(Almost throwaway)* It's only sex.
DEXTER: Only.
CARYS: Lots of marriages work without it.
DEXTER: Not this one.
CARYS: Good marriages.

*ENTER MRS. CORCORAN, AN ATTRACTIVE WOMAN IN
MIDDLE AGE, WITH A GENTLE IRISH ACCENT. SEAN FOL-
LOWS; STARTS BRUSHING AGAIN.*

MRS. CORCORAN: Mr. and Mrs. Juffs?
DEXTER: Yes.
CARYS: No.
MRS. CORCORAN: No?
CARYS: We're not Mr. and Mrs.
DEXTER: I'm Dexter Juffs and this is my . . . my fiancee—
MRS. CORCORAN: Oh.
DEXTER: Carys.
CARYS: Skinner.
MRS. CORCORAN: I'm Mrs. Corcoran.

DEXTER: Pleased to meet you.

MRS. CORCORAN: I'm sorry about the confusion. I thought you were married.

DEXTER: Well, we're almost married.

CARYS: It was supposed to be tomorrow. But we've decided to talk about it for a couple of years.

MRS. CORCORAN: It doesn't matter two hoots to me. *(To the boy)* Sean! *(To Dexter and Carys)* I've put you at the front overlooking the—

*SEAN HAS APPROACHED THE GROUP.*

SEAN: Sand.

MRS. CORCORAN: Beach. Will you take up Mr. Juff's case for him? Number 9. You do still want a double room?

DEXTER: Certainly.

MRS. CORCORAN: Sean.

*SEAN DOESN'T MOVE.*

CARYS: Just as a point of interest: where *is* the sea?

SEAN: Twenty minutes by taxi.

MRS. CORCORAN: Will you *please* take the cases up?

SEAN: That's Ulysses' job.

MRS. CORCORAN: Well, where's Ulysses?

SEAN: Search me.

MRS. CORCORAN: *(Gently threatening)* Would you find him please, Sean?

*SEAN EXITS.*

DEXTER: I came here as a boy. I remember the sea being closer somehow.

MRS. CORCORAN: It's the low autumn tides.

DEXTER: Oh.

SEAN: *(Off, yelling)* ULYSSES!

MRS. CORCORAN: It looks as though the weather's brightening up a bit.

DEXTER: Yes.

MRS. CORCORAN: It was quite squally last night. Come far?

DEXTER: Manchester.

SEAN: *(Off)* ULYSSES!

MRS. CORCORAN: You'll be wanting a bath and a change of clothes. Where's the boy got to? Would you like to sign the register, Mr. Juffs, on behalf of you both?

*MRS. CORCORAN EXITS; CARYS EXHALES, SLOWLY.*

CARYS: It's stifling here.

DEXTER: Is it?

CARYS: There's no air conditioning.

*DEXTER HAS TAKEN OUT HIS PEN, BUT CAN'T GET IT TO WRITE.*

CARYS: Did you ask for a room with a view of the sea?

DEXTER: My pen doesn't work.

CARYS: You don't hear a word I say.

DEXTER: Got a pen?

CARYS: *(Vehemently)* Jesus Christ!

DEXTER: *(Blandly)* You haven't.

CARYS: I could scream.

DEXTER: Scream then. Go on. Make a spectacle of yourself.

*SHE OPENS HER MOUTH TO SCREAM. A SCREAM FILLS THE STAGE; BUT NOT HERS. WHEN SHE CLOSES HER MOUTH, FURIOUS THAT HER THREAT MEANS NOTHING, THE SCREAM GOES ON. SHE STANDS IGNORING DEXTER, STARING OUT AT THE AUDIENCE, WHILE DEXTER, BACK TO US, TRIES TO GET HIS PEN TO WORK BY SCRIBBLING WITH IT.*

*UNSEEN BY BOTH OF THEM (AND APPARENTLY UNHEARD), A LARGE GORILLA ENTERS, TRAILING SHATTERED SHACKLES FROM ITS WRISTS, AND CARRYING A SCREAMING GIRL OVER ITS SHOULDER. NEITHER DEXTER NOR CARYS FLINCH; THIS SPECTACLE IS CLEARLY NOT VISIBLE TO THEM.*

VIRGIN: Let me be, you heartless brute! I'm technically still a virgin!

*THE GORILLA PUTS THE GIRL DOWN, STILL HOLDING ON TO HER. SHE THRASHES IN ITS ARMS, BEATING AT ITS FACE AND CHEST. THERE'S SOMETHING CURIOUSLY FORMAL ABOUT THE DISPLAY: LIKE A SCULPTURE COME TO LIFE.*

VIRGIN: I'll never love you! Not if you were the last thing on earth! I'll die first!

*THE GORILLA PULLS HER CLOSE.*

VIRGIN: Rape! Rape!
DEXTER: *(Looking up from the register, which he is now signing)* What did you say?
VIRGIN: You're heartless and repulsive!
CARYS: What?
DEXTER: You said something.
CARYS: No.
DEXTER: Oh.
VIRGIN: *(Overwhelmed now)* Oh God . . . God in Heaven . . .

*SEAN HAS FOUND HIS WAY ONTO THE PATIO. HE CALLS OUT ACROSS THE DUNES.*

SEAN: Ulysses!
CARYS: My watch has stopped.
VIRGIN: I want to die! Oh! Oh!
CARYS: Probably got sand in it.
DEXTER: *(As if he's being blamed)* Don't look at me.
SEAN: Ulysses!
CARYS: Damn.
MR. FOSS: *(In his sleep)* Somebody help her. Piggily-pot! Man in a white shirt. Shoot the simianky beast!
SEAN: What?

*THE GIRL SCREAMS ONE FINAL TIME, WRAPPED IN THE GORILLA'S EMBRACE.*

MR. FOSS: *(In his sleep)* Too late!
SEAN: *(Shaking him)* Mr. Foss!

*THE SCREAM STOPS.*

MR. FOSS: Oh!

*HE WAKES. THE GORILLA DROPS THE GIRL.*

SEAN: Mr. Foss! Are you all right?
MR. FOSS: What? *(Sees Sean)* Oh.
SEAN: You were talking in your sleep.
MR. FOSS: Was I?

*HE STANDS UP; GLANCES INTO THE HOTEL AT THE GORILLA AND THE GIRL, WHO WAIT LIKE ACTORS ANTICIPATING THE NEXT LINE.*

SEAN: Were you dreaming?
MR. FOSS: What did I say?
SEAN: Something about a simi . . . simi-something beast.
MR. FOSS: Nonsense.
SEAN: Beg pardon?
MR. FOSS: It was all . . . just nonsense. I'm forgetting already.

*THE GORILLA AND THE GIRL WANDER AWAY IN OPPO-SITE DIRECTIONS.*

MR. FOSS: Foolishness.
SEAN: Was it dirty?
MR. FOSS: Not that I recall. Just the usual banalities. You'd think
    a man my age'd have a decent catalogue to rummage
    through. Puerile rubbish. I disgust myself.

*MR. FOSS IS IN FACT EDWARD LEAR, WATERCOLORIST AND WRITER OF NONSENSE, LIVING AT THE ATLANTIC UNDER THE ASSUMED NAME OF HIS FAVORITE CAT. HE IS AN IMPRESSIVE MAN; WIDE, DOMED FOREHEAD, A DARK THATCH OF A BEARD. THOUGH HIS MANNER IS POLITE TO A FAULT, IT BARELY CONCEALS RAGES AND PASSIONS OF WAGNERIAN PROPORTIONS. HE WEARS MODERN CLOTH-ING: SUBDUED, ELEGANT. HE CARRIES A HALF-SMOKED CIGAR. OFTEN IT IS UNLIT, BUT HE SELDOM IS WITHOUT*

*IT FOR THE REST OF THE PLAY. ON OCCASION HE USES IT
TO PROVIDE A SMOKE-SCREEN FOR HIMSELF. IN FRONT OF
HIM IS A SMALL EASEL, AND PAINTING EQUIPMENT.*

SEAN: Have you seen Ulysses?
MR. FOSS: How old are you, boy?
SEAN: I'm nineteen.

*MR. FOSS WASHES OUT A PAINT BRUSH.*

MR. FOSS: Traveled much?
SEAN: I've been around. Newcastle. Glasgow.
MR. FOSS: *(Contemptuous of these boasts)* Ah. Go abroad. There's
   nothing left here.

*HE PICKS UP THE GLASS THAT CONTAINS HIS WATER-
COLOR WATER.*

MR. FOSS: Did you know there were tides in a glass of water? Oh
   certainly. Dominion of the moon, this tumble glass. And the
   waters of my eyes. Tides there, even. And what do I do, surrounded by such wonders? I dream banalities. Loveless, the
   soul goes to dust.
SEAN: I'll remember.
MR. FOSS: You do that, nineteen.

*HE GIVES THE GLASS TO SEAN.*

SEAN: And you haven't seen Ulysses?
MR. FOSS: Oh, but I have. Half an hour ago, he went down onto
   the beach, accompanied by a shovel. I think it must be serious.
SEAN: What?
MR. FOSS: Between him and the shovel. They wanted to be alone
   together, no doubt, so that he could canoodle with the curve of
   her handle. You don't have a clue what I'm talking about, do you?
SEAN: Not much.
MR. FOSS: And quite right too.

*FOSS STEPS THROUGH INTO THE HALL, LEAVING SEAN
ON THE PATIO.*

SEAN: *(Shouts)* ULYSSES!

*FOSS LOOKS AT CARYS; CARYS STARES BACK.*

MR. FOSS: Oh. I'm sorry.

*HE WITHDRAWS AND TAKES COVER ON THE PATIO.*

MR. FOSS: *(Hissing)* Psst! Sean! People. Flesh and blood. D'you see them?
SEAN: Newlyweds.
MR. FOSS: Now there's a profession. I'll go round the back. Young love is all I need.

*FOSS GATHERS UP HIS BELONGINGS AND DISAPPEARS AROUND THE BACK OF THE HOTEL.*

CARYS: Did you see that man?
DEXTER: No.
CARYS: Didn't he have sad eyes?
DEXTER: I didn't see him.
CARYS: He was staring. Like I had three heads.
DEXTER: Maybe he thought you were beautiful.

*SHE ALMOST SMILES; TURNS TO MEET HIS GAZE; HE IS LOOKING AWAY.*

*ENTER MRS. CORCORAN.*

MRS. CORCORAN: Everybody seems to have disappeared. I can't even find the boy now.
CARYS: There was a man in here. With a beard.
MRS. CORCORAN: Oh, that's Mr. Foss.
CARYS: I thought I . . . his face rang a bell.
MRS. CORCORAN: He stays here every year, late in the season. When everybody else has gone home.
CARYS: Foss.
MRS. CORCORAN: Says it reminds him of the Holy Land, being here. Of all places.

*SEAN ENTERS.*

MRS. CORCORAN: Have you found him?
SEAN: He's buggered off somewhere.
MRS. CORCORAN: Well, you'll have to take the bags up yourself.
SEAN: Typical.
DEXTER: Carys was wondering . . . can we see the sea from our room?
MRS. CORCORAN: Well, not exactly; but you have a panoramic
    view of the dunes.
SEAN: You lucky people.

*SEAN PICKS UP THE BAGS AND LEADS OFF BEFORE MRS.
CORCORAN CAN GIVE HIM ANOTHER LOOK.*

MRS. CORCORAN: Will you be wanting dinner tonight?
DEXTER: Please.
MRS. CORCORAN: If you need anything, just dial through to me
    on the phone beside the bed. And if it's not working just yell
    down the stairs.
DEXTER: Thank you.
MRS. CORCORAN: I must say, it's lovely to have you here.

*DEXTER AND CARYS FOLLOW SEAN UPSTAIRS. MR. FOSS,
WHO HAS COME ALL THE WAY AROUND THE BACK OF
THE HOTEL, NOW ENTERS BY THE FRONT DOOR.*

MR. FOSS: Mrs. Corcoran.
MRS. CORCORAN: Mr. Foss.
MR. FOSS: I wonder, has there been any communication for me?
    A telegram perhaps?
MRS. CORCORAN: Not to my knowledge.
MR. FOSS: *(To himself)* I'm forgotten.
MRS. CORCORAN: Are you all right? You look tired.
MR. FOSS: I'm not sleeping well.
MRS. CORCORAN: Is it the pillows?
MR. FOSS: Oh no, the pillows are miracles of duck down.
MRS. CORCORAN: Only I can easily change them for you. Maybe
    something with a bit more spring.
MR. FOSS: *(To himself)* A boy.
MRS. CORCORAN: Sorry?

MR. FOSS: A buoyant thought. But no, really. No.

*HE STARTS TO GO, LEAVING MRS. CORCORAN BEWIL-
DERED, AS EVER. SUDDENLY, HE BRIGHTENS.*

MR. FOSS: There is something.

MRS. CORCORAN: Yes?

MR. FOSS: I'd turn somersaults for a pot of coffee. Turkish coffee.
So thickadicorice you can stand your spoon in it.

MRS. CORCORAN: Now?

MR. FOSS: My tongue has more fur than the back of a cat. I swear
if I stroked it, the thing would purr.

MRS. CORCORAN: It's probably all the coffee which is keeping
you awake. Are you having nightmares?

MR. FOSS: I wish I were.

MRS. CORCORAN: Don't say that.

MR. FOSS: I wish once in a while my empty head could drum up
a few terrors. Blue bottle cities, rains of flaborous fire, men
with nutmeg graters for hands scratching at the door.

MRS. CORCORAN: Sounds like one of Sean's books.

MR. FOSS: You don't like bad dreams?

MRS. CORCORAN: When Mr. Corcoran and I bought the hotel—
this is almost eleven years ago now—I dreamt somebody
pulled the plug out of the sea and it all drained away. I think
it was prophetic, don't you? In those days the sea used to
come within twenty yards of the back door. In eleven years,
it's receded so far you can't even see it. All caused by move-
ments in the earth's crust—

MR. FOSS: Taken away your bread and butter.

MRS. CORCORAN: I'm glad Edwin isn't here to see it. The sand
everywhere. It would have distressed him terribly.

MR. FOSS: I rather like it.

*HE REACHES INTO HIS POCKET AND TAKES OUT A
HANDFUL OF SOFT, DRY SAND, WHICH FALLS BETWEEN
HIS FINGERS.*

MRS. CORCORAN: It gets in everything. In the linen cupboard,
in the carpets. I think it wants to bury us alive.

*SEAN COMES DOWNSTAIRS. MRS. CORCORAN SEES THE
SAND MR. FOSS HAS JUST LET FALL FROM HIS HAND.*

SEAN: No tip.
MRS. CORCORAN: There's sand on the floor, Sean.
SEAN: What do I do? Applaud?
MRS. CORCORAN: I'll make your coffee, Mr. Foss.

*MRS. CORCORAN EXITS.*

SEAN: Lugged their stuff up two flights.

*HE GETS BROOM OUT AND STARTS BRUSHING UP THE
SAND AGAIN.*

SEAN: It's slavery.
MR. FOSS: I was thinking, nineteen—
SEAN: Huh?
MR. FOSS: We could perhaps be of some use to each other. Do
    you dream?
SEAN: Sometimes.
MR. FOSS: Vividly?
SEAN: *(Smiles)* Oh yeah.
MR. FOSS: Dreams of some faraway tomorrow, are they? Futurial
    visions?
SEAN: I hadn't thought. Suppose so. Yeah.
MR. FOSS: And do you remember them? In detail? Colors? Faces?
SEAN: When I bother to.
MR. FOSS: I'll pay you for them.
SEAN: Are you kidding?
MR. FOSS: Deadly serious. You bring me a fistful of nightflights—
    erotic, traumatic, apocalyptic—I'll buy them all off you.
SEAN: Any kind of dream?
MR. FOSS: Anything. Except gorillas. Shall we shake on it, nineteen?

*THEY SHAKE.*

MR. FOSS: Good.

*AS HE EXITS.*

MR. FOSS: *(As he exits, jubilant)* GOOD, GOOD, GOOD.

*SEAN GOES BACK TO BRUSHING UP THE SAND, A RHYTHMICAL BRUSHING THAT IS QUIET AND CALMING.*

*MUSIC. SLOWLY, THE LIGHTS CHANGE. LIGHT COMES THROUGH A VENETIAN BLIND. THE CASE WHICH DEXTER WAS CARRYING IS OPEN ON A CHAIR. DEXTER IS STANDING IN THE MIDDLE OF THE ROOM, SMOKING.*

*CARYS ENTERS. SHE'S CHANGED FROM THE RATHER TOO PRISSY CLOTHES SHE WAS WEARING; SHE'S BATHED: SHE FEELS CLEAN AND OPTIMISTIC.*

CARYS: *(A joke)* Well, at least there was no sand in the taps.
DEXTER: Um.
CARYS: It doesn't matter, does it really, not having a view of the sea? We wouldn't have looked at it anyway.

*A BEAT.*

DEXTER: You were right: we shouldn't have come.
CARYS: *(Ignoring his pessimism)* I was thinking while I was in the bath. Everything's going to be all right.
DEXTER: Oh.
CARYS: Why don't you have a bath too? You'll feel better.
DEXTER: We *could* go back. Tell them it was all a joke.
CARYS: What's brought this on?
DEXTER: Being here. Talking's not going to change anything. We'll get married. What the hell. We'll raise kids, the way they want us to. What the hell. We'll raise bloody whippets if your father prefers.
CARYS: This is Rob's fault. This whole cynical routine. I can hear him now.
DEXTER: I'm not being cynical, I'm just saying you're right. What more do you want? Let's get married, for Christ's sake, next week could be too late.
CARYS: Bloody Rob.
DEXTER: You're talking about our best man.

CARYS: Best rat.

DEXTER: Cheap.

CARYS: Shall we have an argument, is that what you want?

DEXTER: No.

CARYS: Isn't it? Wouldn't you like to have one almighty row, 'cause I would. I'd really love that.

DEXTER: All right. You're on.

CARYS: No holds barred.

DEXTER: Where shall we start? Sex?

CARYS: Sex is good.

DEXTER: Ladies first.

CARYS: You're lousy in bed.

DEXTER: I'm not used to screwing for an audience.

CARYS: What?

DEXTER: Your mother taking a sperm count.

CARYS: Now *that's* cheap.

DEXTER: Your whole bloody family's cheap, paper bags, whippets and all.

*LIGHTS HAVE BEGUN TO COME UP ON ANOTHER PART OF THE STAGE, GENTLY ILLUMINATING THE "AUDI-ENCE" FOR THIS ARGUMENT. MR. FOSS ON HIS BAL-CONY, DRINKING TURKISH COFFEE, POT IN HAND TO TOP UP HIS CUP. SEAN LEANING ON THE DOOR FRAME OF THE FRONT DOOR, SUNNING HIMSELF, SWEATING. MRS. CORCORAN INSIDE THE HOTEL. THE GORILLA ON THE PATIO READING* PLAYBOY.

CARYS: It always comes back to my mother.

DEXTER: Oh, you've noticed that too.

CARYS: What about your holy family?

DEXTER: You leave them out of it.

CARYS: Then you leave my family out of it. Just because they've got money.

DEXTER: Paper bags.

CARYS: So they sell paper bags. Somebody has to sell paper bags. At least they're not afraid of living it up a bit.

DEXTER: Flaunting their money, that's all it is. It's not life.

CARYS: You know the trouble with you—

DEXTER: Do tell.

CARYS: Everything makes you guilty. You're afraid any minute God's going to strike you dead.
DEXTER: (*Near tears*) I wish he would. I bloody wish he would—

*DEXTER STARTS TO EXIT.*

CARYS: Where are you going?
DEXTER: To drown myself.
CARYS: The sea's that way! (*Pointing*)

*DEXTER EXITS.*

CARYS: (*Shouts after him*) If you can find it!

*THE LIGHT FADES ON CARYS, AS HER FACE BEGINS TO CRUMPLE. THE FOUR WATCHERS GO ABOUT THEIR BUSINESS. MRS. CORCORAN WATERS THE CACTI. FOSS RETURNS TO HIS COFFEE DRINKING. DEXTER EXITS FROM THE HOTEL BY THE FRONT DOOR, NUDGING SEAN ASIDE.*

SEAN: Excuse me.
DEXTER: What?
SEAN: How about "excuse me"?
DEXTER: Sorry. I didn't mean to—sorry.

*DEXTER EXITS.*

*SEAN WHISTLES GENTLY TO HIMSELF. THE SUN BEATS DOWN ON HIS FACE. THE GORILLA CROSSES THE STAGE AND LOOKS UP LONGINGLY AT FOSS ON THE BALCONY. FOSS STANDS UP AND RETURNS THE STARE.*

MR. FOSS: I tried to conjure up a dream of pure energy, pure sexuality. Pure life. Something to prove my potency. And what do I get? An adhesive and love-lorn Gorilla. (*To the Gorilla*) Please fade away, there's a good fellow. Dreams should fade away once you've woken from them.

*THE GORILLA SIGHS AND EXITS.*

*AT THE FRONT DOOR, SEAN IS STRIPPING OFF HIS T-SHIRT, STRETCHING AND WIPING SWEAT OFF HIS CHEST. MRS. CORCORAN, STILL AT THE CACTI, SEES HIM.*

MRS. CORCORAN: You haven't forgotten the rest of the hallway have you, Sean? There's still sand. And those lights.

SEAN: No, I haven't forgotten.

MRS. CORCORAN: Another night like last night and they'll be blown down.

SEAN: I'm getting some sun while it lasts.

MRS. CORCORAN: Five minutes.

*MRS. CORCORAN EXITS.*

*SEAN CLOSES HIS EYES. FOSS, THROUGH THE INVISIBLE WALLS OF THE HOTEL, WATCHES HIM, TRANSFIXED.*

MR. FOSS: We possess two bodies. The physical and the subtle.

*MRS. CORCORAN COMES BACK. SHE CALLS ACROSS THE HALLWAY.*

MRS. CORCORAN: Sean?

SEAN: Five minutes, you said.

MRS. CORCORAN: Did you ever find Ulysses?

SEAN: No.

MRS. CORCORAN: He's supposed to be serving dinner at six-thirty.

*MRS. CORCORAN EXITS.*

SEAN: It's not my fault. *(No answer. He shrugs.)*

MR. FOSS: The subtle body is our dream-self. By day, it is discreet. Like a flame in sunlight, burning yet invisible.

*SEAN SHIFTS TO CATCH THE SUN BETTER, FLITTING AWAY A FLY FROM HIS FACE. THE MOVEMENT CATCHES MR. FOSS' ATTENTION.*

MR. FOSS: But by night, the subtle body goes, at the speed of thought, into . . .

*HE'S LOSING CONCENTRATION.*

MR. FOSS: . . . into . . .

*SUDDENLY THE ANGER IN FOSS BREAKS OUT.*

MR. FOSS: Go on, strip off your shirt if you must. Strip off your pants while you're at it. I don't care. I'm quite unmoved. You see?

*RAISES HIS HANDS.*

MR. FOSS: Scarcely a tremor. What do I care what's between your legs? No doubt your ears are unwashed, your fingernails bitten, no doubt you are entirely viliacious. Pumpy and slumpy and . . .

*SEAN, WHO HAS OF COURSE HEARD NOTHING OF THIS, FLITS AWAY ANOTHER FLY.*

MR. FOSS: Where was I? I get misled. It's so very easy to forget invisible things. The life of the mind.

*SEAN STRETCHES.*

MR. FOSS: *(Re: Sean)* This'll decay. Even this. But the subtle body dreams on.

*MR. FOSS WATCHES SEAN FOR A WHILE.*

*THE SOUND OF GULLS.*

*SEAN'S EYES HAVE CLOSED.*

MR. FOSS: Asleep, boy?

*APPARENTLY HE IS. THE SEA SOUND IS CLOSER NOW.*

MR. FOSS: Bring me something back, will you? Something bright and dangerous.

*LIGHTS CHANGE. IN THE CHANGE, ENTER ULYSSES. HE'S FIFTY (AT LEAST); WEATHER-BEATEN; BLOODY-MINDED, AND A LITTLE SLOW. HE IS WEARING BOOTS AND WIND-CHEATER AND IS CAKED IN MUD AND WET SAND. AS HE CROSSES THE STAGE THE PHONE RINGS.*

SEAN: *(Opens his eyes)* Shit!

*HE GOES INSIDE. ULYSSES PICKS UP THE PHONE.*

SEAN: Ulysses?
ULYSSES: Shhh!

*SEAN WANDERS BACK TO THE FRONT DOOR.*

ULYSSES: *(Into phone)* Hello? Yes, this is the Atlantic Hotel. Huh? Will you speak up? Juffs? No, there's nobody here name of Juffs. Sorry.

*SEAN HEARS. POINTS TO THE REGISTER.*

ULYSSES: Wait a minute.

*ULYSSES LOOKS AT REGISTER.*

ULYSSES: Sorry. My mistake. A Mr. and Mrs. Juffs booked in sometime this afternoon. You want a word with them? Uh? Oh I see. Yeah. How many? Is that all singles? Two doubles, rest singles. No problem. Fine. Yeah.

*ULYSSES PUTS DOWN THE PHONE.*

SEAN: Who was it?
ULYSSES: Wrong number.
SEAN: Where have you been?
ULYSSES: Watching a lady do very slow striptease.
SEAN: Lady? You don't know no ladies.

*ULYSSES STARTS TO EXIT.*

SEAN: Who is it? Eh? Ulysses. What are her tits like?

*AT THIS MOMENT CARYS ENTERS WITH HER BAG, THE WORSE FOR A BOUT OF CRYING. SEAN CRINGES AND GOES OUTSIDE.*

ULYSSES: How do.

*ULYSSES EXITS. CARYS STANDS, LOOKING LOST, THEN GOES TO SPEAK TO SEAN.*

CARYS: Have you seen Mr. Juffs?
SEAN: He went out a while back.
CARYS: Which way?
SEAN: I wasn't watching.

*SHE GOES BACK INSIDE, AS MRS. CORCORAN COMES BACK IN. SHE SEES THE SAND ULYSSES HAS TRODDEN IN, AND THE MUD ON THE PHONE.*

MRS. CORCORAN: *(To Carys)* Can I help you with something, Mrs. Juffs?
CARYS: I'm leaving. Sorry it's been such a short stay. It's not the room or the view or anything like that—
MRS. CORCORAN: Oh.
CARYS: And I'm not Mrs. Juffs. I'm not going to *be* Mrs. Juffs either. He's a pig.
MRS. CORCORAN: Mr. Juffs, is this? The pig.
CARYS: I'd rather not talk about it if you don't mind.
MRS. CORCORAN: Fine.

*A BEAT.*

CARYS: We were going to get married tomorrow. They're all waiting in Manchester—
MRS. CORCORAN: *(Shocked)* You mean you didn't cancel it before you came here?
CARYS: The reception was for a hundred and thirty people. We were going to Malta for two and a half weeks.
MRS. CORCORAN: Mr. Foss said Malta's very hot.

CARYS: It doesn't matter anyway, not now. It's all wrecked. I had a lovely dress, cream silk satin, lace on the bodice and the cuffs, tiers of lace on the skirt. It cost a small fortune. Daddy always called me Princess, you see. Wanted to look that way on my wedding day. (*Furious*) It's all that bloody Rob's fault.

MRS. CORCORAN: Who's Rob?

CARYS: I'm not sure I should be telling you all this. (*A beat*) He's the best man. I can't bear him. When he's with Dexter they never stop laughing, like a couple of school kids. It's pathetic. They laugh at such stupid things.

MRS. CORCORAN: I think maybe men have got a different sense of humor. Edwin, my husband, never laughed at the same things I did.

CARYS: Does he run the hotel with you?

MRS. CORCORAN: He's dead. Cancer of the lung. He was fifty-three. We never really found the same things funny, right from the wedding-night. I suppose we were compatible in everything but that.

CARYS: And was it important?

MRS. CORCORAN: We managed. He'd tell his silly stories, and I suppose I'd pretend to laugh.

CARYS: I do the same. With sex.

MRS. CORCORAN: Pretend to laugh.

CARYS: Pretend. Just pretend. Sex is so important to him. It's like work.

MRS. CORCORAN: With Mr. Corcoran it was more of a hobby. On the whole I think he preferred telling jokes. I still hear his laugh you know. All the time. Of all the things to remember. After the funeral I got panicky. I couldn't bring his face to mind. You know? I thought: I've forgotten what he looks like. A few days gone and I can't even remember his face. And then the laugh came back. I just heard it in my head.

*CARYS HAS CLOSED HER EYES.*

MRS. CORCORAN: Are you all right?

CARYS: I'm trying to think what Dexter looks like. Oh God. You know, I can't picture him.

MRS. CORCORAN: Well, he hasn't died, has he?

*CARYS SMILES.*

CARYS: No.
MRS. CORCORAN: Of course he hasn't. He hasn't died.

*MRS. CORCORAN SMILES. CARYS SEEMS TO SEE THE HUMOR OF IT. THEY LAUGH TOGETHER.*

MRS. CORCORAN: You should wait at least to tell him you're going.
CARYS: *(Warming to this idea)* Maybe spend the night.
MRS. CORCORAN: That's right.
CARYS: It could be all right here without his bloody self-righteous family.
MRS. CORCORAN: A little sea air.
CARYS: He's such a child.
MRS. CORCORAN: They all are.

*MR. FOSS APPEARS, CIGAR IN HAND.*

MR. FOSS: A call for me, perhaps? I heard the telephone ring a while ago.
MRS. CORCORAN: No. This is Carys—
CARYS: Skinner.
MRS. CORCORAN: Carys Skinner. Mr. Foss.
MR. FOSS: How do you do?
MRS. CORCORAN: I must start dinner. Excuse me.

*MRS. CORCORAN EXITS.*

MR. FOSS: Leaving?
CARYS: . . . no. Tomorrow maybe.
MR. FOSS: The beds are terrible.
CARYS: Are you leaving, then?
MR. FOSS: Oh no. I love it. Reminds me of the Holy Land. Sand in the bed. In the food. I miss the company of an occasional scorpion, otherwise it's home away from home.
CARYS: You've lived in the Holy Land?
MR. FOSS: Lived all over.

CARYS: May I ask . . . what do you do? Only, the face . . .

MR. FOSS: I'm a minor poet. I have a small income from rhymes. For children.

CARYS: Oh. You're not on the television.

MR. FOSS: Thank the Lord, no. There's been nothing, while you've been down here, in the way of a message for me?

CARYS: Not that I saw.

MR. FOSS: Only the widow Corcoran forgets.

CARYS: Are you expecting good news?

MR. FOSS: Good or bad. I'm open to suggestions. Anything at all, really. I'd just like some news. I feel . . .

CARYS: Lost.

MR. FOSS: Well now, there's a word.

CARYS: Not lost.

MR. FOSS: No, you're right. Lost.

CARYS: Are you really a poet?

MR. FOSS: After my peculiar fashion.

CARYS: Go on then.

MR. FOSS: Go on what?

CARYS: Recite something.

MR. FOSS: My memory's a sieve, I'm afraid. I have holes in my past large enough to drive a life through.

CARYS: Make something up.

MR. FOSS: I can't. Not remotely.

CARYS: You're not much of a poet if you can't—

MR. FOSS: Wait. Your name is . . . ?

CARYS: Carys . . . Skinner.

MR. FOSS: (*He concentrates and produces a limerick with evident difficulty*) There was a young person called Skinner
Who ate two small dogs for her dinner
Once inside . . . Once inside, at a pace—
The dogs had a race, And the one that got out was the winner.

CARYS: That's stupid.

MR. FOSS: (*Pleased*) Yes, it was, wasn't it? Well, it's been perfectly splendiferous chatting with you. I'll wish you a good afternoon and make myself scarce.

*HE EXITS. CARYS STANDS STILL, TRYING TO THINK WHERE SHE'S SEEN HIS FACE BEFORE. DEXTER COMES IN. HE'S WALKED A FAIR DISTANCE.*

DEXTER: Are you staying or going?

*SHE LOOKS AT HIM, EXPRESSIONLESS.*

CARYS: We're waiting for news.
DEXTER: What?
CARYS: Oh. Staying.
DEXTER: Good.

*ULYSSES APPEARS, DRESSED NEATLY NOW; HAIR COMBED, FACE WASHED. HE STILL WEARS HIS BOOTS, SAND ENCRUSTED. HE HAS A TRAY, A CLOTH OVER HIS ARM: AN IMPERFECT COPY OF A WAITER. HE ALSO HAS A GONG, WHICH HE STRIKES WITH UNNECESSARY VIGOR.*

ULYSSES: Dinner will be served in half an hour.
DEXTER: I'll go and wash.

*HE KISSES CARYS AND EXITS.*

DEXTER: (*As he leaves*) White tie and tails, I presume.

*SEAN COMES IN AS CARYS PICKS UP HER BAG AND FOL-LOWS DEXTER UPSTAIRS.*

SEAN: You look a sight!
ULYSSES: And you don't?
SEAN: You're the maitre d'. I'm the dogsbody.
ULYSSES: If I'd had a dog with a body like yours, I'd have shot it.
SEAN: (*Taking aim with two fingers*) Bang!
ULYSSES: Missed.
SEAN: Who's the stripper?
ULYSSES: I'm not telling you.
SEAN: Come on. Someone taking a swim, was it?
ULYSSES: It's my secret.
SEAN: You're too old for secrets.
ULYSSES: Foss said that to me once. I'd watch the old bugger you
     know. He's got his eye on you.
SEAN: Never.
ULYSSES: Gawps at your bum all the time. God knows why.

SEAN: (*Faintly embarrassed*) Lay off, will you?

ULYSSES: You like it, don't you?

SEAN: You think he's a pederast?

ULYSSES: No, pederasts are obsessed with feet.

SEAN: They are not. Pederasts like boys. I read it.

ULYSSES: Get off. Pederasts like feet. Same as pedestrian: that's feet. Or pedicure.

SEAN: Bet you.

ULYSSES: You're on.

SEAN: Two quid.

ULYSSES: All right.

SEAN: Much you know.

*SEAN PUTS ON HIS T-SHIRT.*

SEAN: Getting a bit breezy.

*ENTER MRS. CORCORAN.*

MRS. CORCORAN: Ulysses.

ULYSSES: His mistress' voice.

MRS. CORCORAN: Finish the hall will you, Sean?

*EXIT MRS. CORCORAN. ULYSSES FOLLOWS.*

ULYSSES: Feet.

SEAN: Boys.

*ULYSSES EXITS. SEAN RELUCTANTLY GOES TO FETCH THE BROOM. LIGHT CHANGES, SLOWLY. AMBER LIGHT, ALL FROM ONE DIRECTION, FAR ON THE HORIZON, POURS THROUGH THE HOTEL. IT'S SUNSET. SOME-WHERE, MUSIC IS PLAYING. SEAN FINISHES BRUSHING. ON THE BALCONY, MR. FOSS.*

MR. FOSS: How the sun sets. Treacle clouds and a syllabub sea. Too picturesque for a man of refined tastes. It's shameful to be moved by such a crass display. But I watch the pelicans skim, and my heart wants to burst.

*THE AMBER LIGHT BEGINS TO FADE.*

MR. FOSS: It's going, see? Entirely jellified, down in slumbers. At one stride comes the dark. Not mine, that. Coleridge.

*THE SUN HAS GONE. A WIND HAS STARTED. WE ARE MOVING INTO A DREAM-SPACE NOW.*

MR. FOSS: Another wind tonight, oh yes. That'll breeze its way into a few dreams.

*A YELLOW LIGHT WASHES THE STAGE NOW; THE WIND IS HOWLING. APES CHATTER IN THE DISTANCE. MR. FOSS HAS GONE. IN THE MIDDLE OF THE STAGE THERE IS NOW A MULTI-COLORED BEACH UMBRELLA, LOOKING SINGULARLY OUT OF PLACE. A YOUNG MAN ENTERS, ALMOST NAKED, HIS BODY PAINTED. HE CARRIES A BOW AND ARROW. THE WIND IS WHISTLING LIKE A SAND STORM, DEAFENINGLY LOUD. THE YOUNG MAN WHOOPS, DELIGHTED BY THE STORM.*

YOUNG MAN: Come on out! Come on—

*HE SEARCHES AROUND THE STAGE, FAILS TO FIND WHOEVER HE'S SEARCHING FOR, AND EXITS; AS A BEACH BALL ROLLS ON TO THE SAND, FOLLOWED BY TWO LAUGHING PEOPLE, DRESSED FOR THE BEACH, WHO CHASE IT OFF.*

*ENTER DEXTER. HE IS IN EVENING DRESS TO HIS WAIST, BUT HE WEARS NEITHER TROUSERS NOR SHOES.*

DEXTER: Oh God, God, someone help me!

*HE IS YELLING AGAINST THE WIND, WHICH MORE OR LESS DROWNS OUT HIS WORDS.*

*THE YOUNG MAN ENTERS.*

YOUNG MAN: Ah!
DEXTER: Oh Christ, no!
YOUNG MAN: Come to Daddy.
DEXTER: You can't do this. I haven't any trousers. You can't!

*THE YOUNG MAN POINTS THE BOW AT HIM. HE
SCREAMS. IN THE STORM, CARYS ENTERS, TOWEL AND
BOOK IN HAND. SHE WEARS SUNGLASSES.*

DEXTER: Carys.

*SHE DOESN'T SEE OR HEAR HIM. THE YOUNG MAN STILL
HAS THE BOW POINTED AT HIM. CARYS LAYS THE
TOWEL UNDER THE BEACH UMBRELLA.*

DEXTER: Carys! It's me! Dexter! It's Dexter!

*SHE IGNORES HIM.*

DEXTER: Help me, Carys!

*SHE LIES ON THE TOWEL, FACE DOWN, AND SLEEPS.
THE YOUNG MAN ADVANCES ON DEXTER, WHO RUNS
OFF. THE YOUNG MAN FIRES.*

*THE STAGE IS SUDDENLY FULL OF PEOPLE, ALL
DRESSED (OR UNDRESSED) FOR THE BEACH; BALLS,
BOOKS, TOWELS, GLASSES, SUNSHADES. THEY ARE ALL
TALKING, BUT WE CAN HEAR NOTHING OF WHAT
THEY'RE SAYING. THEY SIT DOWN IN GROUPS, FILLING
THE STAGE; AN EXPANSE OF OILED FLESH AND GRIN-
NING FACES. SOME EAT; SOME DRINK.*

*THE STORM DIES, ABRUPTLY, AND WE HEAR THEM ALL
TALKING, VERY LOUDLY, TO EACH OTHER, GOSSIPING,
SHOUTING, ARGUING, MAKING LOVE. SEVERAL RADIOS
ARE PLAYING SIMULTANEOUSLY; DOGS ARE BARKING,
BABIES CRYING. INTO THIS CROWD COMES DEXTER
FROM BACK CENTER-STAGE. HE PICKS HIS WAY THOUGH
THE MORASS, STAGGERING A LITTLE.*

DEXTER: Carys . . . Carys!

*HE COLLAPSES, AN ARROW IN HIS BACK. SOMEONE SCREAMS. CHAOS. EVERYONE STANDS UP, AND LOOKS AT THIS DEAD MAN.*

*THEY ALL START TO DRIFT AWAY, PICKING UP THEIR BELONGINGS. CARYS IS STILL SUNNING HERSELF.*

*NO WIND NOW; JUST A DISTANT RADIO, PERHAPS.*

DEXTER: (Dying) Carys . . .

*THE YOUNG MAN COMES BACK CARRYING HIS EMPTY BOW.*

DEXTER: Oh God . . . Carys . . .

*THE YOUNG MAN STANDS A LITTLE WAY OFF; SCRATCHES HIS CROTCH; INSOLENT. CARYS GETS UP. SEES HIM.*

CARYS: What are you doing, Dexter?

*SHE PUTS ON A DRESSING GOWN SHE'S BROUGHT WITH HER.*

DEXTER: Help me. He's killed me.

*TECHNICIANS TAKE THE UMBRELLA AND OTHER PROPS AWAY.*

CARYS: Do you know what you look like?
DEXTER: I'm dying, Carys.

*THE YOUNG MAN CROSSES IN FRONT OF DEXTER, AND THEN PULLS OFF HIS JACKET. THE ARROW COMES OFF, TOO.*

CARYS: No, you're not. You're dreaming.

*THE YOUNG MAN EXITS. NOW ALL THAT'S LEFT ON STAGE IS DEXTER IN A SHIRT AND TIE, AND CARYS, LOOKING DOWN AT HIM, IN HER DRESSING GOWN.*

*THE LIGHTING HAS CHANGED SUBTLY SO THAT NOW IT IS MOONLIGHT IN THE HALLWAY OF THE ATLANTIC HOTEL.*

CARYS: You're dreaming, Dexter. Wake up.

*DEXTER OPENS HIS EYES.*

DEXTER: Oh! Oh God . . . *(Sits up)* I was in a desert; full of people: all families.
CARYS: Never mind.
DEXTER: When did I put my shirt on?
CARYS: In your sleep, presumably. Come back to bed.

*HE IS HELPED TO HIS FEET BY CARYS AND GOES WILLINGLY; LIKE A LAMB. THE YOUNG MAN WANDERS BACK ON AND WATCHES HIM GO. AS HE CROSSES, OTHER FIGURES EMERGE FROM THE SHADOWS, WHERE THEY HAVE BEEN WATCHING THE SPECTACLE OF DEXTER'S DREAM. ONE WE RECOGNIZE: MR. FOSS. THE OTHER TWO ARE STRANGERS. AN IMPERIOUS WOMAN IN PURPLE AND BLACK: MRS. MOCATTA; AND FURTHER IN THE SHADOWS THE DIMINUTIVE MR. TREADAWAY, A BOWLER-HATTED, MIDDLE-AGED MAN WITH WHITE GLOVES. HE HAS THE PEDANTIC MANNER OF A FICTIONAL DETECTIVE. HE CARRIES A BRIEFCASE.*

MRS. MOCATTA: What are you doing, Edward?
MR. FOSS: So you arrived. At last.
MRS. MOCATTA: Of course I arrived.
MR. FOSS: No telegram; no telephone call. I've been on tenterhooks.
MRS. MOCATTA: I've been busy. I'm not staying, Edward. So please say your piece and have done with it.
MR. FOSS: It's all in my letter of jellification. I thought it would be a fine thing, once I was dead, to join the Bureau and work in the sleep of men. And women. But I can't . . . do it . . . any longer.

MRS. MOCATTA: Your request to be relieved was duly noted and filed.

MR. FOSS: So I'm discharged?

MRS. MOCATTA: Good God no.

MR. FOSS: My resignation wasn't accepted?

MRS. MOCATTA: It was looked on sympathetically, but—

MR. FOSS: (*Mournfully*) Not accepted.

MRS. MOCATTA: The Dream Bureau is overworked, pressed to the limits. We need reliable agents in the field. If we lose you, we need to find somebody to replace you.

MR. FOSS: But I'm incompetent. That dream that Dexter just created?

MRS. MOCATTA: What about it?

MR. FOSS: I couldn't have choreographed a Freudian spectacle like that. I haven't got the wit left. I'm reduced to stealing ideas from juveniles.

MRS. MOCATTA: I'm sympathetic. Really I—

MR. FOSS: (*Furious now*) You are not! You don't give a damn for me. As long as you have your agents burrowing in the dream life of the nation, you're quite content. Bugger me! I'm just a cog! Well I won't do it! I won't!

MRS. MOCATTA: (*Unmoved*) You will, Edward. You signed a contract.

MR. FOSS: I've got a good mind to spill the beans.

MRS. MOCATTA: Now you're being silly.

MR. FOSS: Tell the world about this conspiracy.

MRS. MOCATTA: It's not a conspiracy, it's a science. What would your so-called dream-life of the nation be like without our nurturing it, shaping it? Once upon a time you thought it would be a fine sport to paddle in the collective unconscious.

MR. FOSS: Well, I've got my feet wet and it wasn't as advertised. Most of the minds I peer into are awash with trivia.

MRS. MOCATTA: Not everyone can dream the *Iliad*.

MR. FOSS: They make up shopping lists, and re-run soap operas. Its banality grinds me down.

MRS. MOCATTA: I'm truly sorry. But there's nothing I can do.

MR. FOSS: (*A warning*) I'll abscond. I will.

MRS. MOCATTA: I don't doubt you're perfectly capable of doing so. That's why Mr. Treadaway here—

*TREADAWAY GETS UP AND COMES FORWARD TO SHAKE FOSS' HAND. FOSS IGNORES HIM.*

MRS. MOCATTA: —will be staying to keep you company.

MR. FOSS: Prisoner, you mean. Why can't you release me, let him take over?

MRS. MOCATTA: He's not adequately qualified.

MR. TREADAWAY: I'd like to learn, Mr. Lear. From a genius such as yourself.

MR. FOSS: Don't call me Mr. Lear. I live here under the assumed name of my deceased and much missed cat, Foss. Mister. Foss.

MRS. MOCATTA: *(Taking Mr. Foss aside)* Edward. In the long run it's in everybody's interest that you be replaced. You're passé.

MR. FOSS: Mildly, she crushes me.

MRS. MOCATTA: On your own admission. The archetypes are constants, but the forms obviously leave you confused. At your age, I don't wonder.

MR. FOSS: Gently, she hammers me into the ground.

MRS. MOCATTA: Be assured, I'll do my best to hurry the bureaucrats up. Find someone to relieve you. In the meanwhile . . .

MR. FOSS: In the meanwhile?

MRS. MOCATTA: Sweet dreams.

*SHE TURNS HER BACK ON MR. FOSS, WHO CLOSES HIS EYES, AND THE GORILLA ENTERS, CHARGING IN WITH AN AXE TO KILL HER.*

*WHEN THE WEAPON IS POISED ABOVE HER HEAD, SHE TURNS AROUND AND FREEZES THE GORILLA IN ITS TRACKS.*

MRS. MOCATTA: *(As to an errant child)* Really, Edward.

MR. FOSS: It was worth a try.

*THE GORILLA DROPS ITS AGGRESSIVE POSE AND STANDS, HANDS AT ITS SIDE, WATCHING MRS. MOCATTA EXIT. TREADAWAY CONFISCATES THE AXE AND ESCORTS MRS. MOCATTA OUT.*

MR. FOSS: *(Pretending as if nothing has happened)*
    Mrs. Jaypher said it's safer

If you've lemons in your head
First to eat a pound of meat
And then to go at once to bed.

*MR. TREADAWAY RETURNS. THE GORILLA GROWLS AT HIM.*

MR. FOSS: *(To Treadaway)* I'll be a sensible prisoner, Treadaway.

*MR. TREADAWAY DOESN'T ANSWER.*

MR. FOSS: *(Needling him politely)* This is my Gorilla, by the way. But I'm embarrassed to admit I don't even know what sex it is. You haven't had any Gorilla-sexing experiences I suppose? No. Why should you? It's not much of a hobby. Can't get rid of it. The Gorilla. It lingers around like a discarded lover, even when I'm wide awake. Do you have those dreams? The ones you can't shake off? You do speak?

MR. TREADAWAY: On occasion.

MR. FOSS: Well, that's something. Shall we be friends?

MR. TREADAWAY: I have my orders. To keep you in my little eye.

MR. FOSS: Yes, it is a little eye. Positively piggy, in fact. What shall I call you? The Pobblesquat? The Pumpkibble? *(With sudden vehemence)* Or maybe just plain *PIG*?

MR. TREADAWAY: Where are you going?

MR. FOSS: To bed.

MR. TREADAWAY: Aren't you going to see how the house is dreaming?

MR. FOSS: I'm on holiday.

*THE YOUNG MAN IS STILL WANDERING AROUND. MR. FOSS SEES HIM.*

MR. FOSS: One indulgence, perhaps.

*MR. FOSS WHISPERS IN THE YOUNG MAN'S EAR. THE YOUNG MAN CROSSES TO THE GORILLA AND KISSES IT. THE GORILLA PICKS HIM UP AND CARRIES HIM OFF. MR. FOSS GRINS.*

MR. FOSS: *(Sighing)* Ah. Love.

*MR. TREADAWAY IS ALREADY MAKING NOTES IN HIS BLACK BOOK ABOUT THIS OUTRAGEOUS BEHAVIOR, SHAKING HIS HEAD. FOSS BEGINS TO LAUGH, AS THE LIGHTS GO DOWN, SLOWLY.*

*END OF ACT ONE.*

# Act 2

# Act 2:

*SLOWLY, LIGHTS UP ON THE HOTEL. IT IS NOW MIDDAY, SATURDAY, SEPTEMBER 23RD. THE HOTEL IS QUIET, EXCEPT FOR ULYSSES BRUSHING UP THE SAND.*

*THE GORILLA SITS OUT ON THE PATIO, SMOKING A CIGARETTE. SUDDENLY THE SOUND OF: A MUSICAL CAR HORN; THREE CARS DRIVING UP OUTSIDE; SLAMMING CAR DOORS; SHOUTING; LAUGHTER; VOICES NOW, ABRA-SIVE. THE WEDDING PARTY ERUPTS ONTO THE STAGE.*

*FIRSTLY THE SKINNER FAMILY. PHOEBE SKINNER: OVER-DRESSED, A NATURAL ORGANIZER AND BULLY. LIND-BERG SKINNER, A SELF-MADE MAN WHO MADE HIS FOR-TUNE IN PAPER BAGS, BOMBASTIC, OVER-HEARTY, UNTRUSTWORTHY. DONNA-MARIE SKINNER, CARYS' YOUNGER SISTER, A MENTALLY DISTURBED GIRL WHOSE DISTURBANCE IS NOT HELPED BY THE AGGRESSION OF HER PARENTS.*

*THE JUFFS PARTY. MELBA JUFFS, A SHARP, CLEVER WOMEN WHO'S NOT THE EQUAL OF PHOEBE IN VOL-UME, BUT MAKES UP FOR THAT IN VITRIOL. FRANK, HER HUSBAND, A QUIET, GOD-LOVING LIFE-HATER, WHO IS WEARING A NECK BRACE THAT SWELLS HIS NECK OUT TO THREE TIMES ITS REAL SIZE, INHIBITING MOVEMENT.*

*THERE ARE THREE OTHER GUESTS. ROSE GIDDY, WHO*

*ASPIRES TO BE ANOTHER PHOEBE, BUT SUCCEEDS ONLY IN BEING IN HER SHADOW; VINCE BURROUGHS, ALREADY THE WORSE FOR SEVERAL BEERS, HANDS THRUST INTO HIS POCKETS TO PLAY WITH HIS BALLS: A SLOB OF THE FIRST RANK; ROB KIDD, THE BEST MAN, HIS HANDSOME, BESPECTACLED FACE BETRAYING THE IRRITATION OF HAVING TRAVELED WITH THESE PEOPLE ALL MORNING. DONNA-MARIE HAS LATCHED ON TO HIM TODAY, LOOKING CONSTANTLY FOR HIS APPROVAL.*

*ULYSSES WITHDRAWS IN HORROR AS THEY DUMP THEIR HAND-LUGGAGE AND FEW CASES DOWN. SUDDENLY THE STAGE, WHICH WAS ALMOST EMPTY, IS CRAWLING WITH PRIMARY COLORS AND BUZZING PEOPLE. EXTRAORDINARY DETAILS ABOUND. WHY IS PHOEBE WEARING A FUR COAT? WHAT IS FRANK'S INJURY? WHY SO MANY BAGS, PAPER AND PLASTIC?*

*THE FOLLOWING CONVERSATIONS, NUMBERED I, II, III, ARE GOING ON MORE OR LESS SIMULTANEOUSLY.*

I.

MELBA: How's your neck, Frank?
FRANK: I'm fine. Really.
MELBA: Only Vince can take the bags—(*Frank is loaded down*)—can't you Vince?

*VINCE, EMPTY-HANDED, WALKS AWAY.*

VINCE: Laden, love, laden.
MELBA: I'll swing for that man, I swear it.
FRANK: Just ignore him.

II.

LINDBERG: Bit of a dive for the Princess to have chosen, isn't it?
PHOEBE: Donna-Marie—

DONNA-MARIE: Yes?

PHOEBE: Leave Rob alone. (*To Lindberg*) She didn't choose it, *he* did.

ROB:(*Re: Donna-Marie*) She's all right.

PHOEBE: *Leave Rob alone,* Donna-Marie.

LINDBERG: Oh for Christ's sake, leave the girl be. How about the booze, Vince?

VINCE: I'm game. Past opening time.

III.

DONNA-MARIE: I've never been to sea before. Have you been to sea?

ROB: Not for a long time, no.

DONNA-MARIE: Will we go swimming? I hope we can go swimming. Do you think we can?

I.

MELBA: Please put the bags down, Frank, before you do yourself some damage. We'll get somebody to take them upstairs.

FRANK: Is it really sixteen years? Seems longer, doesn't it?

MELBA: I think it's flown by.

FRANK: Oh.

MELBA: It's rather sweet bringing her here. Not like Dexter to be sweet.

II.

LINDBERG: Vince is going out for the drinks. Coming, Rob?

MELBA: And the sandwiches, if you will, Mr. Juffs.

LINDBERG: Oh Christ. The ever open door.

PHOEBE: Humor her.

LINDBERG: Rob?

ROB: Huh?

PHOEBE: Donna-Marie, will you *please* not bother Rob.

VINCE: She's quite taken to you, hasn't she?

PHOEBE: (*To Donna-Marie*) And I'm not going to tell you again.

III.

DONNA-MARIE: Go swimming with wimmin. Swimming with wimmin.

ROSE: Picture, everybody!

*ROSE IS NEVER WITHOUT HER CAMERA. THE CONVERSATION HALTS. THERE IS SOME MOVEMENT TOWARDS ROSE FOR A PHOTOGRAPH TO BE TAKEN.*

PHOEBE: (*With absolute authority*) Not now, Rose.

*ROSE WITHERS. CONVERSATION STARTS AGAIN, BUT NOW IN A MORE ORDERLY FASHION, WITHOUT THE SAME OVERLAPPING.*

LINDBERG: Are you coming Vince? Get the stuff unloaded or we'll be standing around all day.

VINCE: Good thinking, chief.

*VINCE DOESN'T MOVE.*

PHOEBE: They may not even be here.

MELBA: Oh but he said on the phone. Mr. and Mrs. Juffs.

PHOEBE: They could have gone back by now. Could be a different Juffs.

MELBA: It's not a common name.

PHOEBE: Meaning Skinner is?

MELBA: Meaning it's not a common name, Mrs. Skinner. We came here when Dexter was a boy: he obviously thought we wouldn't remember.

DONNA-MARIE: Swimming with wimmin.

LINDBERG: Shush Donna. Rob?

ROB: Yes. I'm coming.

MELBA: He thought he'd hide away for a while. He was always a hider.

LINDBERG: I don't blame him. Phoebe, sort that bloody child out before she drives us to drink.

VINCE: Too late.

*VINCE EXITS, PATTING ROSE ON THE BACKSIDE AS HE GOES BY. ROB IS DISENGAGING HIMSELF FROM DONNA-MARIE.*

ROSE: She's very clingy today, isn't she?
PHOEBE: She always gets like this on long journeys.
ROB: I'll be back in a moment.

*ROB EXITS. MELBA JUFFS HAS SEEN ULYSSES.*

MELBA: Excuse me. Where's the manager?
PHOEBE: Ah!
ULYSSES: I don't know anything.
PHOEBE: We're booked in. Two doubles, four singles.
ULYSSES: I don't know anything about it. Sorry.
MELBA: Wasn't it you I spoke to?
ULYSSES: No.
PHOEBE: There must be *somebody* in authority.
MELBA: We've got our reservations.
ULYSSES: That makes two of us.

*ULYSSES EXITS.*

PHOEBE: What a place to come to.
FRANK: It's changed hands since we were here.
MELBA: We don't know that.
PHOEBE: Running away.
ROSE: It's rather romantic.
PHOEBE: *(Forbidding)* Rose.
ROSE: Well, I think so.
FRANK: I'm sure they had their reasons.
PHOEBE: The boy doesn't know his own mind half the time.
MELBA: How would you know?
PHOEBE: I would have left them to it, but Lindberg's always let Carys run over him. Especially since Donna-Marie.

*DONNA-MARIE IS SITTING OPEN-MOUTHED, OPEN-LEGGED, ON A CHAIR, STARING INTO MIDDLE-DISTANCE.*

PHOEBE: It broke my heart. I didn't want to see that happen

again. But I'm not going to find it easy to forgive this little drama. All the cancellations, it's humiliating. And expensive.

FRANK: Don't you see a little of yourself in them? Far from the maddening crowd?

PHOEBE: They've thrown it all back in our faces. That's all I can see.

*ROB RETURNS WITH THE FIRST CRATE OF DRINK.*

PHOEBE: I can't bear ingratitude.

ROSE: Hold it!

*SHE SNAPS ROB IN THE DOORWAY. VINCE FOLLOWS WITH TWO CANS OF BEER, ONE OPENED AND BEING DRUNK.*

VINCE: What about me?

*HE POSES. ROSE IGNORES HIM. ROB GOES OUT FOR SOME MORE. DONNA-MARIE FOLLOWS.*

PHOEBE: Donna.

ROB: It's all right, I'll watch her.

ROSE: Sandwiches! Mrs. Juffs wanted sandwiches.

MELBA: It doesn't matter if you can't—

*ROSE FOLLOWS ROB OUT TO FETCH SOME FOOD. LINDBERG ENTERS, BOTTLES IN ARMS.*

LINDBERG: Anyone turned up yet?

*ENTER MRS. CORCORAN, FACING A SPRAWLING MASS OF PEOPLE, CASES, HANDBAGS, BOOZE, ETC.*

MRS. CORCORAN: Oh my God.

LINDBERG: Ah! We *are* in the land of the living.

MRS. CORCORAN: Can I help you?

MELBA: I rang last night. Juffs—

LINDBERG: We've been waiting here—

PHOEBE: We're the Wedding Party.

MELBA: We rang last night; booked the rooms.

PHOEBE: Skinner.

MELBA: Juffs.

MRS. CORCORAN: Juffs? Are you sure you booked?

LINDBERG: 'Course we're bloody sure. We've driven sixty miles this morning—

PHOEBE: We're the Wedding Party.

MELBA: They are here, aren't they? The children?

FRANK: Our son Dexter.

MRS. CORCORAN: Yes, they're both here.

LINDBERG: So there you are. The mountain has come to Mohammed.

PHOEBE: We're the Wedding Party.

MRS. CORCORAN: So I see.

LINDBERG: She's a willful little so-and-so. But if she wants to have her wedding in the middle of nowhere, so be it.

PHOEBE: The point is, we've booked.

MELBA: Yes. Quite definitely. No doubt about that.

MRS. CORCORAN: Well, there must be some error.

PHOEBE: We need six rooms.

MELBA: Two doubles and four singles.

LINDBERG: I assume you've got the space?

MRS. CORCORAN: Well, yes.

LINDBERG: Good enough. Right: we'll get the rest of the stuff. If we get cracking we can have the afternoon on the beach.

*LINDBERG GOES OUT WITH ROB. VINCE STAYS PUT, MAKING EYES AT ROSE. THE CONVERSATION BREAKS DOWN AGAIN, THE THREE PARTS OVERLAPPING.*

I.

MELBA: I knew they'd be here.

FRANK: Of course.

MELBA: Stands to reason. Why don't you put the bags down, Frank? You look uncomfortable.

FRANK: I am uncomfortable.

MELBA: I think you enjoy it sometimes.

II.

VINCE: Nice camera.
ROSE: Mm.
VINCE: You're the official photographer, are you?
ROSE: I suppose I am. I hadn't thought.
VINCE: Ever do nudes, do you?

*ROSE IS STONY-FACED.*

VINCE: Take pictures of yourself in the bathroom mirror?
ROSE: No, I don't.
VINCE: Lovely woman like you. You ought.
ROSE: No.

III.

PHOEBE: We'll need one of the singles adjacent to our room for
    Donna-Marie.
MRS. CORCORAN: Oh. Yes.
PHOEBE: She'll probably be all right. But you know. And you
    want a double, don't you?
FRANK: I'm sorry?
PHOEBE: You want a double room?
MELBA: Oh yes. Of course.
MRS. CORCORAN: I'll have to put one of the singles in a double
    bed, I'm afraid.
PHOEBE: Rose. You'll have to go in a double bed.
ROSE: Oh.
VINCE: Never mind.
PHOEBE: That's all right, isn't it?
VINCE: We'll work something out.
ROSE: Where's Rob gone?

*TO SHAKE OFF VINCE, SHE GOES TO THE DOOR, AS ROB
COMES IN WITH MORE LUGGAGE. SHE RELIEVES HIM OF
SOME OF IT, A DESPERATE SMILE PLASTERED ON HER
FACE.*

VINCE: We're not going on a bloody world cruise, are we? *(To*

*Lindberg, who comes in with more luggage)* I just said: we're not going on a bloody world cruise, are we? Anyone found the kitchen sink?

*LINDBERG SMILES THINLY.*

VINCE: Mine used to pack for a cruise every time she left the house.
PHOEBE: *(Acid)* But of course, eventually she went on one, didn't she, Vince? Permanently.

*THIS SHUTS HIM UP.*

ROSE: Is there a beach? Safe for swimming, I mean?
MRS. CORCORAN: Oh yes.
ROSE: *(To Rob)* Can you swim?
DONNA-MARIE: *(To herself)* Swim.
ROB: A little.
MRS. CORCORAN: *(Sorting out the keys)* Well, one double is Number 7; that's for Mr. and Mrs. Juffs; 6 is for you, Mrs. Skinner, with your daughter in Number 5. All right? Would you like to sign the register? The other double is on the middle floor: Room 2. And there's 12 and 13, the other singles.
ROSE: *(To Rob)* I'm having the double bed.
MRS. CORCORAN: I'll get someone to help with the bags.
FRANK: I can manage.
MRS. CORCORAN: There's a lot.
MELBA: Anyone want a sandwich?

*SHE HAS UNVEILED A PLATE OF SMALL TRIANGULAR SANDWICHES, PRESUMABLY CUT FOR THE RECEPTION. SHE IS ALREADY PLOWING THROUGH THEM.*

MELBA: They're salmon and water-cress on this side, and ham on the other.
MRS. CORCORAN: Ulysses. The bags. And then a word.
ULYSSES: I don't know anything about it.
MELBA: Sandwich? *(To Rob. He takes one)* Take one of each. There's plenty.
FRANK: Any chance of lunch?

MRS. CORCORAN: Lunch. Well . . . we might run to a light buffet. Only we weren't anticipating—

VINCE: *(To Melba)* You missed me. *(She offers him a sandwich)* Ta.

ULYSSES: *(To Rose)* Is this your case?

ROSE: No, that one.

MELBA: *(To Ulysses)* Want a sandwich? They're salmon and watercress on this side and ham on the other.

MRS. CORCORAN: I'll see what I can sort out.

LINDBERG: Much appreciated.

*MRS. CORCORAN EXITS. ULYSSES LOADS HIMSELF UP WITH BAGS.*

MELBA: We may as well go up. *(To Frank)* You're late for your tablets.

ULYSSES: I'll lead off, eh?

*ULYSSES LEADS MELBA JUFFS, FRANK JUFFS AND ROSE UPSTAIRS.*

PHOEBE: What a pair of killjoys.

LINDBERG: Now, now.

PHOEBE: How could Carys marry into a family like that?

LINDBERG: As I remember, your family weren't too keen on me 'til the business flourished.

PHOEBE: It makes me boil. They haven't paid for a penny. Not a bloody penny! Not even the cars.

LINDBERG: Don't make such a song and dance.

*SHE DESPAIRS OF HIM.*

PHOEBE: Vince.

VINCE: Um?

PHOEBE: Bring up my bag, will you? Donna-Marie.

DONNA-MARIE: What?

PHOEBE: Not "what," "pardon."

DONNA-MARIE: Pardon.

PHOEBE: Come with me. And wipe your mouth. *(To Lindberg)* She's getting worse.

DONNA-MARIE: Mam.

PHOEBE: What?
DONNA-MARIE: *(By rote, no insolence)* Not "what," "pardon."
PHOEBE: Come on!
DONNA-MARIE: Can't I stay with Rob?
PHOEBE: No you can't.

*UNWILLINGLY DONNA-MARIE JOINS HER MOTHER, STARTING TO CRY AS THEY EXIT TOGETHER. VINCE OPENS ANOTHER BEER.*

VINCE: *(Picks up a mock leopard-skin bag)* This hers?
LINDBERG: It looks tasteless enough.
VINCE: I'm in with Rose, eh? No trouble. No trouble.
LINDBERG: *(Suddenly weary of all this, he sighs heavily)* Never have kids, Rob.
ROB: No?
LINDBERG: More bloody trouble than they're worth. You wait and see.
ROB: It's not . . . very likely.
LINDBERG: That's what I used to say. Never catch me married, not in a month of Sundays. You know, these few days, I've watched you. You don't get ruffled, do you? Stay out of things unless you've got something worth saying. I like that. Ever thought about working for Skinners?
ROB: A career in paper bags?
LINDBERG: If I had a penny for every time I've heard that joke, I'd be even richer than I am.
ROB: I'm happy where I am, thank you. Really. I like research.
LINDBERG: That's a bad sign at your age. Being happy. Doesn't leave you much room for ambition, does it?
ROB: Oh, I've got my ambitions. They're just not . . . fiscal. Thanks for the offer anyway.
LINDBERG: Bit of a balls-up this, isn't it? I'm only doing it for Phoebe, she worships the girl. Especially since Donna-Marie. Personally—I know he's a friend of yours, but better out than in—I've never taken to Dexter. Or the family. The father's a bit of an odd-ball, don't you think? Too much religion. It buggers you up.
ROB: Dexter's his own man.
LINDBERG: I'm sure he is, I'm sure he is, and the sooner he's out

from under those two the better all around. Anyway, it's what Carys wants. You'll see. You do anything for them. Even give them away. That's the pity of it.

*SEAN ENTERS AND CROSSES THE STAGE, EXCHANGING A GLANCE WITH ROB.*

LINDBERG: Eh! Eh! Eh!

*SEAN STOPS, STARING AT LINDBERG.*

LINDBERG: There's bags here. For upstairs. It's about time we got a little service.

*SEAN LOOKS PUZZLED.*

LINDBERG: (*As to an idiot*) Bags. Upstairs. Up. Stairs.

*SEAN SHRUGS AS THOUGH HE DOESN'T UNDERSTAND.*

LINDBERG: Oh for Christ's sake, can't you understand plain pigging English? (*To Rob*) Is he foreign, is that it? (*Slowly*) I want the bags taken upstairs.

*SEAN MAKES A SIGN TO SIGNIFY HE CAN NEITHER HEAR NOR SPEAK.*

LINDBERG: What? Speak up.
ROB: I think he's telling you he's deaf and dumb.
LINDBERG: Oh Christ.

*LINDBERG NOW STARTS AN ABSURD MIME ROUTINE TO ACCOMPANY HIS INSTRUCTIONS.*

LINDBERG: I want the bags taken upstairs. Up. Stairs. Bloody imbecile.
ROB: I don't think you're getting through.
LINDBERG: What is this, a hotel or a home for the bloody disabled? Where's the manager?
ROB: I'll take the bags. It's no problem.

LINDBERG: Will you hell as like. We're paying for the bloody service.

*HE EXITS TO FIND MRS. CORCORAN. SEAN AND ROB EXCHANGE LOOKS.*

SEAN: There's nothing like playing hard to get.
ROB: I see.
SEAN: Was that in poor taste?
ROB: Yes.
SEAN: I'm Sean.
ROB: I'm Rob.
SEAN: Are you with him?
ROB: In a manner of speaking.
SEAN: My commiserations.

*ROSE ENTERS.*

ROSE: Could you bring up Phoebe's other case, Robert? It's the blue one. Only Vince left it down here.
ROB: Surely. *(To Sean)* Maybe see you around.

*ROB PICKS UP THE CASE, WHICH IS VERY HEAVY.*

SEAN: Watch it. You'll strain your groin.
ROB: Wouldn't want that.

*ROB EXITS WITH ROSE.*

SEAN: *(To himself)* Queer.

*HE IS ABOUT TO EXIT WHEN MR. FOSS ENTERS. HE HAS BEEN LINGERING ON THE PATIO UNTIL THE CROWD DISPERSES.*

MR. FOSS: Sean. Sweetness. A moment.
SEAN: Mr. Foss.
MR. FOSS: I wondered—
SEAN: You always come up from behind. Why d'you do that?
MR. FOSS: No reason.
SEAN: Well, I'm watching you. How can I help?

MR. FOSS: We had a small transaction planned. The dreams?
SEAN: Oh yeah. Yeah. I've got one.
MR. FOSS: Erotic?
SEAN: No, the other one. The long one.
MR. FOSS: Apocalyptic? Tell me.

*SEAN STARTS AN ELABORATE LIE.*

SEAN: Well, I don't know what brought it on. I had this dream about the sea—
MR. FOSS: What about it?
SEAN: I dreamt a wave came. A hundred feet high. At least. Frigging huge, it was. Roaring like a herd of lions.
MR. FOSS: Pride of lions.
SEAN: Who's telling the story, you or me? It came, right? Everyone was running around with their hair on end; and I was just standing on your balcony, watching.
MR. FOSS: Just watching.
SEAN: I wasn't afraid. There were ships on its crest, and huge fish, and islands, it had islands on it, swept up. White foam, spitting everywhere, Christ, and it kept coming and coming—
MR. FOSS: And?
SEAN: And nothing.
MR. FOSS: That's it?
SEAN: Suppose I woke up.
MR. FOSS: My God. And I dream gorillas.
SEAN: Well, you would. Is that worth something, then?
MR. FOSS: Oh indeed. *(He takes out his wallet)* Shall we say five pounds?
SEAN: *(Incredulously)* For that?
MR. FOSS: Ten then.

*MR. FOSS APPROACHES HIM. GIVES HIM THE MONEY. THEN HE CAN'T RESIST IT, HE TOUCHES SEAN'S FACE.*

MR. FOSS: You. Shame. Me.

*HE WANTS TO KISS SEAN; THE CONFUSION ON HIS FACE IS AGONIZING.*

MR. FOSS: Shame. Me.

SEAN: It's all right.

MR. FOSS: No, it isn't all right. Not at all.

*HE DROPS HIS HAND.*

MR. FOSS: Thank you for the flight.

*MR. FOSS EXITS.*

SEAN: All my own work.

*ENTER MR. TREADAWAY.*

MR. TREADAWAY: Where's he gone now?

SEAN: Mr. Foss? He went out.

MR. TREADAWAY: As soon as I close my eyes, he's off.

*ROB HAS COME BACK FOR MORE CASES. SEAN FOLLOWS TREADAWAY TO THE FRONT DOOR TO SEE WHAT'S GOING ON. ROB WATCHES HIM GO. AS HE PICKS UP A CASE OF BOOZE, DEXTER AND CARYS ENTER FROM THE PATIO.*

ROB: Hello.

DEXTER: Christ.

CARYS: What are you doing here?

ROB: *(Unenthusiastically)* Surprise, surprise.

DEXTER: *(Looking at the remaining cases)* You're not alone?

ROB: No.

CARYS: Who's here?

ROB: Your mother and father; his mother and father; Donna-Marie, Rose, Vince, Uncle Tom Cobbly and all.

CARYS: Oh Jesus.

ROB: Don't look at me, it wasn't my idea.

CARYS: *(To Dexter)* It was your mother. *(To Rob)* Wasn't it? She guessed.

ROB: Yes. But it was Phoebe who led the expedition.

CARYS: I knew we weren't safe here.

DEXTER: We'll pack our bags; get out before they find us.

ROB: You'll have to face them sooner or later.

DEXTER: I vote later.

CARYS: I'll pack. You pay Mrs. Whatzit.

ROB: You can't run out on them again.

CARYS: Listen, Rob. We're just beginning to sort something out here. Don't interfere. (*To Dexter*) Five minutes.

*CARYS EXITS.*

ROB: Nothing's this bad.

DEXTER: Want to bet?

ROB: It's absurd. Hiding away.

DEXTER: Don't talk to me about hiding away. Not you.

ROB: Oh listen, I'm ready to announce my bed-manners to the assembled company anytime you like. I've had it up to here with "And when are you going to get married, Rob?" and fending off innuendos from Cousin Vince and come-ons from Rose. You took the easy way out, Dex. I've had twenty-four hours of hysterics, mutual recriminations and family cannibalism and it's been an illuminating experience. Nothing would give me more pleasure than to tell them I do it with men. I would happily provide diagrams at this point.

DEXTER: Cool down.

ROB: You ask a lot in the name of friendship, Dexie.

DEXTER: Look, I came here to sort this mess out. To tell Carys that you and I had . . . had . . .

ROB: It was so good it leaves you speechless.

DEXTER: Slept together. (*A qualification*) On occasion. (*Another*) When I was drunk.

ROB: The first time, you were drunk.

DEXTER: I couldn't marry her without explaining.

ROB: What's to explain, Dex? You're not gay. You just sleep with men.

DEXTER: It's all right for you. You know what you want.

ROB: Whereas you go where the wind blows.

DEXTER: That's not fair.

ROB: You want her. You want me. Maybe both. Maybe neither. Probably neither. If you're not careful, Dex, you're going to end up on your own, and oh boy, are you going to be sorry.

*DEXTER CROSSES TO ROB.*

DEXTER: Don't say that, Rob. About being on my own.

*DEXTER SUDDENLY WRAPS HIS ARMS AROUND ROB.*

DEXTER: Please.

*ROSE HAS COME IN. SHE WATCHES.*

ROB: (*Disentangling himself*) No you don't.
DEXTER: I was going to drown myself yesterday, but I couldn't even find the bloody sea.

*ROB STARTS TO LAUGH. DEXTER BEGINS TO LAUGH. THEY HUG EACH OTHER.*

DEXTER: I love you.

*ROSE MAKES A SMALL NOISE.*

DEXTER: (*Unhanding Rob*) Oh! Rose!
ROSE: Dexter.
DEXTER: Just saying hello to Rob.
ROSE: (*Coldly*) I saw.

*SHE'S WATCHING ROB, NOT DEXTER. HER EMOTIONS ARE ONLY JUST HELD IN CHECK.*

DEXTER: It's wonderful, wasn't I just saying, Rob, I was just saying to Rob it's wonderful everybody being here. It's like home away from home.

*ROSE JUST STARES AT ROB. ENTER CARYS, AT A RUSH, WITH CASE.*

CARYS: Dexter. Quickly! Have you paid—

*SEES ROSE.*

CARYS: Rose.
ROSE: Hello.

*ENTER LINDBERG AND PHOEBE WITH DONNA-MARIE.*

LINDBERG: Princess.
PHOEBE: It was her.
LINDBERG: We called after you!
CARYS: *(Face forward)* Oh God. *(Turns, smiling)* Daddy!
PHOEBE: You ran straight past us in the corridor.
ROB: Excuse me. I get sentimental.

*DEXTER POINTS TO THE CASE CARYS BROUGHT DOWN.*
*ROB PICKS IT UP AND TAKES IT UPSTAIRS AGAIN.*

*THE CONVERSATION SPLITS INTO TWO.*


I.

PHOEBE: What's the meaning of this?
CARYS: It's good to see you. No, it really is.
PHOEBE: Answer me, please.
CARYS: We thought it was for the best.
PHOEBE: This has been the worst two days of my life, Carys.
    Your father might be forgiving, but I'm not. After all the
    preparations. The expense.
CARYS: I didn't want to. It was Dexter.
PHOEBE: I'll have words with him later.

II.

LINDBERG: Not an ideal place to elope to, Dexter.
DEXTER: No.
LINDBERG: Stealing her away, were you?
DEXTER: In a manner of speaking.
LINDBERG: I had this same thing when I married your mother-
    in-law; couldn't face it all. We ran away too; but we were a
    little better at hiding ourselves. It was your mother who
    remembered this place. You used to talk about it, she said.

*ENTER VINCE, AND THE JUFFS. FURTHER GREETINGS; KISSES, HANDSHAKES. VINCE TAKES NO NOTICE OF DEXTER OR CARYS. HE'S SEEN ROSE, WHO IS SITTING BY HERSELF TRYING TO HOLD BACK TEARS. THE CONVER-SATION SPLITS AGAIN.*

*LINDBERG HAS CROSSED TO CARYS.*

I.

LINDBERG: Take no notice, Princess.
PHOEBE: Don't interfere.
LINDBERG: I understand, baby.
CARYS: *(Suddenly starts to cry)* Oh Daddy!
LINDBERG: And now—
PHOEBE: *(Despairing)* Butter wouldn't melt.
LINDBERG: It's all right. It's all right, Princess. We'll have the wedding another day. As long as you're all right. I don't want my Princess crying.

II.

MELBA: Are you well?
DEXTER: Of course.
FRANK: We've had to take a lot of flak about this, Dexter. I hope you've got an explanation.
DEXTER: It all just happened.
FRANK: Nothing just happens. There's always reasons.
MELBA: Has she been difficult? She's like her mother. Highly strung.
DEXTER: It's not her.

III.

VINCE: You all right?
ROSE: Fine.
VINCE: Want a drink?
ROSE: No. Yes.

*VINCE GRINS. HE'S WINNING HER OVER, HE THINKS. HE OPENS A CAN OF BEER FOR HER.*

VINCE: There. That'll put hairs on your chest.
ROSE: Thank you. Very much.

*SHE DRINKS, VINCE WATCHING HER LIKE AN OVER-SEXED HAWK.*

LINDBERG: I think we should have a photograph, now we're all back together again.
CARYS: No, Daddy, I look a sight.
LINDBERG: Rose! Everybody! Photograph.
PHOEBE: Rose.
ROSE: Yes?
PHOEBE: Photograph.

*ROSE LOOKS UNWILLING.*

PHOEBE: Come on.

*EVERYBODY STARTS TO ORGANIZE FOR A PHOTO.*

DONNA-MARIE: Rob!
PHOEBE: Ssh!
DONNA-MARIE: Where's Rob?
DEXTER: He went upstairs.
PHOEBE: Dexter, you slot in beside Carys.
DEXTER: What about Rob?
DONNA-MARIE: I'll go.
PHOEBE: Donna!

*SHE IGNORES HER MOTHER AND EXITS.*

PHOEBE: Rose. Snap out of it.
ROSE: I'm sorry. I've got a headache.
PHOEBE: It's that beer. She's not used to drink. (*Accusingly, to Vince*) You should know better.

*VINCE SHRUGS.*

VINCE: We thought it was a celebration.
PHOEBE: We can celebrate sober.

*THE GROUP STARTS TO ARRANGE ITSELF, AND IS DULY REARRANGED, BY PHOEBE. ROSE IS A LITTLE DIZZY FROM THE BEER, AND STILL THREATENING TEARS. THE SCENE IS AD-LIBBED AS THE PHOTOGRAPH IS ORGANIZED.*

PHOEBE: All right; are we ready?
VINCE: Where's the best man?

*DONNA-MARIE ENTERS WITH ROB.*

DONNA-MARIE: *(Triumphantly dragging Rob)* I've brought him! I've brought him!

*THE TWO NEWCOMERS ARE FITTED INTO THE PICTURE. ROSE, WHO HAS SET HER CAMERA ON A TRIPOD, VIEWS THE ASSEMBLED COMPANY.*

ROSE: Everybody squeeze up a bit. More. Phoebe, you're obscuring Carys. Mr. Juffs, in a bit. A bit more. All right. Smile everybody. Smile!

*SHE SETS THE TIME-RELEASE, AND STEPS INTO THE PICTURE BESIDE DONNA-MARIE.*

ROSE: Say cheese!
ALL: Cheese!
VINCE: Danish Blue.
PHOEBE: *(Volcanic)* Vince.

*THE CAMERA FLASHES, THE LIGHTS CHANGE. FIXED IN THE GLARE OF THE FLASH BULB, DESPERATION, FEAR AND LOSS REGISTER BEHIND THE FROZEN SMILES. HELD IN THIS FUGUE STATE, THEY SPEAK THEIR MINDS, UNFREEZING TO SAY THEIR PIECE, THEN FREEZING AGAIN.*

MELBA: I hate smiling.
FRANK: I'm in torment. Absolute torment.
MELBA: It shows my gums.
FRANK: My spine is simply going to dust.

MELBA: And my nose casts a shadow; it'll look as though I've got a moustache.

PHOEBE: She looks like Hitler in this light.

MELBA: I'll look like Hitler.

PHOEBE: Carys must be out of her mind.

DONNA-MARIE: Swimmin with wimmin! Swimmin with wimmin!

PHOEBE: Still, who are we to pick and choose?

DONNA-MARIE: Swimmin with wimmin!

PHOEBE: We'll have Donna-Marie hanging round our necks all our lives. We should be grateful to have got rid of one.

ROB: Poor child.

DONNA-MARIE: Swimmin with wimmin!

ROB: Doesn't stand a chance. Nobody stands a chance in this mob.

VINCE: She was trembling when I touched her. I've never had a girl tremble before.

ROSE: They were going to kiss one another. On the mouth. Animals! Animals!

VINCE: She likes the animal in me. That's what it is.

DEXTER: If she says a word, I'm finished.

CARYS: Secrets. Everybody's got secrets. God, I'm unhappy.

LINDBERG: As long as she's happy.

DEXTER: I don't want this.

CARYS: I don't want this.

LINDBERG: This is what she wants.

ROSE: They were going to kiss.

CARYS: I'm going to scream.

DEXTER: I'm going to scream.

ROB: Sooner or later—

LINDBERG: Everybody's happy. Look at them smiling.

DEXTER: Hate it!

CARYS: God!

ROB: Bang!

MELBA: Gums!

PHOEBE: Bitch!

FRANK: Ah!

DONNA-MARIE: Oh!

CARYS: I am going to—

ROSE: Smile!

*THE SMILES BROADEN, THE FLASH BRIGHTENS AND*

*GOES OUT. DARKNESS FOR AN INSTANT, THEN EVERY-
BODY IS TALKING AT ONCE, VERY LOUDLY, AS THE
GROUP BREAKS UP. SEAN ENTERS WITH A MEGAPHONE.
HE COUGHS THROUGH IT. THEY ALL FALL DEAD SILENT
AND LOOK AT HIM.*

SEAN: Ladies and gentlemen, luncheon is served.

*EXPECTANT BUZZ FROM THE GROUP, BAGS ARE PICKED
UP, PEOPLE START TO MAKE THEIR WAY TOWARDS THE
EXIT.*

LINDBERG: Wait a minute ! *(Points to Sean)* You were a deaf mute
    ten minutes ago!
SEAN: *(A revelation)* Hallelujah! It's a miracle!

*LIGHTS OUT. MUSIC. THE SCENE CHANGES. FOUR
TABLES ARE PUT ON THE STAGE; THREE OF THEM HAVE
NOTHING ON THEM, AND THE CHAIRS ARE PLACED
CHAOTICALLY AROUND THEM. ONE, AT WHICH MR.
FOSS SITS (IN EVENING DRESS), IS SET FOR TWO, BUT
THE OTHER PERSON HAS OBVIOUSLY NOT BOTHERED
TO COME DOWN FOR DINNER.*

*IT IS EVENING NOW. THE LIGHTS COME UP SLOWLY. DIS-
TANT MUSIC.*

*MR. FOSS HAS SCARCELY EATEN ANY OF HIS DINNER,
BUT HE DRINKS HIS TURKISH COFFEE.*

*A CANDLE BURNS AT HIS TABLE.*

*ULYSSES, DRESSED AS A WAITER BUT STILL WEARING
HIS WELLINGTON BOOTS, RUNS AROUND WIPING
DOWN THE TABLES AND TAKING THE CHAIRS OFF-
STAGE, AS THE SCENE GOES ON.*

MR. FOSS: I see you traipsing down to the beach with a shovel
    and wearing those boots of yours. Why?
ULYSSES: Been spying on me?

MR. FOSS: It's difficult to miss you, going dressed as you do.

ULYSSES: I've got a woman.

MR. FOSS: On the beach?

ULYSSES: That's right.

MR. FOSS: And you go in boots carrying a spade? She must have strange tastes.

ULYSSES: Can you keep a secret?

MR. FOSS: I'm a bearded clam. Trust me.

ULYSSES: The dunes . . . are moving in the night. The wind shifts them and when the sand moves, it uncovers things.

MR. FOSS: Such as?

ULYSSES: Wrecks.

MR. FOSS: A dog?

ULYSSES: Ship wrecks.

MR. FOSS: Oh. Your woman is a ship.

ULYSSES: My ship is a woman. She's called *Providence*. Went down in 1866. All hands lost. Now the sea's withdrawn, and the sand's shifting, and she's uncovering herself, inch by inch. It makes me want to weep to look at her.

MR. FOSS: Well then, it must be love. A ship, eh?

ULYSSES: A frigate.

MR. FOSS: (*An idea is flickering into life in his head*)) Suppose a ship . . .

*A BURST OF LAUGHTER; ENTER VINCE, VERY DRUNK, WITH LINDBERG, NOT QUITE AS FAR GONE, BUT STILL CLEARLY WELL LUBRICATED.*

VINCE: (*Shouting*) Bring me meatballs, mother!

*THIS REMARK STARTS LINDBERG AND VINCE LAUGHING AGAIN. LINDBERG SEES MR. FOSS.*

LINDBERG: Hey. You.

ULYSSES: What?

LINDBERG: I'm talking to the organ-grinder, not the monkey.

*VINCE GIGGLES.*

LINDBERG: Come and join the party, eh? Celebration.

MR. FOSS: Thank you for the invitation, but no.
LINDBERG: You've got to. It's a bloody wedding.

*VINCE FILLS ONE OF MR. FOSS' WINE GLASSES UP WITH
BEER. IT FOAMS AND SPILLS OVER.*

VINCE: Come on, come on, you don't want to insult the bride, do
　　　you?
LINDBERG: Drink up. Health to the happy couple.
MR. FOSS: Thank you, no.
ULYSSES: Now listen, you. If Mr. Foss doesn't want to drink—
VINCE: You stay out of this, fairy boots.

*ULYSSES EXITS.*

LINDBERG: Come on, Vince; we don't want to bicker with the
　　　old fart.
MR. FOSS: That's right, you leave the old fart be, eh? Because he's
　　　already had a bellyful of your celebrations.
VINCE: Oh yeah?
MR. FOSS: To my ear it verges on a civil disturbance. Your crass
　　　songs and your dirty jokes bawled down the corridors. Is
　　　that really a way to celebrate?
VINCE: What the hell's he talking about?
LINDBERG: Leave him be.
VINCE: *(Insistent)* What are you talking about? Are you a fucking
　　　lunatic? What do you know about enjoying yourself, eh?
　　　You keep your fat nose out of it.
MR. FOSS: Don't insult my nose.
VINCE: Fat nose. *(To Lindberg)* Isn't it?

*MR. FOSS IS VERY SENSITIVE ABOUT HIS NOSE. HE IS
FURIOUS.*

MR. FOSS: May I warn you—
VINCE: Fat, ridiculous, frigging nose.
MR. FOSS: You cretin!

*VINCE GETS HOLD OF MR. FOSS AND PULLS HIM OUT
OF HIS SEAT.*

VINCE: What did you call me?
LINDBERG: Hey, whoa there, Vince.
MR. FOSS: Cretin.
VINCE: I'm going to sort out your nose once and for all, pal.

*MR. TREADAWAY APPEARS, JUST AS VINCE PREPARES TO BEAT MR. FOSS UP.*

MR. TREADAWAY: Unhand him.
VINCE: Eh?

*MR. TREADAWAY HAS TAKEN UP A BOXING STANCE, WHICH LOOKS FOOLISH IN HIS MAGRITTE-LIKE OUTFIT. VINCE LETS FOSS GO, AND AIMS A BLOW AT TREAD-AWAY.*

MR. FOSS: Oh I beg you, no.

*A FIGHT BEGINS AMONGST THE TABLE.*

MR. FOSS: Please! Stop it! Mr. Treadaway!

*MR. TREADAWAY TURNS TO LOOK AT FOSS AND VINCE CATCHES TREADAWAY A HEAVY BLOW. TREADAWAY FALLS OVER GROANING. MR. FOSS GOES TO HELP HIM. AS HE DOES SO A RIOTOUS CONGA LINE ENTERS, MADE UP OF PHOEBE, MELBA, FRANK, DEXTER, DONNA-MARIE, ROB, ROSE, SEAN AND CARYS. THEY WEAVE IN AND OUT OF THE TABLES, SINGING THE CONGA SONG AT THE TOPS OF THEIR VOICES, OBLIVIOUS OF THE SPRAWLING FIGURE OF MR. TREADAWAY. VINCE, FLUSHED WITH GLORY, DRAGS ROSE FROM THE LINE AND KISSES HER, GRAPPLING WITH HER TO DO SO. SHE PUSHES HIM OFF AND FOLLOWS THE DISAPPEARING CONGA LINE.*

LINDBERG: Vince!

*VINCE CHASES ROSE OFF, BOTH IN PURSUIT OF THE CONGA, WHICH CAN STILL BE HEARD OFF-STAGE, WEAVING ITS WAY AROUND.*

LINDBERG: *(Re: Treadaway)* Is he all right?
MR. FOSS: Go to hell!

*MRS. CORCORAN ENTERS WITH ULYSSES. LINDBERG EXITS, MUTTERING TO HIMSELF. TREADAWAY IS NOW SITTING UP AT THE TABLE: HIS NOSE IS MASHED, FOSS' BLOODY HANDKERCHIEF PRESSED TO HIS FACE.*

MRS. CORCORAN: Fighting?
MR. TREADAWAY: It's nothing.
MRS. CORCORAN: Let me see. *(Looks at Mr. Treadaway's nose)*
ULYSSES: Is it broken?
MRS. CORCORAN: No.
MR. FOSS: I must protest, Mrs. Corcoran. These people are savages. I couldn't eat a mouthful of dinner for their riotous ways.
MRS. CORCORAN: Are you feeling dizzy at all?
MR. FOSS: No, luckily I had a good lunch.
MRS. CORCORAN: Not you, *him!*
MR. TREADAWAY: I'm all right. Thank you. You're most kind.

*THE SINGING IS GOING ON AS LOUDLY AS EVER, OFF-STAGE.*

MRS. CORCORAN: I'll try and calm them down.
MR. FOSS: Much obliged, Mrs. Corcoran. Much obliged.

*MRS. CORCORAN EXITS.*

MR. TREADAWAY: Some fresh air, maybe . . .
MR. FOSS: Yes. Yes. Of course. One more hour of this, I'll go mad.

*MR. FOSS WAVES AWAY ULYSSES' HELP, AND TAKES MR. TREADAWAY ONTO THE PATIO. ULYSSES BUSIES HIMSELF WITH CLEARING THE TABLE; FIRST DRINKING THE BEER VINCE POURED. ENTER ROSE, WITH MELBA JUFFS AND CARYS. ROSE HAS DRUNK A GREAT DEAL, AND WANTS TO BE SICK.*

ROSE: Leave me alone. Just let me lie down. I want to lie down.
MELBA: It's best if you make yourself sick.
ROSE: No! I hate being sick.
MELBA: Get it out of your system. You'll feel much better.
ROSE: I told you, no.
CARYS: Melba's right, Rose. It'll only take a minute.
MELBA: Just put your fingers down your throat. I'll do it if you like.
ULYSSES: Not in here you don't.

*ULYSSES EXITS WITH TRAY OF STUFF FROM MR. FOSS' TABLE.*

*ENTER LINDBERG WITH ROB.*

LINDBERG: How's she doing?
ROSE: *(On the verge of tears)* No, no. Go away. I don't want you to see me.
CARYS: Go on.
ROSE: Leave me alone. Everybody. Leave me alone!
LINDBERG: Come on, love. I brought a bag. For you to be sick in. It's one of my double-lined specials.

*THE VERY PROXIMITY OF LINDBERG SEEMS TO MAKE IT WORSE.*

MELBA: There? *(As to a child)* Isn't that kind?

*ROSE SNATCHES THE PLASTIC BAG AND EXITS.*

LINDBERG: Come on, Melba, back to the party. Rob—
ROB: Yes. Coming.

*EXIT MELBA WITH LINDBERG; ULYSSES RE-ENTERS.*

ROB: Any chance of some coffee?
ULYSSES: Help yourself.

*ULYSSES EXITS.*

*ROB POURS A CUP OF COFFEE, AND DRINKS IT. IT'S BIT-TER, BUT GOOD. DEXTER ENTERS; HE TOO IS THE WORSE FOR WEAR.*

DEXTER: How about a kiss from the best man?
ROB: Drunk?
DEXTER: Yeah.
ROB: That makes it all right, huh?
DEXTER: We can go up to your room. Nobody'll notice. Few minutes.
ROB: This is your wedding night, Dex.
DEXTER: All the more reason to celebrate.
ROB: No.
DEXTER: No?
ROB: Not tonight, not tomorrow night.
DEXTER: You fucking queens are too much, you know. You really are.

*VINCE ENTERS.*

VINCE: I wondered where the boys had gone. *(He's conspiratorial)* Can I ask a favor? I'm in with a chance with Rose, you know. I don't have any . . . you know, protection on me. Wouldn't like to get the girl in trouble. Rob? You packed anything? I'll pay for it. Or I'll wash it out, give it you back. Whatever suits.
ROB: Christ.

*ROB TURNS AWAY FROM VINCE AND GOES TOWARDS THE FRONT DOOR.*

VINCE: What did I say?

*ROSE ENTERS CRYING; SHE CONFRONTS ROB, LOOKS UP AT HIM FROZEN FOR A MOMENT, THEN EXITS UPSTAIRS, SOBBING.*

*CARYS FOLLOWS ON IN WITH A WEIGHED-DOWN PLASTIC BAG.*

*ROB EXITS.*

CARYS: *(To Vince)* Present from Rose.
VINCE: For me?

*VINCE PLUNGES HIS HAND IN THE BAG. HIS FACE REGIS-
TERS DISGUST; HE LOOKS INTO THE BAG, WITHDRAWS A
DRIPPING HAND.*

VINCE: Oh Jesus Christ.

*HE EXITS WITH BAG. DEXTER IS LAUGHING. ULYSSES
COMES BACK, FINISHES THE TIDYING.*

DEXTER: Good one.
CARYS: Enjoying yourself?
DEXTER: As much as can be expected.
CARYS: Don't get too drunk. Tonight . . . tonight we're going to
    be all right, Dex. We are. We're going . . . *(Whispers in his
    ear)*

*AS SHE WHISPERS, THE CONGA LINE REAPPEARS,
DRUNKER AND SMALLER THAN BEFORE, BUT MORE
BOISTEROUS THAN EVER.*

CARYS: *(Hisses to him, demanding)* Kiss me.

*DEXTER KISSES HER, AWARE THAT THIS IS A PERFOR-
MANCE FOR THE WEDDING PARTY. THE CONGA LINE
WINDS ITS WAY ON WHILE DEXTER AND CARYS KISS
PASSIONATELY CENTER-STAGE. THE GORILLA HAS
TAGGED ALONG AT THE END OF THE CONGA. PHOEBE
SEES THE KISS; THE CONGA BREAKS. WHOOPS, WHIS-
TLES, APPLAUSE. DEXTER AND CARYS ARE SHOWING
OFF NOW; THE WHOLE PARTY IS TAKING A DIFFERENT
TONE. MUSIC PLAYS FROM SOMEWHERE. VINCE CLIMBS
ONTO A TABLE AND STARTS TO DO A STRIPTEASE,
INEPTLY. MELBA, PISSED OUT OF HER HEAD, APPLAUDS.
SO DOES THE GORILLA. ENTER MR. FOSS, WITH TREAD-
AWAY, WHOSE FACE IS A BLOODY MESS. HE TAKES A*

*DRINK FROM MELBA.*

MR. FOSS: Is there no end to this?
LINDBERG: Have a drink and shut up.
MR. FOSS: I don't want a drink, damn you.
PHOEBE: Snooty little prick. Where's Rose? Has anyone seen
    Rose?
CARYS: She went upstairs.
MELBA: She was sick.
CARYS: And she went upstairs.
PHOEBE: We should have a photograph! Somebody fetch Rose.
FRANK: I'll go.

*EXIT FRANK. VINCE HAS STRIPPED DOWN TO HIS
UNDERWEAR NOW, AND IS GIVING HIMSELF A BEER
SHOWER. ROB COMES BACK IN. MR. FOSS WATCHES THE
PERFORMANCE, DISGUST ON HIS FACE. TREADAWAY HAS
TAKEN TO DRINKING, HEAVILY, HAVING ACCEPTED
LINDBERG'S APOLOGIES, UNHEARD OVER THE BABBLE
AND MUSIC. ENTER FRANK.*

FRANK: Quickly! Somebody! Quickly!
LINDBERG: What is it?
FRANK: Rose! It's Rose! You, boy! Quickly!

*HE GRABS SEAN AND THEY EXIT.*

PHOEBE: What's she done now? Damn woman.
CARYS: She could have had an accident.

*CARYS EXITS TOO. VINCE, PAST NOTICING, STILL PER-
FORMS, COVERING AND UNCOVERING HIS NIPPLES
WITH HIS FINGERS, MOCK-TEASING. THE MUSIC GRINDS
TO A HALT. THE CROWD PARTS AS FRANK AND SEAN
BRING ROSE IN, SOAKING WET, AND LAY HER DOWN.
HER EYES ARE CLOSED.*

FRANK: There was water coming from under the bathroom door.
SEAN: We had to kick it in.

*ULYSSES HAS COME IN TOO. THEY ALL GATHER AROUND HER. SHE IS MOANING SLIGHTLY.*

CARYS: She tried to drown herself.
PHOEBE: Rose! How dare you!
FRANK: Can anyone give the kiss of life?
VINCE: I'll do it!

*ROSE SITS UP QUICKLY, HEARING VINCE'S OFFER.*

ROSE: No! Keep away from me! All of you, keep away from me!
LINDBERG: For a minute there—
CARYS: Thank God.
ROSE: You stopped me! Why did you stop me?
PHOEBE: All right, have you had all the attention you need now?
LINDBERG: Phoebe.
ROSE: I want to die!
CARYS: Ssh! It's all right; really.
MELBA: Everybody throws up once in a while.
CARYS: Can somebody fetch a towel? She's shivering.
ROSE: I'll die of pneumonia. I'm not fussy.
PHOEBE: What have you got to die about?
CARYS: Leave her be, mother.
PHOEBE: She's spoilt the whole atmosphere.
VINCE: Silly bitch. *(To himself)* I wouldn't have touched her.
LINDBERG: Come on, Rose, what's all this about?
DEXTER: *(He's guessed)* Don't bully her. She was just feeling sick.
      Isn't that it, Rose? You were just feeling sick.
PHOEBE: Rose? I want an answer.
ROSE: *(Teeth chattering now)* I can't tell you.
LINDBERG: Come on, love.
CARYS: It's all right, Rose. Whatever it is. Tell us. We'll understand.
ROSE: *(Glowering at Dexter)* He knows.
CARYS: Dexter?
ROSE: Ask him. Ask them both. Him and Rob.
FRANK: Rob?
DEXTER: Oh Christ.
ROSE: Ask both of them. They'll tell you.

*DEXTER LOOKS GLASSY-EYED.*

ROSE: I saw them. My Rob, my lovely Rob—
PHOEBE: He's not your Rob.
ROSE: They were kissing.
PHOEBE: Who were— (*Looks up*) kissing?
CARYS: Dexter?
MELBA: I don't understand.
DEXTER: What do you care?
LINDBERG: I do. I bloody understand.
CARYS: She's mistaken.
LINDBERG: I bloody understand right enough.
ROSE: My Robert—
CARYS: She's mistaken, right?
DEXTER: No.
VINCE: Fuck a duck.
PHOEBE: She's a lying bitch.
ROB: She's got eyes in her head.
LINDBERG: You! Shut up!
FRANK: Does that mean—?
MELBA: Oh God, Frank.
PHOEBE: (*To Carys*) What did I tell you? From the beginning. Don't get involved, I said.
LINDBERG: You're a homosexual; is that it, Dexter?
CARYS: Is it?
DEXTER: I don't know.
PHOEBE: (*White with fury*) Well, isn't it about time you made up your fucking mind?
LINDBERG: Oh Princess.
CARYS: Don't Princess me. I'm not your Princess.
LINDBERG: Ssh! Ssh! Don't cry.
CARYS: I'm not going to cry.
ROSE: I'm sorry.
CARYS: (*Calmly*) It's all right, Rose. It's perfectly all right.

*THE PARTY BEGINS TO BREAK UP.*

DEXTER: I'm sorry.
LINDBERG: It's not your fault, is it? I mean, you've been messed about with, that's all. It happens—
PHOEBE: Why didn't you tell me, Rose? There was no need to make a public display of it, was there?

ROSE: Tell you? You're so . . . you're so . . . carnivorous.

PHOEBE: Well, there's thanks.

LINDBERG: The bloody best man. That's a laugh. I'm just appalled I didn't see it earlier.

ROB: See what?

LINDBERG: Your nancy ways, son, your bloody nancy ways.

ROB: What would you know?

DEXTER: Don't.

LINDBERG: I've seen a damn sight more than you'll ever see. Oh, I daresay you think you're a bit of a wit, eh?

ROB: No—

LINDBERG: Coming in here, spoiling a young couple's chances together.

CARYS: Dad.

ROB: No, let him rant a bit.

LINDBERG: You don't care; your type never does. Lower form of bloody humanity! And it's about time the rest of us stood up and got counted.

*ROSE STARTS TO CRY AGAIN. DONNA-MARIE IS CRYING IN SYMPATHY.*

LINDBERG: You make me want to puke.

ROSE: I'm going to be sick.

*SHE GETS UP, IGNORED, HANDS CLAMPED TO HER MOUTH.*

LINDBERG: Better we found out what was going on. You've done us a service here, Rose, and I'm grateful. Rose?

*ROSE IS EXITING.*

LINDBERG: *(To Phoebe)* Go with her, love.

*PHOEBE EXITS. VINCE IS PUTTING ON HIS CLOTHES, DRUNKENLY TRYING TO GET BOTH LEGS INTO ONE TROUSER-LEG.*

MELBA: Dexter.

DEXTER: Carys—

*HE MAKES A MOVE TOWARD HER. LINDBERG CUTS HIM OFF.*

LINDBERG: No. *(A beat)* Not now.
MELBA: Dexter. How could you do this to us?

*MELBA JUFFS EXITS.*

FRANK: I suppose . . . it's some kind of judgment, or other. God moves in mysterious ways.
DEXTER: Spare me the heavenly details, Dad.

*FRANK JUFFS EXITS.*

ROB: *(To Carys)* Nothing was going on. Nothing was going to go on. It was in the past.
CARYS: I don't want to know.
LINDBERG: *(Quietly, to Rob)* You are shit.

*ULYSSES FADES AWAY; SEAN TOO. TREADAWAY, NOW DRUNK, IS ASLEEP ON A CHAIR. VINCE EXITS, STILL HALF-DRESSED.*

VINCE: Has anyone seen the other leg of my trousers?

*FOSS DOESN'T MOVE.*

LINDBERG: You are still my Princess.

*LINDBERG TAKES CARYS OFF.*

ROB: Go with her. Stop him making it worse.
DEXTER: Why?
ROB: She's in agony.
DEXTER: I don't have anything reassuring to say.
ROB: You were going to marry her.
DEXTER: Well, I'm well out of that then, aren't I?

*DEXTER EXITS. THE LIGHTS CHANGE; A DEEP GLOOM NOW, PIERCED BY FRAGMENTS OF LIGHT. SEAN HAS RE-ENTERED. HE IS STANDING, DRINKING MILK FROM A BOTTLE.*

SEAN: Are you really queer?

ROB: Really.

SEAN: You never did it with a woman?

ROB: *(Very quietly)* Once or twice. Not very successfully.

SEAN: I think it's really . . . dirty. What you do. It's really dirty.

ROB: You've tried it?

SEAN: Me? . . . no. I just heard.

ROB: They why don't you stop flirting and go to bed; or I might just show you the real thing.

*SEAN EXITS, EMBARRASSED, HIS BLUFF CALLED.*

ROB: *(To himself)* You stupid bastard.

*MR. FOSS EMERGES FROM THE SHADOWS.*

MR. FOSS: So much for rage.

ROB: *(Drained)* So much for rage.

MR. FOSS: The error, you think, is yours?

ROB: In part.

MR. FOSS: More convenient.

ROB: Huh?

MR. FOSS: Than to take them on.

ROB: There's no way to do that. You'd have to turn them inside out. Get beyond their performances.

MR. FOSS: Is my nose, would you say, abnormally large?

ROB: I beg your pardon?

MR. FOSS: My nose was a bone of contention. I ask for your opinion.

ROB: It's an average nose.

MR. FOSS: Sir, you're a gentleman. *(Beat)* And do they have secrets?

ROB: What do you think? Goodnight, Mister . . .

MR. FOSS: Lear. Edward Lear.

ROB: Like the poet?

MR. FOSS: Like the poet. Goodnight, Mr. Kidd.

*ROB EXITS. FOSS SITS AT THE TABLE AGAIN. TREADAWAY
IS ASLEEP IN THE CHAIR OPPOSITE HIM.*

MR. FOSS: One last dream. You and I, Treadaway; the Wedding
Party, perhaps the boy, all sharing one . . . apocalyptic . . .
dream.

MR. TREADAWAY: *(Eyes still closed)* No.

MR. FOSS: You're listening.

MR. TREADAWAY: I'm always listening.

MR. FOSS: What a way to go.

MR. TREADAWAY: It's out of the question. The rules forbid collective dreams. They're dangerous.

MR. FOSS: *(Innocently)* Are they?

MR. TREADAWAY: They encourage fascism and hysteria.

MR. FOSS: I'll do it anyway, with or without you. Hugo. Where's
your spirit of adventure?

MR. TREADAWAY: I told you: *no.*

MR. FOSS: Should I report you as a drunkard? That would stymie
your hopes for advancement.

*TREADAWAY TRIES TO HIDE THE BOTTLE HE'S NURSING.*

TREADAWAY: Are you blackmailing me?

MR. FOSS: Suppose a ship—

MR. TREADAWAY: A ship. Oh Lord. *(Sighs)* Yes?

MR. FOSS: And the sea. The way Sean dreamed it. Foamy and
vast.

MR. TREADAWAY: What sort of ship?

MR. FOSS: We'll need dream technicians. Not the usual herd.
Iconoclasts, who want to do something a little off-beat. Real
illusionists, ready to conjure some sights.

MR. TREADAWAY: You can't mean tonight.

MR. FOSS: Of course tonight. While this mob are sweating in
their beds, we'll pick them up and dress them for a voyage.
Take off your hat, Hugo. Let your head breathe a bit.

MR. TREADAWAY: *(Takes his hat off)* Oh.

MR. FOSS: Better?

MR. TREADAWAY: Not much.

MR. FOSS: Think of it. All of us on one final cruise into frenzical
waters.

*THE SOUND OF WAVES, DISTANTLY.*

MR. TREADAWAY: It could be a disaster.
MR. FOSS: *(Smiling)* Yes, I believe it could.

*THE NOISE OF THE SEA GROWS.*

MR. FOSS: I can already hear the sea. The wind is with us.
MR. TREADAWAY: Oh God.
MR. FOSS: *(Fired with an almost visionary zeal)* The sea, Treadaway, do you hear it? Do you hear it?
MR. TREADAWAY: I'm afraid I do, I'm afraid I do—

*THE NOISE OF THE SEA BLOTS OUT TREADAWAY'S VOICE. AS THE LIGHTS FADE.*

*END OF ACT TWO.*

# Act 3

# Act 3:

*BLACKNESS.*

*THE DOUBLE BOOM OF THE FOG-HORN OF THE GREAT SHIP BEAR OF AMSTERDAM PIERCES THE BLACKNESS, FOLLOWED BY THE RHYTHMICAL CHURNING OF ITS ENGINES IN THE BOWELS OF THE VESSEL. THE SEA CAN ALSO BE HEARD; AS CAN DISTANT MUSIC. A SINGER; PIANO. THE LIGHTS COME UP ON THE INTERIOR OF THE HOTEL, TRANSFORMED. IT IS NOW THE MAIN DECK OF A LUXURY LINER. A RAILING HAS BEEN PUT UP IN FRONT OF THE ACTING AREA; LIFE PRESERVERS, ALL WITH THE "BEAR OF AMSTERDAM" NAME ON THEM, HANG AT INTERVALS. THE BALCONY, UPON WHICH THE CAPTAIN OF THIS SUBTLE SHIP STANDS, IS ALSO EQUIPPED WITH A LIFE PRESERVER, AS WELL AS A WHEEL AND SPEAKING TUBE. THE CAPTAIN IS DRESSED IN A LARGE OVERCOAT, LEATHER GLOVES, A PEAKED HAT. IT IS STILL QUITE DISTINCTLY MR. FOSS. HIS FEATURES SUIT THIS TRANSFORMATION.*

*ON THE LOWER DECK, WHICH IS AT PRESENT NOT AS WELL ILLUMINATED AS THE BRIDGE, THERE ARE SIGNS OF PARTYING. STREAMERS FESTOON THE RAILING, BALLOONS LITTER THE DECK. THE COLORED LIGHTS BURN BRIGHTLY. THE SCENES WHICH FOLLOW ARE ALL "STAGE-MANAGED" IN QUITE OBVIOUS MANNER BY THE DREAM TECHNICIANS FOSS SUMMONED AT THE END OF ACT TWO.*

*IT IS THEY WHO OPERATE THE MECHANISM OF THE DREAM: THEY WHO CHOREOGRAPH THE PANIC AND THE CHAOS OF THE SINKING SHIP; THEY WHO GIVE US A BRIEF POIGNANT IMAGE OF THE BEAR OF AMSTER-DAM DISAPPEARING INTO THE ATLANTIC OCEAN; THEY WHO ROCK THE LIFE-BOAT, THEY WHO SPIRIT AWAY THE DROWNED, ETC. THEIR PRESENCE, NEEDLESS TO SAY, IS NOT ONCE NOTICED BY THE PROTAGONISTS; TO THEM, THE SCENES OF TERROR THAT WILL DEVELOP LATER IN THE ACT HAVE ALL THE FORCE OF REALITY; AS INDEED DO THE EVENTS WHICH ARE EVEN NOW UNFOLDING ON THE SHIP.*

MR. FOSS: *(Binoculars to eyes)* Mr. Treadaway.

*TREADAWAY CLIMBS UP TO THE BRIDGE. HE HAS A BAN-DAGE ON HIS NOSE AND HE STILL WEARS HIS BOWLER HAT.*

MR. TREADAWAY: This is terribly wrong.

MR. FOSS: I'm in charge of this vessel, Mr. Treadaway. Should you wish to question my sanity, you may do so to the proper authorities when we're safely docked at dawn. But for tonight, Mr. Treadaway, for tonight—the ship is mine; and God help all who sail in her!

MR. TREADAWAY: *(Defeated)* Yes.

MR. FOSS: Yes *sir!*

MR. TREADAWAY: Yes sir!

MR. FOSS: Don't fret so much. We have a fine night for a cruise. A little fog maybe, a few icebergs—

MR. TREADAWAY: *(Terror-stricken)* Icebergs?

MR. FOSS: We are sailing the Arctic Ocean, didn't I tell you? This promises to be a positively Titanic experience for us all.

MR. TREADAWAY: *(Very quietly)* Oh Christ.

MR. FOSS: Take the wheel, I'm going below to join the Captain's table. *(Kindly, as he exits)* Keep a stiff upper lip, Mr. Tread-away, worse things happen at sea.

MR. TREADAWAY: *(A desperate plea)* But we *are* at sea!

*FOSS DISAPPEARS.*

MR. TREADAWAY: Sir!? Sir . . .

*THE LIGHTS GO DOWN ON TREADAWAY IN PANIC, AND COME UP ON THE DECK. PEOPLE STROLL TO AND FRO, ARM IN ARM, CARRYING DRINKS. SOME, AS WILL BE DESCRIBED, ARE IN ELABORATE FANCY-DRESS. ROB, IN A TUXEDO, IS LEANING ON THE RAILING; THE WATER THROWS PATTERNS ONTO HIS FACE. A DOOR OPENS, MUSIC FROM DISTANT ROOMS, THE SOUND OF LAUGHTER. ENTER DEXTER. HE STANDS WATCHING ROB.*

DEXTER: I wondered where you'd got to.

ROB: Oh?

DEXTER: They're going to judge the fancy-dress competition in a few minutes. Should be a riot. Do you have any idea where we're going, by the way?

ROB: What?

DEXTER: Only I can't even . . . I know this sounds daft, but I can't even remember getting on this bloody ship. I mean, I know I must have done it. I just don't remember. And my pockets are full of sand. Have you seen Carys?

ROB: What's she dressed as?

DEXTER: The Bride of Dracula.

ROB: No I haven't.

DEXTER: I've decided . . . I'm going to use the voyage to propose to her. Then I'll marry her when we cross the Equator. How's that? I'm a groom, see? The shirt's painted on.

*DEXTER UNBUTTONS HIS JACKET. A SHIRT AND TIE ARE PAINTED ON HIS BARE TORSO.*

DEXTER: The waiter did it.

ROB: Did he paint on underwear too?

DEXTER: Wouldn't you like to know?

*ENTER ROSE, AS A MERMAID.*

ROSE: Yoohoo!

*SHE WADDLES ACROSS THE DECK.*

ROSE: You're here.
DEXTER: What the hell are you dressed as? Half a haddock?
ROSE: Guess. Rob?
ROB: You're a mermaid.
ROSE: That's right. What are you dressed as?
ROB: An escapologist.
ROSE: Oo. What do you escape from?
ROB: Fancy-dress parties.

*DEXTER GIGGLES.*

ROSE: Was that a joke?
ROB: Not so's you'd notice.
DEXTER: (*Backing off*) Well, I feel a bit of a gooseberry right now.
ROB: Don't go, Dex.
DEXTER: (*Maliciously*) The moonlight, the sea. Love's young dream. See you around.

*DEXTER EXITS.*

ROSE: Why are you watching the sea?
ROB: I saw lights.
ROSE: In the sea?
ROB: That's what I thought.
ROSE: Do you want to kiss me?
ROB: Would you take it personally if I said no?
ROSE: Actually, yes. (*She touches his face*)

*A DOOR OPENS. OUT TUMBLES CARYS, DRESSED AS THE BRIDE OF DRACULA; MELBA, DRESSED AS A FLOWER; AND DONNA-MARIE, DRESSED AS A FROG.*

CARYS: Break it up! Break it up!
MELBA: It's quite chilly.
CARYS: Rose isn't cold; are you Rose?
DONNA-MARIE: I'm a frog.
CARYS: So you keep saying.
DONNA-MARIE: A green frog! Look at me.
CARYS: Look at her, Rob.
DONNA-MARIE: I'm a green frog.

ROB: I can see.

CARYS: And I'm the Bride of Dracula, and Melba's a hardy perennial. Only she's out of season.

ROB: Dexter was looking for you.

CARYS: So, let him look. I don't care.

*ENTER LINDBERG AND PHOEBE. THE FORMER AS NAPOLEON, THE LATTER IN A SUMPTUOUS EVENING DRESS, AND MASK.*

PHOEBE: Rose?

ROSE: *(Without turning)* Phoebe.

PHOEBE: Should you be out here dressed like that? You'll catch a chill.

ROSE: Well, that's my business, isn't it?

PHOEBE: We're the ones who have to put up with you when you're sniveling.

DONNA-MARIE: I'm a green frog.

PHOEBE: Just remember that. Lindberg and I are going on a tour of the deck. Will you watch Donna-Marie? Make sure she doesn't fall overboard.

MELBA: What are you dressed as?

PHOEBE: Josephine. Lindberg is Napoleon.

*PHOEBE STARTS TO GO OFF.*

LINDBERG: I came, I saw, I conquered.

PHOEBE: No you didn't. That was Julius Caesar.

LINDBERG: Well, what did I do?

ROB: You were a pain in the arse to all of Europe.

LINDBERG: *(Brightly)* That sounds right.

*LINDBERG EXITS WITH PHOEBE. ROB IS WANDERING AWAY.*

ROSE: Maybe later we could dance. Do you think?

ROB: I don't see why not.

ROSE: You've got secrets, haven't you?

ROB: Have I?

ROSE: You're a man of mystery. It's very sexy.

ROB: Oh hell.

*ROB EXITS.*

ROSE: We're going to dance.
CARYS: Grow up, Rose.
ROSE: He said he saw lights in the sea.
DONNA-MARIE: We could go swimming.
CARYS: You are such a wet. Why don't you stand up to my mother?
ROSE: She's been very good to me.
CARYS: Only when it suits her.
MELBA: I saw an iceberg. In the mist, I'm sure.
CARYS: *(Bored)* Fascinating.

*SEAN ENTERS, WITH A BOTTLE OF CHAMPAGNE IN EITHER HAND. HE IS DRESSED AS A STEWARD.*

CARYS: Oh, we wondered where the drink had got to.
SEAN: Champagne for the lady?
CARYS: Champagne and more champagne.

*HE POURS CHAMPAGNE INTO HER GLASS.*

CARYS: You've got your hands full, haven't you?

*SHE REACHES FOR HIS FLY. HE BENDS OUT OF THE WAY.*

MELBA: Carys.
CARYS: What's the problem?
SEAN: Anyone else for a glass of bubbly?
ROSE: Me.
DONNA-MARIE: Me too.
CARYS: None for the frog.

*SEAN MOVES OFF.*

MELBA: He's got a nice bottom.
CARYS: He's a fruit.
ROSE: What sort of fruit?
CARYS: He's gay.
MELBA: How can you tell?
CARYS: Bet you he can't whistle.

*VINCE HAS COME ON, UNSEEN. HE HAS A MONSTER MASK ON.*

ROSE: What does that mean?
CARYS: If a man can't whistle he's a fairy. Don't you know anything, Rose?

*SEAN EXITS, WHISTLING.*

MELBA: Oh God. Rose. Watch it. It's that man again. The sex maniac.
VINCE: *(Pulls off mask)* Hello, ladies.

*DONNA-MARIE SHRIEKS.*

CARYS: Oh that's horrible . . . horrible . . .
VINCE: Wait, ladies! Ladies!

*THEY EXIT SHRIEKING AND LAUGHING.*

VINCE: Damn you then. Damn you all to hell.

*HE SEES ROB ENTERING, AND TURNS AWAY, TO GO BACK THE WAY HE CAME.*

*SEAN CROSSES TO ROB.*

SEAN: Drink, sir?
ROB: No thank you. Question though.
SEAN: Yes sir?
ROB: I keep seeing lights in the sea. Look.

*THEY GO TO THE SIDE OF THE SHIP.*

SEAN: They're fish, sir. Luminous fish. They live at the very bottom of the ocean, see, where there's no sun. So they make their own light.
ROB: Why can I see them if they live so deep?
SEAN: Maybe they come up to see the ship. Maybe they think it's a big fish.

*ENTER MR. FOSS, NOW TOTALLY DISGUISED AS THE INVISIBLE MAN: BANDAGES, GLOVES, DARK GLASSES.*

SEAN: 'Evening.

*THE INVISIBLE MAN NODS.*

SEAN: *(To Rob)* He's been following me round all night. Do you know who's in it?
ROB: Can't say I do.

*THE INVISIBLE MAN CROSSES TO SEAN.*

SEAN: I think he's got designs on my body.

*SEAN EXITS, THRUSTING A BOTTLE INTO THE INVISIBLE MAN'S HANDS.*

SEAN: Don't drink it all at once.

*THE INVISIBLE MAN WATCHES SEAN GO, AND LEANS ON THE RAILING NEXT TO ROB.*

ROB: Nice boy.

*THE INVISIBLE MAN LOOKS AT ROB. PHOEBE ENTERS, AT A RUSH.*

PHOEBE: Have you seen Lindberg? He went off to get some drinks and he didn't come back.
ROB: No he hasn't come past here—
PHOEBE: I have this terror of him falling overboard. The sea looks so . . . *(She puts her fear out of her mind)* Who's he?

*SHE APPROACHES THE INVISIBLE MAN AND PEERS AT HIM.*

PHOEBE: Lindberg? Is that you in there? *(To Rob)* Do you know who this is?
ROB: No.

PHOEBE: Lindberg? It is you, isn't it?

*SHE GETS HOLD OF THE INVISIBLE MAN'S HEAD, AND TRIES TO PULL OFF THE MASK. THE MAN FIGHTS BACK.*

PHOEBE: Take that off! Lindberg! Take that off this minute!
ROB: I think you might be making a mistake.

*PHOEBE AND THE INVISIBLE MAN WRESTLE.*

PHOEBE: Take that off, I said!

*THE INVISIBLE MAN PICKS HER UP, MORE TO STOP HER THAN ANYTHING ELSE.*

PHOEBE: Oh!

*THROWS HER OVER HIS SHOULDER.*

PHOEBE: *(The tone changes)* Oh Lindberg! Yes! Yes! I'm ready.

*THE INVISIBLE MAN STARTS TO CARRY HER OFF.*

PHOEBE: Hurry up, Lindberg. Anywhere! Anywhere!

*ENTER LINDBERG, WITH VINCE.*

PHOEBE: Ravish me.
LINDBERG: Here?
PHOEBE: Lindberg!

*SHE REALIZES HER MISTAKE.*

PHOEBE: Oh God!
LINDBERG: Put my wife down!
ROB: She thought it was you.
LINDBERG: She has this effect on the blind! Put her down!

*THE INVISIBLE MAN EXITS WITH HER.*

LINDBERG: The bloody nerve! *(To Vince)* Fetch my gun!

ROB: Wait a minute. It's just a simple mistake.

LINDBERG: What would you know? Fetch my bloody gun, Vince. It's in my cabin.

*ROSE ENTERS.*

ROSE: Donna-Marie's been sick. Where's Phoebe?

LINDBERG: She's been abducted!

ROSE: Who by?

LINDBERG: The Invisible Man.

ROSE: I didn't see him—

*ENTER CARYS AND MELBA JUFFS WITH FRANK, DRESSED AS THE POPE.*

LINDBERG: *(To Frank)* Christ, what do you look like? Everybody, spread out. We'll find him, if we're systematic.

FRANK: What are we looking for?

LINDBERG: My wife, you bloody fool. We've got to find her before he does something terrible to her.

FRANK: Like what?

ROB: Like giving her some pleasure.

LINDBERG: *Shut up*!

*LINDBERG STARTS TO ORGANIZE THE SEARCH, AD-LIBBING THE DIVIDING UP OF THE SHIP, WHILE LIGHTS COME UP ON THE BRIDGE, WHERE SEAN STANDS WITH MR. TREADAWAY. THE HORN SOUNDS.*

MR. TREADAWAY: I don't like the look of the weather up ahead. The fog's closing in. Where's the captain?

SEAN: I looked for him, but I can't find him.

MR. TREADAWAY: I don't know what to do. If we stop all engines, we'll drift, maybe strike an iceberg. If we go on, we'll sail straight into that. Look again. Search high and low, but find him. We haven't got much time. *(He starts to pray)* Holy Mary, Mother of God, pray for us sinners, now and at the hour of our death.

*THE PRAYER IS LOST IN BABBLE FROM THE LOWER DECK. PEOPLE TO AND FRO; THE ACTION IS ACCELERATING. EVERYBODY SPREADS OUT TO LOOK FOR THE KIDNAPPER, LEAVING ROB AND LINDBERG ALONE.*

LINDBERG: I blame you for this.

ROB: Why me?

LINDBERG: You just watched her snatched away.

ROB: She seemed to be enjoying herself.

LINDBERG: What would you know? You've never loved a woman. Have you? You don't know what it's like. Having to watch over them, protect their virginity, their bodies, their teeth. A man has to be a tower of strength.

ROB: Bollocks!

*SEAN APPEARS ON THE LOWER DECK. HE STARES OUT OVER THE RAILING.*

SEAN: *(Shouts up)* Sir! Mr. Treadaway!

LINDBERG: Bollocks?

MR. TREADAWAY: Found him?

SEAN: No. He's disappeared. But sir—

MR. TREADAWAY: *(Through a megaphone)* Will Captain Foss please return to the Bridge immediately? Captain Foss. To the Bridge. Immediately.

ROB: You talk rubbish most of the time, Lindberg. You open your mouth and shit spews out.

*VINCE ENTERS WITH GUN.*

VINCE: Here.

LINDBERG: About time.

*HE TAKES THE GUN AND POINTS IT AT ROB.*

*ENTER DEXTER.*

DEXTER: Where's Carys?

LINDBERG: Not now, son; I'm shooting the sodomite.

SEAN: (*At the railing*) There's something in the fog! Mr. Tread-away! *There's something in the fog!*

DEXTER: You can't.

LINDBERG: Just watch me. On your knees, son. I'll make it quick.

ROB: Fuck off.

SEAN: Dead ahead!

*ENTER MELBA.*

MELBA: We've found them!

LINDBERG: What?

*ENTER CARYS.*

CARYS: Quickly!

*SEAN CROSSES THE STAGE AND CLIMBS ONTO THE BRIDGE.*

SEAN: Do you see? Do you see? It's a wave. A hundred feet high. Do you see?

MR. TREADAWAY: That's no wave. It's an iceberg, boy!

LINDBERG: (*Rob is forgotten*) Where are they?

MELBA: We cornered them on the second-class deck.

DEXTER: Carys!

CARYS: Not now, Dexter.

LINDBERG: My wife? In second class? The bastard!

*HE EXITS WITH VINCE.*

DEXTER: I want to propose to you.

CARYS: Later! Later!

DEXTER: The captain can marry us. When we dock at Mozam-bique.

ALL: Mozambique??

DEXTER: Say yes.

CARYS: Yes! Now let me go. I have to go with Dad.

DEXTER: No you don't.

CARYS: Yes! I do!

*CARYS EXITS.*

ROB: Well?
DEXTER: Well what?
ROB: What are you looking at me for?
DEXTER: She's going to marry me.
ROB: So?
DEXTER: So aren't you . . . jealous? Be *something* at least.
ROB: Would that make you feel better?
DEXTER: Yeah.
ROB: Poor Dex. Poor bloody Dex. *(He kisses Dex, lightly)* There.

*ENTER PHOEBE, STILL BEING CARRIED BY THE INVISIBLE MAN.*

PHOEBE: Oh Christ! Put me down! Put me down!

*HE PUTS HER DOWN.*

PHOEBE: *(Disappointed)* I didn't mean actually put me down!
SEAN: What's going on down there?
MR. TREADAWAY: Never mind the guests. Watch the fog!

*DONNA-MARIE ENTERS.*

DONNA-MARIE: Mamma.
PHOEBE: Oh little one, don't look.
DONNA-MARIE: What's happening?

*DEXTER COVERS DONNA-MARIE'S EYES.*

PHOEBE: Mamma's going to be ravished. Fore and aft.

*VOICES OFF. LINDBERG SHOUTING. THE INVISIBLE MAN EXITS WITH PHOEBE, PURSUED BY VINCE, MELBA, FRANK, CARYS, ETC. THE SHIP'S HORN BLOWS.*

DEXTER: Listen! Something's happening to the engines. Oh Christ! What's going on?
DONNA-MARIE: *(Breaking away from Dexter)* Ice-cream! Ice-cream!

DEXTER: Ice-berg! Oh God! Ice-berg!

*THE LIGHTS CHANGE AS THE SHADOW OF THE ICEBERG PASSES BY. A TERRIBLE GRATING SOUND.*

DEXTER: Christ! That was a near thing. What's going on? (*He yells up at the Bridge*) I'm going to complain to the Captain.
MR. TREADAWAY: We can't find the Captain.

*THE SHIP'S HORN BLOWS AGAIN.*

DONNA-MARIE: I see fishes. (*To Rob*) Look! Fishes.

*ULYSSES ENTERS. GUESTS COME BACK ON, AS THE HORN CONTINUES TO BLOW. CARYS ENTERS.*

DEXTER: Carys darling—
CARYS: Have you seen my Dad?
DEXTER: Never mind your Dad. Let's get to the life-boats.

*GUESTS HEAR THE WORD "LIFE-BOATS." CONSTERNATION. EVERYONE STARTS YELLING "LIFE-BOATS! LIFE-BOATS!"*

ULYSSES: It's all right. It's all right. No need for panic. Ladies and gentlemen; please return to the celebrations.
DONNA-MARIE: Fishes! Fishes!
ULYSSES: (*Through gritted teeth*) Never mind the fishes, little girl. Frogs get eaten by fishes.

*NOW EVERYBODY HAS GATHERED ON STAGE EXCEPT PHOEBE, VINCE, LINDBERG AND THE INVISIBLE MAN. PEOPLE ARE MILLING AROUND WHILE ULYSSES TRIES TO GET THEM BACK INTO THE BALLROOM FOR THE PARTY. HE HASN'T A HOPE IN HELL. THERE IS AN AIR OF PANIC GROWING BY THE MINUTE. PEOPLE ARE START-ING TO SHOUT; PRAY; CURSE.*

ULYSSES: Please!! There's nothing to worry about. Go back to the ballroom. (*To Rob*) And you, sir, all of you—

*ENTER THE INVISIBLE MAN WITH PHOEBE.*

PHOEBE: Either do it or don't do it. But make up your mind.

*THE INVISIBLE MAN GETS HALFWAY ACROSS THE STAGE WHEN LINDBERG ENTERS WITH VINCE. HE POINTS THE GUN AT THE INVISIBLE MAN.*

LINDBERG: Stop!

*THE OCCUPANTS OF THE STAGE ALL FREEZE.*

VINCE: Shoot the bugger!
PHOEBE: Don't you dare! Lindberg? You hear me? *(To the Invisible Man)* For God's sake, run! He's blind with jealousy.

*THE INVISIBLE MAN STARTS TO EXIT.*

*EVERYBODY DUCKS AS LINDBERG FIRES. ABSOLUTE SILENCE. THE INVISIBLE MAN STAGGERS; DROPS PHOEBE'S HAND, STAGGERS SOME MORE, AND FALLS DOWN. THE CROWD STARTS TO GET UP AGAIN; A CHAOS OF COMMENTS.*

VINCE: You got him!
LINDBERG: Damn thug!
CARYS: Mother!
PHOEBE: You shot him, Lindberg!
MR. TREADAWAY: What's going on? What's going on?
FRANK: You shot him. He was defenseless, and you shot him.
LINDBERG: He had hold of my wife.
FRANK: You don't even know who it is.

*TREADAWAY HAS COME DOWN FROM THE BRIDGE, LEAVING SEAN UP THERE WITH THE BINOCULARS.*

MR. TREADAWAY: Clear out of the way. Are you all animals?
ULYSSES: *(Officious)* Clear the way for the officer!
MELBA: He shot that man!
MR. TREADAWAY: This is murder—

LINDBERG: I was provoked.

SEAN: *(Looking up)* Oh God . . . Sir! Look!

MR. TREADAWAY: *(To Sean)* Shut up! *(To the crowd)* Who is he?

SEAN: Sir! It's another iceberg! Twice as big!

LINDBERG: I was protecting my wife.

MR. TREADAWAY: You! *(To Dexter)* Take off his mask.

*THE MASK COMES OFF. A SHOCKED RESPONSE FROM THE CROWD AS MR. FOSS' FACE IS REVEALED.*

MR. TREADAWAY: Oh no. You shot the Captain! Oh no, no, no, no, no . . .

PHOEBE: Well, who's steering the ship?

MR. TREADAWAY: I am not by nature an hysterical man. *(Hysterically)* YOU SHOT THE CAPTAIN!!

LINDBERG: Are you sure?

MR. TREADAWAY: I'd know that nose anywhere.

SEAN: Iceberg dead ahead! Just . . . telling anybody who's . . . interested.

*NOBODY IS.*

MR. TREADAWAY: He was in charge! What do I do now?

FRANK: *(Brightly)* Photo, everyone.

*OH, SAYS EVERYONE, ENCHANTED BY THE IDEA OF A PHOTOGRAPH. THEY GATHER AROUND THE DEAD MAN. LINDBERG PUTS HIS FOOT ON THE CAPTAIN'S CHEST: THE TRIUMPHANT HUNTER. THE REST GATHER AROUND ADMIRINGLY.*

ROSE: Smile, everyone.

SEAN: Twenty yards!

FRANK: We're all going to die.

SEAN: Ten yards!

ROSE: Closer in, everyone.

SEAN: Five! Four! Three! Two!—

ROSE: Freeze!

*THEY FREEZE.*

*CRASH!*

*THE STAGE IS SUDDENLY PANDEMONIUM AS THE BEAR OF AMSTERDAM PLOWS, BOW FIRST, INTO AN ICEBERG. THE SOUND EFFECTS TELL ALL: THE CRUNCH OF IMPACT, THE SCREECH OF TORTURED METAL AS THE 'BERG TEARS A GASH IN THE SIDE OF THE VESSEL; THE RUSH OF WATER INTO THE HOLD; THE THUNDER OF ICE ON THE DECK.*

*SCREAMS. THE LIGHTS FLICKER OUT; EMERGENCY LIGHTS, BRIGHT YELLOW(?) FLICKER ON. THE PASSENGERS FALL OVER AS THE SHIP LURCHES.*

*TREADAWAY CLIMBS BACK UP TO THE BRIDGE, YELLING. "HE SHOT THE CAPTAIN! HE SHOT THE CAPTAIN!"*

*OTHER VOICES—THE DREAM TECHNICIANS—CALL IN THE DARKNESS, OVERLAPPING, LOST, HEARD AGAIN, WASHED AWAY IN SCREAMS AND THUNDER.*

FIRST VOICE: We're sinking!

MR. TREADAWAY: Damage report?

SECOND VOICE: Front compartment's gone. The bulk-heads won't hold.

FIRST VOICE: She's going down by the bow.

MR. TREADAWAY: How long?

FIRST VOICE: Help! Help!

MR. TREADAWAY: How long, Mr. Melville?

SECOND VOICE: Minutes! Minutes!

MR. TREADAWAY: *(Through megaphone)* Ladies and gentlemen, I've some bad news and some very bad news. The Captain is dead. In addition, the ship has hit an iceberg and will sink in approximately three and a half minutes. Give or take three minutes. Please do not panic. Instead, proceed in an orderly fashion to the life-boats on the upper decks, as you were instructed in the Boat Drill.

MELBA: What Boat Drill? I don't remember a Boat Drill!

CARYS: This is like some bad dream.

ROB: *(Looks at her)* That's the first intelligent thing you've said in the last . . . how long have I known you?

DONNA-MARIE: Fishes! Fishes!

LINDBERG: Oh shut up!

MR. TREADAWAY: *(Through megaphone)* Do not, repeat, do not attempt to return to your cabins for belongings. The lower decks are already flooding, and you will most assuredly drown.

*THE TECHNICIANS HAVE APPEARED AND ARE HELPING TO CHOREOGRAPH THE CONFUSION.*

MR. TREADAWAY: Simply make your way, in an orderly fashion, to your allotted life-boat. *DO NOT PANIC.* There is no need to panic. Women and children first! Women and children first!

*TREADAWAY CONTINUES TO GIVE AD-LIBBED ORDERS THROUGHOUT THE FOLLOWING EXCHANGES.*

VINCE: Why women and children first? That's not fair.

ULYSSES: You'll have to take your turn with the rest of the men. Women and children always go first.

VINCE: I paid my money. I've got as much right to a life-boat as any of them.

ULYSSES: I'm sorry. Don't make me hit you very hard across the face.

VINCE: Bugger!

*VINCE EXITS.*

LINDBERG: Are you all right, sweetheart? Do you know which life-boat you're going to?

PHOEBE: You damn fool! This is all your fault!

*SHE GOES TO EXIT.*

LINDBERG: Where are you going?

PHOEBE: To get my fur coat.

LINDBERG: He said we shouldn't go below.

PHOEBE: I want my coat!

LINDBERG: Phoebe. We can buy another coat. Come back here.

(*He catches hold of her*)
PHOEBE: Oh Lindberg. I don't want to die—

*THEY EMBRACE.*

ULYSSES: (*To Technicians*) Get this useless body out of the way.

*TECHNICIANS REMOVE THE BODY OF MR. FOSS.*

CARYS: Where's Dexter?
ROB: I haven't seen him.
CARYS: He was here! He was going to marry me when we got to
Mozambique. Dexter!

*SHE GOES OFF LOOKING FOR HIM.*

ROB: (*Calling after her*) Don't waste your time!
ULYSSES: You. Lend a hand with the boat.
ROSE: Rob . . .
ROB: Go and find your boat, Rose.
ROSE: But I want to stay with you. If I drown, I drown.
FIRST TECHNICIAN: Stand back, please. Everyone stand back.

*THE TECHNICIANS BRING ON A LIFE-BOAT, AIDED BY
ROB. THERE IS A GREAT RUSH FOR THE BOAT. THE TECH-
NICIANS FIGHT THE GUESTS BACK. TRUNCHEONS ARE
WIELDED. HYSTERIA IS HIGH.*

FIRST TECHNICIAN: Not yet! Not yet!
MR. TREADAWAY: Do not rush the life-boat! (*Through megaphone*)
Repeat: do *not* rush the bloody life-boat! Wait your turn!
Wait your turn! Mr. Skinner—
LINDBERG: Yes.
MR. TREADAWAY: Use your gun.
LINDBERG: (*Delighted*) Yes?
MR. TREADAWAY: Yes!

*LINDBERG POINTS HIS GUN AT THE PANICKING PASSENGERS.*

LINDBERG: Stay back! You morons!

MR. TREADAWAY: Thank you, Mr. Skinner.

FRANK: Everybody pray to the Lord! He alone will protect us! On your knees, sinners!

*SOME OF THE GUESTS FALL TO THEIR KNEES.*

FRANK: Our Father, we are unworthy sinners who don't deserve to lick the mud off your tap-shoes—

LINDBERG: Did he say tap-shoes?

MR. TREADAWAY: Try the Lord's prayer, Mr. Juffs. Or else shut up!

*FRANK CONTINUES TO LEAD THE LORD'S PRAYER, WHILE IN THE BACKGROUND, A STRING QUARTET PLAYS ON. DISTANT SHOTS.*

*SCREAMS. THE CONTINUING SOUND OF CHURNING ENGINES, OF STEAM ERUPTING IN THE ENGINE ROOM, OF WATER CLAIMING THE LOWER DECKS; THE TERRIBLE CREAKING OF THE SHIP'S PLATES AS THEY ARE WRENCHED APART. DEXTER ENTERS. HE HAS LOST HIS JACKET, HIS "SHIRT" IS SMEARED, HIS HEAD IS BLOODY.*

CARYS: Dexter! I thought you were dead.

DEXTER: I got lost in the dark.

ULYSSES: I'm sorry, sir, you'll have to stand back, this boat is for women and children only.

CARYS: Oh Dexter—

ULYSSES: *(Hitting him)* I said: stand back!

*ULYSSES PARTS THE LOVERS BEFORE THEY CAN KISS.*

ULYSSES: You'll see each other again. In some dimension or other.

*PEOPLE ARE SAYING GOODBYE EVERYWHERE. TEARS; EXCHANGES OF KEEP-SAKES. DONNA-MARIE AND PHOEBE GET INTO THE LIFE-BOAT; SO DOES CARYS.*

MELBA: Come on, Frank.

FRANK: You go! The Lord will protect me!
MELBA: You're a damn fool, Frank. You're wearing a skirt! Get in!
FRANK: I'd rather drown than deny my masculinity.
MELBA: It's not much to deny, Frank. Get in!
FRANK: No!

*MELBA GETS INTO BOAT.*

ROB: Go on, Rose.
ROSE: I'm frightened.
ROB: We're all frightened.

*ROSE KISSES ROB, AND GETS INTO THE LIFE-BOAT.
ULYSSES BRINGS ANOTHER WOMAN FORWARD, IN A
HEAVY FUR COAT, DARK GLASSES, AND A HAT WITH A
VEIL. IT IS VINCE, HEAVILY DISGUISED.*

ULYSSES: Gangway! Gangway!
VINCE: *(High-pitched voice)* Thank you, my man.

*VINCE GETS INTO THE BOAT. THERE IS A TERRIBLE
CRASH. DISTANT SCREAMS.*

MR. TREADAWAY: *(Through megaphone)* Ladies and gentlemen,
    the ship is going down. Repeat: the ship is going down. Boy,
    find yourself a life-boat.
SEAN: Yes, sir.

*SEAN EXITS, TREADAWAY COMES DOWN FROM THE
BRIDGE. THE SOUND OF RUSHING WATER IS MOUNTING.*

ULYSSES: Any more for any more?
LINDBERG: Look. Here's a donation for the Old Sailor's Home.
    *(Thrusts money at Ulysses)* Let me go in the boat. My wife's in
    there.
ULYSSES: I'm sorry, I never accept small bribes.
LINDBERG: It's all I've got.
ULYSSES: No exceptions.

*LINDBERG HITS ULYSSES, WHO FALLS BACK.*

LINDBERG: *(To Dexter)* Come on, boy, what are you waiting for?

*MORE CRASHES. LINDBERG GRABS DEXTER AND TOGETHER THEY GET INTO THE LIFE-BOAT.*

MELBA: Frank! Frank!

*FRANK JUFFS IS THE ONLY ONE PRAYING NOW; THE REST HAVE GIVEN UP.*

MELBA: Frank!
DEXTER: It's too late, Mother. He wants to die.
MR. TREADAWAY: *(To Rob)* Come on! The ship's going!
ROB: I don't want to get in there.
MR. TREADAWAY: Ever drowned, sir? I don't recommend it. I've drowned three times. It's horrible, let me tell you. Horrible!
ROB: Shit!

*TREADAWAY DRAGS ROB AND THEY CLING TO THE BOAT AS THE ROAR INCREASES.*

*UTTER, TERRIFYING CONFUSION, WHICH IS REACHING A HIGHER AND HIGHER PITCH. THE LIFE-BOAT, NOW CRAMMED WITH SURVIVORS, IS ROCKED BY THE TECHNICIANS AS THE DARKNESS CLOSES IN. WE CAN HEAR THE STRING QUARTET PLAYING "ABIDE WITH ME"; SEVERAL PEOPLE ON THE SHIP SINGING "SOMEWHERE OVER THE RAINBOW." SOMEBODY ELSE IS MAKING CONFESSION, ANOTHER PERSON YELLS: "THE VORTEX! THE VORTEX!"*

*TREADAWAY, HANGING ONTO THE BOAT, IS TRYING TO ORGANIZE OARSMEN.*

*THE CACOPHONY RISES, DEAFENING, BUT THE NOISE OF THE WATER, THE TERRIFYING ROAR OF THE DEEPS CLAIMING THE SHIP, IS INCREASINGLY DOMINANT. THE SCENE IS JUST LIT BY LIGHTNING NOW. THEN EVEN THAT STOPS.*

*JUST THE ROAR NOW, AND THE DARK. THE ROAR DIES DOWN. IN THE DARKNESS WE CAN HEAR, VERY SOFTLY, GENTLE SOBBING, THE MURMURS OF PRAYERS, AND THE SOFT SLOPPING OF WATER AGAINST THE SIDE OF THE LIFE-BOAT.*

*IN SUMMARY, THE SURVIVORS ARE: MR. TREADAWAY, DEXTER AND MELBA JUFFS, THE SKINNERS (INCLUDING CARYS AND DONNA-MARIE), VINCE (IN DRAG STILL), ROB AND ROSE. LOST ARE: ULYSSES, MR. FOSS, FRANK JUFFS AND SEAN, PLUS SEVERAL UNNAMED PASSEN-GERS. WE CAN SEE NOBODY AT THE MOMENT; ALL IS IN DARKNESS.*

ROB: Send up a distress rocket, Treadaway.
MR. TREADAWAY: Wait a moment; stand clear.

*THERE IS A NOISE OF SPUTTERING FIRE, AND THEN THE SOUND OF A ROCKET TAKING OFF AND THE "WHOOP" OF IT RUSHING OVERHEAD. A PALE LILAC-PINK BLOOMS OVER THE BOAT, AND BY ITS FITFUL LIGHT WE SEE THE SURVIVORS PROPERLY. IN THE BLACKOUT THE ACTORS HAVE PARTIALLY UNDRESSED; THEY LOOK DIRTIED, RUINED. SOME HUDDLE IN BLANKETS. SOME HOLD ITEMS OF SENTIMENTAL VALUE; SHOES, A DOLL, WHAT-EVER. THESE OBJECTS, THE APPEARANCE OF THE SUR-VIVORS, AND THE IMPOSSIBLE WAY THEY ARE CRAMMED INTO THE TINY, PITCHING BOAT, EVOKES THE FINE LINE BETWEEN FARCE AND TRAGEDY WHICH ALL GOOD NIGHTMARES WALK. UNDER COVER OF THE ROCKET-LIGHT, A BLUE, SHIFTING LIGHT COMES UP TO ILLUMI-NATE THE BOAT. WHEN THE ROCKET DIES, THE BLUE REMAINS.*

*ROB AND MELBA HAVE THE OARS.*

MR. TREADAWAY: (*Calling over the water*) Hello! Hello! There must be other boats. Somebody else must have survived. There can't just be us. There can't!
LINDBERG: The whirlpool must have pulled them all down.

MR. TREADAWAY: *(Still calling over the water)* Is there anybody out there?

MELBA: Try another rocket . . .

MR. TREADAWAY: That was the only one that was dry.

PHOEBE: What if a plane comes over? How will we attract attention?

CARYS: I can hear voices. Hush, everyone. I can hear voices!

*THE BOAT HUSHES. VERY DISTANTLY, A VOICE.*

FRANK: *(Off)* Yea, though I walk through the vale of the shadow of death—

MELBA: Frank! It's Frank!

FRANK: *(Off)* I shall fear no evil.

MELBA: Oh Frank. Over here!

VINCE: There's no more room.

MELBA: But that's my husband! Swim, Frank. Follow my voice!

VINCE: There's no room, dammit!

*VINCE STANDS UP.*

MR. TREADAWAY: That woman is a man!

VINCE: What if I am?

LINDBERG: Vince!

*ALL THROUGH THE FOLLOWING EXCHANGE MELBA IS COAXING FRANK TOWARDS THE BOAT.*

VINCE: All right, it's me. Big deal!

ROSE: He's here under false pretenses.

LINDBERG: Of all the tricks.

VINCE: You bought your way on board. Or you tried to! The rest of us have to use the wits God gave us.

FRANK: *(Clambering aboard)* Hallelujah! The Lord has saved the righteous from the flood.

VINCE: Oh shut up.

*THE BOAT LURCHES AS FRANK CLAMBERS IN.*

MR. TREADAWAY: We have to distribute the weight more evenly; move slowly, or we'll roll over.

FRANK: I don't want to worry anybody, but I kept feeling things moving around my legs in the water.

MR. TREADAWAY: You! Skinner. Move down the boat. Slowly; slowly does it.

ROSE: Sharks? Was it sharks?

DEXTER: Not in the Arctic Sea.

VINCE: Polar bears. Oh fuck.

FRANK: God made them all, let's remember that.

PHOEBE: I'm not thanking God for sharks, it's in bad taste.

ROB: What happened to the steward? Anyone see him?

CARYS: He was on the Bridge.

MR. TREADAWAY: I sent him for a life-jacket. I didn't see him after that.

LINDBERG: I intend to sue.

DEXTER: Oh shut up. If it weren't for you we'd still have a Captain.

LINDBERG: I was protecting my wife. That queer was willing to watch her raped. I wasn't.

*THEY'RE ALL LOOKING AT HIM.*

CARYS: So now it's Rob's fault.

LINDBERG: Eying up the children. I saw him! He's the one! Not me! He's the one!

FRANK: This was a judgment. No doubt.

MR. TREADAWAY: Sit down! Will you *please all sit down*!

LINDBERG: What are you staring at, fairy?

ROB: Why don't you just sit down like he says?

LINDBERG: I'll sue. I will.

PHOEBE: Ssh! Ssh!

FRANK: It's a judgment. For our jealousy, our avarice—

DEXTER: Balls!

FRANK: When the children turn on their parents, it's the short road to Sodom.

ROSE: We'll probably all end up going mad. Drinking sea water and going mad. Eating each other.

VINCE: *(To Rose)* You can eat me anytime.

PHOEBE: She'd have to be very desperate, Vincent.

FRANK: I think we should all commend ourselves into the hands of the Lord.

DEXTER: I hope He's washed them.

FRANK: You Godless soul—
MELBA: Frank!
FRANK: How were you ever the fruit of my loins?
VINCE: *(Points at Rob)* No; he's the fruit.
DEXTER: You can talk. Dressed like that.
PHOEBE: Wait a minute; I recognize that coat—
LINDBERG: Not now, Phoebe.
PHOEBE: That's *my* coat! That's my favorite fur coat. Give it here!
FRANK: Oh Lord, whose only son walked on the sea, and calmed
    the raging storms, hear us now in the hour of our need—
DONNA-MARIE: *(Points into the water)* Fishes! Look! Fishes!
PHOEBE: You stole my coat!
VINCE: What if I did?
DONNA-MARIE: Oo. Big fishes.
LINDBERG: Never mind the coat.
PHOEBE: I'm cold, and *I want my coat.*
VINCE: I've got nothing on underneath.
FRANK: —keep us, oh Lord, in your love and mercy—
PHOEBE: I don't care! Lindberg!
LINDBERG: Shut up!
DONNA-MARIE: Little black eyes. Big smiles. They're coming up
    to see us, aren't they?
ROB: Maybe they're coming to have their photograph taken.
MELBA: Sharks?
ROB: I wouldn't be at all surprised.
CARYS: God.

*PHOEBE HAS GOTTEN UP AND IS FIGHTING HER WAY
ALONG THE BOAT TO VINCE. THE BOAT ROCKS AT HER
PASSAGE.*

MR. TREADAWAY: Sit down!
PHOEBE: I want my coat.
LINDBERG: Phoebe!
PHOEBE: Give it to me!

*SHE WRESTLES WITH VINCE, AND PULLS OFF THE COAT;
HE IS INDEED NAKED UNDERNEATH. HE STANDS IN THE
BOAT, COVERING HIMSELF. SHE STEPS BACK WITH THE
COAT, TRIUMPHANT.*

PHOEBE: Got it!
DONNA-MARIE: *(Sing-song)* Fishies! Fishies!
PHOEBE: *(Losing her balance)* Oh!

*SHE FALLS OUT OF THE BOAT. ROSE SCREAMS.*

LINDBERG: Phoebe!
CARYS: Mother!
DONNA-MARIE: Big fishies!
CARYS: Oh Dexter! Help her!
DEXTER: *(Leaning over the side of the boat, arm outstretched)* Let go
    of the coat, Mother.
PHOEBE: I will not!

*ROSE IS STILL SCREAMING.*

DEXTER: It's too heavy. Let go of it, you stupid bitch.
LINDBERG: Don't talk to my wife like that. Let go of it, you daft
    cow!

*TREADAWAY SLAPS ROSE. SHE STOPS SCREAMING AND
SLAPS HIM BACK.*

PHOEBE: I won't! I won't!
LINDBERG: I'll buy you another fucking coat.
MELBA: Sharks! Sharks!
FRANK: For what they are about to receive, may the Lord make
    them truly thankful.
ROSE: I can't live if you die, Phoebe.

*SHE HAS STOOD UP; IS TOTTERING ON THE SIDE OF THE
BOAT.*

DEXTER: No, Rose!
ROSE: I'm coming to join you.

*ROSE DIVES IN THE SEA.*

DONNA-MARIE: Happy fishies! All smiling.
MR. TREADAWAY: They're not smiling. They're biting.

MELBA: There can't be sharks in the Arctic Ocean. They must be penguins.

ROSE: I can't swim. Oh God, I can't swim!

MELBA: *(To herself)* Oh yes. That's it. They're penguins for certain.

DEXTER: Let go of the coat!

MELBA: Penguins can't mean any harm.

PHOEBE: *(Voice fading)* Never! Ever . . .

*SILENCE.*

LINDBERG: Oh God. She's gone.

DONNA-MARIE: *(Merrily)* Bye! Bye!

ROSE: Phoebe . . . Phoebe . . .

DEXTER: Rose.

ROB: She's gone.

LINDBERG: Didn't they look beautiful? The bodies.

DONNA-MARIE: Yes.

LINDBERG: Floating away.

CARYS: Oh Mamma.

LINDBERG: Phoebe was always careful about her appearance.

DONNA-MARIE: *(To Lindberg)* Did you see the fishes?

MELBA: Penguins.

LINDBERG: Come on, darling.

*LINDBERG GETS HOLD OF DONNA-MARIE, WRAPPING HER IN HIS ARMS.*

LINDBERG: We're going swimming.

DONNA-MARIE: Swimming with the fishes. Swimming with the fishes!

*LINDBERG PULLS DONNA-MARIE TO THE SIDE OF THE BOAT.*

DEXTER: *(He tries to stop Lindberg. Carys holds him back)* Oh Jesus . . .

LINDBERG: *(A crazed fatalism has seized him)* It's all right. Life doesn't mean much without her. If that's love . . . then I loved her.

CARYS: Let him go.

LINDBERG: *(To Treadaway)* I shall still sue, of course. From the grave.
CARYS: He's gone mad. Dexter. Listen to me. Let. Him. Go.

*DEXTER LETS LINDBERG GO.*

FRANK: It's the Lord's will.

*LINDBERG AND DONNA-MARIE DISAPPEAR OVERBOARD.*

FRANK: Amen.
DEXTER: *(To Frank)* You bloody stupid man.

*HE GRABS HOLD OF FRANK.*

MELBA: Dexter. You're speaking to your father.
DEXTER: He doesn't feel anything, except a sense of moral superiority.
FRANK: And what do you feel? Is your soul deep and wide? No. It's a mean, narrow, passionless thing, like mine. That's my revenge.
MELBA: There's no need for this, Frank . . .
DEXTER: You're right. You couldn't even put your arms around me—
FRANK: Flesh? Is that all you can think about? You're as corrupt as your mother.
MELBA: Don't bring me into this.
VINCE: Why don't you hit him?
MR. TREADAWAY: Shut up! Sit down and shut up!
CARYS: Dex, let him alone.
FRANK: Corrupt from the womb.
DEXTER: Give it a rest.
FRANK: Rotten, like her stock.
MELBA: *(Outraged)* My family? Rotten?
VINCE: *(To Melba)* Go on; hit him.
FRANK: Syphilitic!

*MELBA HITS FRANK.*

FRANK: Cankerous. To the marrow! To the soul!

*FRANK HITS HER BACK.*

DEXTER: Stop that!

FRANK: *(Turning to Dexter, incensed with hatred)* You may well have been born blind, deaf and dumb. That would have been a judgment. Oh yes! *(Frank crosses the boat to Dexter)* And what would you have lost? Only seeing this dirty flesh, this dirty world. Better you were never born!

DEXTER: Oh fuck off.

*DEXTER PUSHES HIM OVERBOARD.*

MELBA: Dexter! That was your father.

DEXTER: So it was.

MELBA: Tell him you're sorry.

DEXTER: *(Calling)* Sorry, Dad.

FRANK: Oh God! They're eating me.

DEXTER: Who are?

FRANK: The fishes! The bloody fishes!

DEXTER: It's a judgment, Dad.

FRANK: They're between my legs! Ah! Oh! That's my balls you've got there!

*HE SINKS.*

MELBA: Now look what you've done. Your father's been unmanned by penguins.

*FRANK REAPPEARS SUDDENLY AND GRABS MELBA.*

FRANK: Not quite!

MELBA: Oh!

FRANK: Jesus wants you for a sunbeam, light of my life!

MELBA: Oh Christ!

*FRANK PULLS HER OVERBOARD. DEXTER GOES TO THE SIDE OF THE BOAT.*

DEXTER: Gone.

CARYS: This can't be happening. It can't.

DEXTER: Well, I'm glad.

CARYS: Don't say that.

DEXTER: I am. They got on my tits.

VINCE: Good on you. That's it, feed them to the fishes. There's more room for the rest of us then.

ROB: You really are a rat, Vince.

VINCE: All this women and children first crap. Makes me sick. It's survival of the fittest. Always has been, always will be.

DEXTER: So it's you next, is it?

VINCE: What?

*DEXTER STANDS UP.*

DEXTER: I meant you're not fit for anything, 'cept fish food—

VINCE: You wouldn't hit a man with no clothes on?

DEXTER: Try me.

*THEY START TO FIGHT, VIOLENTLY. THE BOAT ROCKS.*

CARYS: Dexter! Behave yourself!

ROB: Let them have their fun. Boys'll be boys.

CARYS: How can you be so calm about this?

ROB: (*Gazing out*) Because it's not . . . quite . . . real.

CARYS: Not real? We just saw them drown; I can still see the blood in the water. There's Mr. Juff's leg . . . floating by. Rose knew. We'll all go mad.

ROB: It's all right, Carys.

CARYS: Don't tell me it's all right! All my life people have been patting me on the head and telling me, "It's all right, Carys!" Well, it isn't. Look at those two: my father's best friend and my husband to be, fighting like mad dogs; us lost at sea, surrounded by sharks, and not even a star in the sky to steer by— (*At this observation, Rob looks up. Indeed there are no stars.*) —and you say it's all right? It isn't! It's never been all right! The lullabies are wrong!

VINCE: Will you please keep your sobs down?

ROB: You're upsetting her. Stop fighting.

DEXTER: Now, you sit down and stay out of this, Robert. Fighting's work for hard men. Not your style at all.

ROB: I hope you remember this. God, I hope we *all* remember this . . . (*He goes to the side of the boat, and peers over*) . . . when it's over.

VINCE: Where were we?

DEXTER: I had you by the nuts.

VINCE: That's right; and I had your hair. Like that.

DEXTER: Okay?

VINCE: Fine!

*THEY START TO FIGHT AGAIN.*

ROB: Which direction are we drifting in?

MR. TREADAWAY: (*Consults his compass*) South south-west.

ROB: Any idea where we are?

MR. TREADAWAY: No.

ROB: So we just sail on until morning.

MR. TREADAWAY: Maybe for weeks.

ROB: (*With calm certainty*) No. Just until morning.

CARYS: I don't follow.

ROB: You were right; they forgot the stars. Silly little oversight. I suppose they thought we'd be too occupied with ourselves to look up. And the sharks. They don't belong in this scenario.

MR. TREADAWAY: Spice things up a bit though, don't they?

CARYS: What?

MR. TREADAWAY: I'm humoring him. The poor man's lost his wits.

CARYS: (*Sorrowful*) Oh Rob. I thought you'd be the last to crack.

ROB: (*To Treadaway*) Why play on?

MR. TREADAWAY: This isn't a game, Mr. Kidd.

ROB: You can admit it. The illusion's almost perfect . . . but not perfect enough.

MR. TREADAWAY: You're too cynical, Mr. Kidd.

ROB: A minute ago I was insane.

CARYS: If you're mad, I can tell you. I never really liked you. I told Dexter you were a conniver. But you're not. I see that now. I'm sorry we didn't get on when you were sane.

ROB: Don't worry.

*DEXTER HAS WON THE FIGHT. HE DRAGS A BLOODIED VINCE TO HIS FEET.*

VINCE: I swallowed one of my teeth.
DEXTER: I won, didn't I?
VINCE: You did.
DEXTER: So I've a perfect right to drown you.
VINCE: Absolutely. Fair's fair.

*DEXTER PUSHES VINCE OVERBOARD.*

CARYS: What did you do that for?
DEXTER: He said I won.
VINCE: *(Calling up out of the water)* I was lying!
DEXTER: What?
VINCE: You couldn't fight your way out of a paper bag—
DEXTER: Come here and say that.
VINCE: You come down here. The water's lovely—
CARYS: No, Dex!
VINCE: And the sharks nibble your toes!
DEXTER: I'm coming!
CARYS: Dexter. Don't you dare!
DEXTER: Oh . . . I dare . . .

*DEXTER JUMPS OVER.*

DEXTER: Chilly!
VINCE: Come here, you little bastard!
CARYS: They're pulling each other down.

*DISTANT CRIES OF DEXTER AND VINCE.*

CARYS: Oh God . . . Rob.

*ROB COMFORTS HER.*

ROB: This has gone far enough, Mr. Treadaway.
MR. TREADAWAY: There's a storm coming up.
CARYS: We're going to die.
ROB: Sooner or later. But not here. Not in this fabrication.
CARYS: We are! The boat'll be swamped!

*THE WIND HAS GOT UP. THUNDER ROARS.*

ROB: Nothing can kill us.

CARYS: Sharks! Sea!

ROB: We'll live forever; in dreams.

CARYS: I don't think I believe you.

MR. TREADAWAY: He's out of his tiny mind.

ROB: No. That's precisely where I am. I'm in my mind.

*HE STANDS UP.*

ROB: I could step out of this boat now. Couldn't I?

MR. TREADAWAY: I wouldn't advise it.

ROB: There's solid ground under here, somewhere. Just over the edge of my bed. I wouldn't sink. Not if I didn't believe it.

MR. TREADAWAY: It's suicide.

ROB: Who's your master, Treadaway?

CARYS: Foss. He's Foss' man.

ROB: Of course, our dead Captain. I'm going to have a few words with him.

MR. TREADAWAY: Don't—

CARYS: If you're wrong—

ROB: I drown. But I'm not.

*ROB STEPS OFF THE BOAT, ONTO SOLID GROUND. CARYS STARES DOWN INTO THE "WATER" THAT SHE STILL SEES.*

CARYS: Oh Rob! He's going down!

MR. TREADAWAY: There; didn't I tell you?

*SHE REACHES OUT.*

CARYS: He's sinking.

ROB: No I'm not.

CARYS: Look at his face; here come the fish!

*SHE LOOKS AWAY.*

CARYS: I can't bear it. He was the last of them.

MR. TREADAWAY: Forget he ever lived. Sit back. We'll ride out the storm. I'll tell you a rhyme. Yes?

*THE LIGHTS START TO GO DOWN ON THE LIFE-BOAT.*

CARYS: Yes.
MR. TREADAWAY: The owl and the pussycat went to sea
    In a beautiful pea-green boat, They took some honey,
      and plenty of money,
    Wrapped up in a five-pound note;
    The owl looked up to the stars above,
    And sang to a small guitar . . .

*TREADAWAY'S VOICE IS FADING. THE LIFE-BOAT HAS DISAPPEARED. A LIGHT HAS COME UP ON SEAN, STANDING IN THE HALLWAY, SMOKING.*

SEAN: . . . O Lovely Pussy! O Pussy, my love,
    What a beautiful Pussy you are,
    You are,
    You are!
    What a beautiful Pussy you are!
ROB: You woke too.
SEAN: I recognized the dream. I sold it to him.
ROB: But you went along with it.
SEAN: I like playing games.
ROB: There's a limit.
SEAN: I'm sorry. I've been stupid. Wasting time.

*ROB APPROACHES SEAN, AND KISSES HIM.*

*MR. FOSS APPEARS. HE WEARS A WHITE SHIRT, BLOODIED BY THE SHOT THAT KILLED HIM. THE LIFE-BOAT HAS BEEN VACATED.*

MR. FOSS: They all drowned, of course.
ROB: Of course.
MR. FOSS: A storm came; it overturned the life-boat. Mr. Treadaway was eaten by a spermacious whale, like Jonah. Carys was carried along the Gulf Stream, and sank somewhere off the coast of Nova Scotia. Nobody's ever defied me before, Mr. Kidd.
ROB: You were being cruel.

MR. FOSS: Why? They're having a fine time now, wandering the bottom of the sea, where the sun never goes. Only drowned cities down there, and maybe their forgotten selves; sunk without a trace.

ROB: Oh, I see. It was me who asked for this. Is that what you're saying?

MR. FOSS: You wanted to turn them inside out. And so they are.

*THE TECHNICIANS HAVE COME ON. THEY START TO REMOVE THE PROPS OF THE DREAM; THE BEAR OF AMSTERDAM IS DISMANTLED, REVEALING THE HOTEL UNDERNEATH. THE LIFE-BOAT IS REMOVED.*

MR. FOSS: *(To Technicians)* Thank you all. You did a miraculous job. *(He gives them money)* Didn't they, though? The sinking was pobbelus. The great wastes of ocean; meticulously evoked.

SEAN: There aren't any sharks in the Arctic.

MR. FOSS: Maybe they lost their way. We all do, once in a while. The general effect was overwhelming. *(Re: Rob)* Even *he* believed it, didn't you? At least for a little time.

ROB: It was beautifully done. I'll say that.

MR. FOSS: It was my swanish song, gentlemen. After tonight I am a legendary poet and nothing more.

*TREADAWAY HAS APPEARED, DRESSED AS HE WAS AT HIS FIRST ENTRANCE.*

MR. FOSS: There's no stopping me, Treadaway, so don't even try. After tomorrow, I shall be a different man.

MR. TREADAWAY: How's that?

MR. FOSS: I have an offer of marriage.

SEAN: Ulysses thought you were a pederast.

MR. FOSS: Only by inclination.

MR. TREADAWAY: Mrs. Mocatta will have to be informed.

MR. FOSS: So. Inform her. Tell her my replacement is here for the hiring. *(Treadaway looks puzzled)* I speak of Mr. Kidd. He beat us at our own game, Treadaway, tell her that.

*BIRDS HAVE STARTED TO SING.*

ROB: That must be the dawn chorus.

SEAN: We'd better get to bed.

MR. FOSS: *(To Rob)* You won't get a better offer than that tonight, Mr. Kidd. I've seen his bed; I spied on him in a moment of blind lust. It's cramped, but you'll find a way to fit the two of you in there somehow or other.

*THE BIRDS ARE GETTING LOUDER.*

MR. FOSS: Go on. No good lover prevaricates.

*HE EXITS.*

SEAN: Don't you want to?

ROB: I'm coming.

SEAN: So's Christmas.

ROB: Who's he marrying, for God's sake?

SEAN: We'll find out tomorrow.

*THEY EXIT TOGETHER.*

MR. TREADAWAY: Tomorrow. What a day it was.

*THE SOUND OF BIRDS RISE.*

*END OF ACT THREE.*

# Act 4

# Act 4:

*ACT FOUR IS A CONTINUATION FROM THE END OF ACT THREE. THE MORNING LIGHT CONTINUES TO INTENSIFY AS THE TECHNICIANS EXIT, ILLUMINATING A SOLITARY LIFE PRESERVER THAT HAS BEEN LEFT, FORLORN, IN THE MIDDLE OF THE STAGE.*

*ONE OF THE TECHNICIANS COMES IN, AND STARES AT IT FOR A MOMENT.*

TECHNICIAN: Untidy.

*THE TECHNICIAN PICKS UP THE LIFE PRESERVER AND EXITS WITH IT AS ROSE COMES DOWNSTAIRS, DRESSED TO LEAVE. SHE CARRIES HER SUITCASE. ULYSSES ENTERS.*

ROSE: Excuse me.

*HE IGNORES HER; WALKS PAST WITH SPADE.*

ROSE: *Excuse me.*

*HE STOPS.*

ULYSSES: She was buried.
ROSE: Who was?

ULYSSES: In the night.

ROSE: Has somebody died?

ULYSSES: Just her ribs, poking up over the sand.

ROSE: Oh my God.

ULYSSES: Can't dig her out now. And by tomorrow morning she'll be covered up completely. The wind's changing.

ROSE: Have you reported this to the police?

ULYSSES: They are not interested. I'm sure there are thousands of them buried out there. What do they care? They're just left to rot. It's a bloody tragedy, if you ask me.

*HE STARTS TO EXIT.*

ROSE: Wait.

ULYSSES: What?

ROSE: I want my bill. I'm leaving.

ULYSSES: *(Consults his watch)* Now? There's only me that's up.

ROSE: Now.

ULYSSES: Well, you'll have to wait until I've served breakfast.

ROSE: I won't be treated like this. You can't get sniffy with me just because my mother called me Rose. I want my bill. Now.

ULYSSES: All right, don't get your knickers in a twist.

*ULYSSES EXITS. ROSE MAKES A SMALL NOISE OF SATIS-FACTION TO HERSELF. SHE GOES TO THE MIRROR IN THE HALL TO ADJUST HER HAIR. ENTER ONE OF THE TECHNICIANS, VIA THE FRONT DOOR. HE/SHE'S DRESS-ING FOR THE WEDDING.*

TECHNICIAN: Have you seen the groom?

ROSE: You mean Dexter?

TECHNICIAN: I mean Mr. Lear.

ROSE: I'm sorry. I don't know anybody called Lear.

TECHNICIAN: But the carriage is waiting—

*THE TECHNICIAN EXITS TO LOOK FOR LEAR. ROSE GOES TO THE FRONT DOOR.*

ROSE: Carriage?

*SHE LOOKS AT THE CARRIAGE WAITING FOR FOSS, AMAZED. VINCE COMES DOWN. HE LOOKS TERRIBLE.*

ROSE: A camel-drawn carriage? Well I never.
VINCE: Christ . . .

*HIS VOICE IS HUSHED. HE HAS A TERRIBLE HANGOVER.*

ROSE: *(Turns)* Oh.
VINCE: *(Without enthusiasm)* Rose.
ROSE: Vince.
VINCE: I don't remember last night at all. What did I do?
ROSE: Well, you danced on the table, you stripped off your clothes. And you stole Phoebe's coat.
VINCE: I did what?
ROSE: *(To herself)* No you didn't.
VINCE: I don't remember a coat.
ROSE: I don't know why I said that. It just sort of came to mind. You in Phoebe's coat.
VINCE: A slob I am. A thief I'm not.
ROSE: No. Of course not. I'm sorry.
VINCE: *(Brightening)* All in all, it's been a good weekend. We should do it again sometime. Maybe just the two of us.
ROSE: I'm sure my photographs won't come out. I feel it in my bones.

*SHE GOES OUTSIDE, LEAVING VINCE ON HIS OWN. VINCE BURPS; SITS DOWN. THE TECHNICIAN COMES IN AGAIN. LOOKS AT WATCH. THE PANIC IS GROWING.*

TECHNICIAN: He's going to be late. Hell! Where in God's name—?

*MRS. CORCORAN ENTERS WITH ROSE'S BILL.*

MRS. CORCORAN: Ulysses said—oh.
VINCE: You looking for me?
TECHNICIAN AND MRS. CORCORAN: No!
VINCE: Don't mind me.
MRS. CORCORAN: I'm after Ms. Giddy.
VINCE: She's outside.

MRS. CORCORAN: *(To the Technician)* Who are you, exactly?

TECHNICIAN: Have you seen Mr. Lear?

MRS. CORCORAN: There's nobody here of that name.

TECHNICIAN: Oh. Foss, then. Mr. Foss.

MRS. CORCORAN: Oh yes, Mr. Foss is eating his breakfast. In the dining room. Do you have a telegram for him?

TECHNICIAN: He's getting married in sixteen minutes.

MRS. CORCORAN: Does he know?

TECHNICIAN: *(As he exits)* This way, is it?

MRS. CORCORAN: *(Calling after the Technician)* Turn right. Straight ahead. *(To Vince)* You look really awful, by the way. What *did* you get up to last night?

VINCE: I'm beginning to wonder.

MRS. CORCORAN: A good breakfast'll help to settle your stomach. I've got some nice fish—

VINCE: Fish?

MRS. CORCORAN: Halibut.

VINCE: *(Bothered by this)* No fish.

MRS. CORCORAN: Tell Ms. Giddy I've got her bill, will you? There's no hurry. *(As she exits)* Did you sleep all right, by the way?

VINCE: I sank like a stone. *(After thought)* . . . log. I slept like a log.

*VINCE GETS UP AND GOES TO THE FRONT DOOR, WATCHES THE CARRIAGE. ULYSSES ENTERS; CHANGED TO SERVE BREAKFAST.*

ULYSSES: I can smell camel shit.

VINCE: Blame me. Go on. I've been blamed for just about everything else this morning.

ULYSSES: *(At front door)* What's that?

VINCE: Someone's getting married, apparently. Lucky sod.

*ENTER SEAN, WITH LADDER.*

ULYSSES: You're late up.

*ULYSSES GOES TO EXIT AS TECHNICIAN ENTERS DRAGGING MR. FOSS, WHO HAS A CUP OF COFFEE IN ONE HAND AND A LETTER IN THE OTHER.*

*THEY BUMP INTO ULYSSES.*

ULYSSES: Watch it!
TECHNICIAN: You're going to be late.
MR. FOSS: There's oodles of time.
TECHNICIAN: Thirteen minutes. I count. Thirteen.
SEAN: A question.
TECHNICIAN: Not now.
SEAN: No, now.
MR. FOSS: What?
SEAN: What's a pederast?
MR. FOSS: As if you didn't know. *(Gives Sean a letter)* This is for
    Mr. Kidd, when next you see him.
TECHNICIAN: Come on.
MR. FOSS: The coffee's a little weak this morning, Ulysses—

*THE TECHNICIAN DRAGS MR. FOSS OFF.*

ULYSSES: What did he mean: "as if you didn't know?"
SEAN: Two quid you owe me.
ULYSSES: *(Exiting)* The place has gone bananas.

*SEAN PUTS THE LADDER ON THE PATIO AND STARTS TO
TAKE DOWN THE LIGHTS, REMOVING THE BULBS ONE
BY ONE AND WRAPPING THEM IN NEWSPAPER.*

*ENTER DEXTER. HE HAS A CRICK IN HIS NECK, FROM SLEEP-
ING IN THE BATH. HE HAS HIS LUGGAGE. HE SEES VINCE,
TURNS HIS BACK ON HIM, AND GOES ON TO THE PATIO.*

DEXTER: Excuse me.
SEAN: Yes?
DEXTER: Any chance of a taxi?
SEAN: Not on a Sunday morning.
DEXTER: Shit.
SEAN: Yeah, I can smell it too.

*HE GOES BACK INTO THE HALL, PUTS DOWN HIS BAG,
AND GOES TO FIND MRS. CORCORAN, AS ROB ENTERS.
HE STOPS.*

ROB: Carys was looking for you earlier.

DEXTER: I can't face her.

ROB: I thought you slept together.

DEXTER: She was in the bed; I was in the bath. It's like I've been thrown out of the human race.

ROB: We shouldn't have come, any of us. I didn't protest at the time and I should have. I think there was some malice there; just wanting to see you cornered.

DEXTER: Well, you've seen. Now I just want to get out before Big Daddy Skinner gets down.

ROB: He'll catch up with you sooner or later.

DEXTER: I want us friends, Rob. Whatever happens. Please.

ROB: We'll be friends. Later. Did you dream?

DEXTER: No. (*A beat*) Yes. Something about trains.

PHOEBE: (*Off-stage*) Come along, for Christ's sake—

DEXTER: See you later.

*DEXTER EXITS. ROB GOES INTO THE PATIO. SEAN HAS COME DOWN THE LADDER.*

SEAN: Want to go swimming?

ROB: Swimming?

SEAN: You know, in the sea.

ROB: They'll be going soon.

SEAN: Oh. And you're going too?

ROB: Dexter may need help.

SEAN: (*Cool*) No problem.

ROB: Doesn't seem fair.

SEAN: And we've got to be fair haven't we? At all fucking costs.

*HE PICKS UP THE BOX OF LIGHTS AND CARRIES IT THROUGH. PHOEBE APPEARS WITH DONNA-MARIE.*

PHOEBE: Boy!

*SEAN STOPS. LOOKS AT PHOEBE.*

PHOEBE: Our bags are on the first landing. Bring them down.

SEAN: Say "please."

PHOEBE: Please.

SEAN: No.

*HE EXITS. PHOEBE LOOKS AT ROB AND CHOOSES TO SAY NOTHING.*

PHOEBE: Where's Rose?

*SHE SEES VINCE, WHO HAS GONE TO SLEEP AT THE FRONT DOOR.*

PHOEBE: Vince!

*SHE CROSSES TO HIM. THE CONVERSATION SPLITS.*

I.

PHOEBE: *(Shakes him)* Vince.
VINCE: What?
PHOEBE: Have you seen Rose?
VINCE: She went out to look at the Wedding Carriage.
PHOEBE: What Wedding Carriage?
VINCE: She said there were camels.
PHOEBE: Find her for me, will you?
VINCE: Jesus. She's a grown woman.
PHOEBE: We don't want a repeat of last night's performance.

*UNWILLINGLY, VINCE GOES TO FIND ROSE.*

II.

DONNA-MARIE: You didn't go swimming, did you?
ROB: No.
DONNA-MARIE: I did.
ROB: No. Donna. We didn't go.
DONNA-MARIE: I did. Last night.
ROB: When?
DONNA-MARIE: Last night, with the fishes.
ROB: Did you?
DONNA-MARIE: All of us went. Don't you remember?
ROB: *(Remembering)* Oh my Lord.

PHOEBE: *(Having dispatched Vince)* This bloody place. *(To Donna-Marie)* Come here. *(She obeys. Then to Rob)* You know, Lindberg and I have never really liked you. It was an instinctive thing. I daresay you're fairly harmless amongst your own, but you've got no place with ordinary people. Watching us. Oh, yes. That's what I didn't like. The way you watch. As if you're learning how to be normal.

ROB: You're lots of things, Phoebe, but normal isn't one of them.

PHOEBE: Oh yes I am. I'm normal. A simple woman, with simple tastes. The thought of your perversions leaves me cold. Physically cold. To think of it. I need my coat. Donna, get my coat. It's with the cases.

*DONNA-MARIE EXITS FOR THE COAT.*

PHOEBE: I suppose you're proud.

ROB: What of?

PHOEBE: I suppose you are. Upsetting the apple-cart. *(We realize slowly that she is very close to tears)* I wanted so much for Carys. I can tell you. It doesn't do to want too much. I married a rock. Lindberg is a rock. It's terrible.

ROB: No wonder you love Rose so much.

PHOEBE: Love her?

ROB: She's gentle.

PHOEBE: I don't love her. Not in the way you're implying.

ROB: You're right, I watch. I'm sorry if it distresses you. It distresses me too sometimes.

PHOEBE: You like other people's pain.

*ENTER ROSE, WITH VINCE.*

VINCE: I found her.

PHOEBE: Rose.

ROSE: Phoebe. What did you want?

PHOEBE: Want?

ROSE: Vince said you wanted something . . .

PHOEBE: Well . . . I just . . . I thought we should have some breakfast.

*ENTER DONNA-MARIE, WITH THE COAT. PHOEBE PUTS IT ON.*

VINCE: Cold?
PHOEBE: It's my coat.
VINCE: I didn't say it wasn't.
PHOEBE: No?
VINCE: No.
PHOEBE: Rose . . . I'm sorry.
ROSE: It's all right.
PHOEBE: I'm sure you didn't mean it.
ROSE: Mean what?
PHOEBE: What you called me. Carnivorous.
ROSE: Did I?

*PHOEBE NODS; FROM APOLOGY TO MARTYRDOM IN TWO MOVES.*

ROSE: Oh, Phoebe.
PHOEBE: Never mind. We'll pretend it never happened. Come to
    breakfast.
ROSE: Yes.

*ROSE KISSES PHOEBE. PHOEBE GET EMBARRASSED IN THE LIGHT OF ROB'S REMARKS, AND HURRIES DONNA-MARIE AND ROSE OUT.*

PHOEBE: Are you coming, Vince?
VINCE: No, it's just the way I walk. (*Laughs, the joke is now on Phoebe, who exits*) Make 'em laugh, I say. (*To Rob*) You don't know what you're missing.

*ROB IS ALONE ON THE STAGE: BELLS START TO RING, DISTANTLY. HE GOES OUT ON THE PATIO AS MR. TREAD-AWAY COMES ON, DRESSED FOR THE WEDDING, FOL-LOWED BY CARYS.*

MR. TREADAWAY: I'm sorry, I don't know what you're talking
    about.
CARYS: Where's Mr. Foss? Let me speak to him.

MR. TREADAWAY: Hear those bells? The old fool's getting married! And I'm the best man!

CARYS: Married? At nine o'clock on a Sunday morning?

MR. TREADAWAY: He's not an easy man to love, but I can't help thinking he's one of God's finest. Despite his poems. Did you ever hear—Ring? Ring? *(He checks his pockets)* Where's the ring?

CARYS: Am I mad, Mr. Treadaway? Just tell me that. Am I?

MR. TREADAWAY: No. You're worth more than the rest of them put together, that's my honest opinion. I've lost the ring!

CARYS: And the dream?

MR. TREADAWAY: Was a dream; and I was flattered I was in it. *(To himself)* There's a hole in my pocket. That'll teach me to play with myself. *(To Carys)* I've lost the ring, damn it!

*ENTER THE JUFFS WITH THEIR CASES. MELBA JUFFS IS WEARING LARGE EARRINGS.*

MELBA: If we're quick—

MR. TREADAWAY: *(Panicking now)* I've lost it!

CARYS: Here. Have my engagement ring.

MELBA: What are you doing?

CARYS: Giving away my ring; what does it look like?

MR. TREADAWAY: No, that's much too small.

CARYS: My fingers are quite thick.

MR. TREADAWAY: The bride's fingers are three times yours.

CARYS: What?

*TREADAWAY SEES THE RINGS IN MELBA'S EARS.*

MR. TREADAWAY: Ah-ha!

MELBA: What are you staring at?

MR. TREADAWAY: *(Advancing on Melba, reciting under his breath) Dear Pig, are you willing—*

MELBA: Keep away from me.

MR. TREADAWAY: *—to sell for one shilling—*

MELBA: Frank!

MR. TREADAWAY: *(Snatches at Melba's ear)—your ring?*

MELBA: Ah!

MR. TREADAWAY: *(Triumphant) Said the Piggy, "I will."* *(Holds up the ring)* Just the job. *(To Carys)* Excuse me.

FRANK: You! You!

*FRANK PURSUES TREADAWAY.*

MELBA: My ear's bleeding.
CARYS: Dear Pig, are you willing to sell for one shilling
    Your ring? said the Piggy,
    "I will."
    So they took it away, and were married next day,
    By the turkey who lived on the hill.
MELBA: What are you reciting?
CARYS: "The Owl and the Pussycat." It's a nonsense poem. By
    Edward Lear. I remember it from childhood.
MELBA: I want to go home.
CARYS: We will. It'll be all right. Have you seen Dexter?
MELBA: We shan't be seeing him again. This has been a terrible
    grief for us both.
CARYS: He's not dead.
MELBA: I don't expect you to understand.
CARYS: Did you dream last night?
MELBA: I never dream.

*ENTER FRANK, BREATHLESS.*

FRANK: He was sprinting like a goat. I lost him.
MELBA: I want to go home.
FRANK: Not on an empty stomach.
MELBA: Tell Dexter goodbye, will you?

*THEY EXIT INTO THE DINING ROOM. ROB STANDS AT
THE PATIO DOOR.*

ROB: None of them will admit to it, except your little sister.
CARYS: They're afraid, that's why.
ROB: They remember though. I'm sure of that.
CARYS: Poor Dexter.

*ENTER SEAN.*

ROB: Why poor Dexter?

CARYS: I love him, you know.

*EXIT CARYS INTO THE DINING ROOM.*

SEAN: Oh, there's a note here for you. From Mr. Foss. I forgot.
ROB: Uh. (*He opens it, reads*) "Mr. Kidd, I meant what I said. Wait a while. Edward."
SEAN: Do you want to leave a reply?
ROB: Maybe I should wait. Enjoy the day.
SEAN: Don't do me any favors.
ROB: You still game for a swim?
SEAN: Now?
ROB: Whenever suits you.
SEAN: You're on.

*ENTER LINDBERG, WITH A SMALL CASE.*

LINDBERG: Boy!
SEAN: Oh Christ.
LINDBERG: Bags!

*MRS. CORCORAN ENTERS, CROSSING THE STAGE.*

MRS. CORCORAN: Nobody seems to want the fish this morning.
LINDBERG: Fish?
MRS. CORCORAN: Your wife's in the dining room, Mr. Skinner.

*DEXTER ENTERS.*

LINDBERG: (*To Sean*) Boy!
DEXTER: (*Sees Lindberg*) Shit.
LINDBERG: Bags!
MRS. CORCORAN: Sean. You heard Mr. Skinner.

*MRS. CORCORAN EXITS. DEXTER HAS TRIED TO SLIP AWAY.*

LINDBERG: Dexter!
DEXTER: I—
ROB: Quickly.

*ROB AND SEAN DUCK OUT.*

LINDBERG: Boy!

*LINDBERG TURNS TO CATCH SEAN, BUT HE'S TOO LATE. ROB AND SEAN HAVE GONE. DEXTER NOW TRIES TO SLIP AWAY.*

LINDBERG: Wait!

*DEXTER TURNS TO FACE LINDBERG.*

DEXTER: Listen, before you start on me—
LINDBERG: No, no.

*MRS. CORCORAN COMES BACK IN.*

MRS. CORCORAN: Did you hear the bells?
LINDBERG: No.
DEXTER: I did.
MRS. CORCORAN: Strange.

*SHE EXITS AGAIN.*

LINDBERG: I'm not in the mood for recriminations. It's too late anyway. I just wanted a word with you. This is strictly between you and I, see, and if I ever hear that this conversation got any further—
DEXTER: It won't.
LINDBERG: *(A confessional; difficult for Lindberg, but he warms to it)* See, before I took over the firm I was a salesman, a damn good one. I used to travel all over the world, selling paper bags. I had money, I was young, about your age, and believe it or not, I was quite good looking. Well. One time I was in a bar in Bangkok and I picked up the most mouth-watering female on God's earth. I had to pay through the nose for her, but I tell you, she was incredible. Ever been with a whore?
DEXTER: No.
LINDBERG: Sex and commerce, it's a very arousing combination. I took her back to my hotel and we started to get down to

business. I remember she was deliciously coy: we even undressed in the dark because she said she was shy. I slung off my clothes in two seconds flat and got into bed. Next thing she was slipping in beside me, smelling of something familiar, like I'd known her all my life, and I ran my hands down over her titties, like a fourteen-year-old's, and over her flat belly down to her pussy. And you know what? She had more between her legs than I did, a right handful, and it was raring to go.

DEXTER: She was a man?

LINDBERG: She was a man.

DEXTER: So what did you do?

LINDBERG: (A beat) I'd paid my money. I screwed him rigid.

DEXTER: Jesus Christ.

LINDBERG: It doesn't mean I'm bent, Dexter. See what I'm saying? You're not the first man who's tasted forbidden fruit and you won't be the last. And if you find you can't live without it, then arrangements can be made. It's not do or die in this life. It's compromise, it's making it work.

DEXTER: That's very enlightened.

LINDBERG: Don't give me that crap. I'm the most benighted son of a bitch in Christendom, and I'm going to stay that way. And if I ever find out, through Carys or anybody else, that your perversions are at all visible, your feet won't touch the ground. Do we understand each other?

DEXTER: Of course.

*DEXTER IS PUZZLED.*

LINDBERG: Spit it out.

DEXTER: I was wondering. Do you still . . .

LINDBERG: Still . . . ?

DEXTER: Make arrangements for yourself?

LINDBERG: Don't push it, son.

DEXTER: Only asking.

*ENTER CARYS.*

LINDBERG: Princess.

CARYS: Mother wants to know are you going to breakfast?

LINDBERG: Why not?

*LINDBERG GOES TO EXIT; CARYS WITH HIM.*

LINDBERG: *(To Carys)* No. Stay. Dexter wants a word.

*LINDBERG EXITS.*

DEXTER: I've been thinking.
CARYS: He's given you a pep-talk.
DEXTER: In a way.
CARYS: Financial inducements?
DEXTER: God no.
CARYS: I don't want to marry you, Dexter.
DEXTER: Oh.
CARYS: Not because of Rob. Like I said, sex isn't everything.
DEXTER: What then?
CARYS: Your parents are going to disown you, you know that?
DEXTER: I can live without them. I don't think I can live without you.
CARYS: I won't marry, Dex.
DEXTER: All right.
CARYS: I like you too much.
DEXTER: God, you're strange.
CARYS: Last night, drifting along, I thought, it's all right. If I
       drown, I drown. It's my life.
DEXTER: I don't know what you're talking about.
CARYS: Don't fret about it.

*SHE KISSES HIM. HE KISSES HER BACK. ENTER ROSE. SHE
WATCHES FOR A MOMENT. SOMEONE APPLAUDS. IT'S
LINDBERG. SUDDENLY, THE WEDDING PARTY COMES
BACK ON. VINCE, LINDBERG, PHOEBE, DONNA-MARIE;
THEN, AFTER A SPACE, MELBA AND FRANK.*

LINDBERG: Congratulations!
CARYS: This doesn't mean a thing.
LINDBERG: All the time in the world.
DEXTER: *(To Melba)* Your ear's bleeding.
FRANK: *(To Melba)* I'm going to get the bill. Get somebody to
       bring the luggage down.
DEXTER: Wait.
FRANK: No.

LINDBERG: Frank—
FRANK: There's nothing to say.
LINDBERG: A moment. Suffer the children.
FRANK: Don't quote the Scriptures to me.
LINDBERG: We came to celebrate a wedding. We end up daggers
    drawn. There's no need.
MELBA: He's right, Frank.
LINDBERG: We've had our share of revelations, but the Bible's full
    of them, Frank, you should be used to them.
FRANK: There's been error on every side.
LINDBERG: My own feelings precisely.
FRANK: I just want to forget this weekend ever happened.
LINDBERG: On that, we also agree.

*LINDBERG OFFERS HIS HAND, FRANK TAKES IT.*

LINDBERG: To forgetting.

*THEY SHAKE.*

VINCE: What about a photograph?
ROSE: No . . .
LINDBERG: It's a good idea.
MELBA: Not with my bleeding ear.
VINCE: Language.
LINDBERG: Reconciliations are always uncomfortable. But they
    should be recorded for posterity.

*MRS. CORCORAN ENTERS WITH SOMETHING IN A
BROWN PAPER PARCEL.*

MRS. CORCORAN: Everybody enjoy their breakfast?
MELBA: Yes, it was lovely.
MRS. CORCORAN: I brought something . . . for Donna. Some
    child left it at the hotel, oh, a long while back.
DONNA-MARIE: For me?
MRS. CORCORAN: They must have had it for the beach. So you
    have it now.

*SHE UNDOES THE PARCEL. IT'S A BOAT. DONNA TAKES*

*IT. EVERYBODY LOOKS, THE MEMORIES BEGINNING TO
FLOOD BACK.*

DONNA-MARIE: Oh.
LINDBERG: A boat.
PHOEBE: Say . . . "thank you."
DONNA-MARIE: Thank you.
MRS. CORCORAN: I suppose it's really a boy's toy.
DONNA-MARIE: For me?
MRS. CORCORAN: Well. I'll fetch your bills.

*ROSE IS SETTING UP THE CAMERA ON A TRIPOD, DOWN
CENTER. VINCE SETS UP SOME CHAIRS, A ROW OF
THEM, VERY FORMAL. PHOEBE ORGANIZES. DONNA-
MARIE STARES AT THE BOAT. YOU COULD CUT THE
ATMOSPHERE WITH A KNIFE. EVERYONE TREMBLES ON
THE EDGE OF SPEAKING.*

DONNA-MARIE: All of us.
PHOEBE: Hurry up, Rose.
DONNA-MARIE: We were in a boat.

*EVERYONE FREEZES.*

ROSE: *(Quietly)* Oh my God.
PHOEBE: Now, shut up, Donna. Or I'll give the boat back to the
     nice lady.
DONNA-MARIE: No!
CARYS: Don't bully her.
ROSE: I dreamt . . . I drowned. Oh God, it was horrible.
PHOEBE: Now look, you've upset Auntie Rose.
ROSE: . . . we were in this life-boat together.
DONNA-MARIE: Fishes in the water.
ROSE: That's right. There were fishes in the water.
PHOEBE: Just hush, Rose. Nobody wants to hear what you
     dreamed about.
VINCE: It's no use pretending. We all know.
LINDBERG: What the hell are you rabbiting on about?
MELBA: You know damn well. Vince is right, for once. We all know.
FRANK: No, I don't.

MELBA: Yes, you do. All of us were in the same boat last night.
LINDBERG: Bollocks!
CARYS: Don't *you* remember?
LINDBERG: No. I do not remember.
DONNA-MARIE: All in a big boat. Then in a little boat.
PHOEBE: Right! That's it, my girl!

*SHE TRIES TO SNATCH THE BOAT FROM DONNA-MARIE, WHO STARTS TO CRY.*

LINDBERG: Phoebe. Let her alone.
PHOEBE: Such a lot of nonsense.
VINCE: I admit it. I drowned.
CARYS: We all drowned.
FRANK: No. I did not drown.
MELBA: You're lying. The girl's right.
DEXTER: We all dreamt the same dream? Everybody?
CARYS: Everybody. It was stage-managed.
MELBA: *(To Lindberg)* You went overboard with Carys.
DEXTER: After Phoebe went down.
LINDBERG: *(Breaking)* Couldn't face living; not without you. I need you in spite of myself.
PHOEBE: What's happened to us?
FRANK: It's not possible. Not the same dream.
DEXTER: The *Bear of Amsterdam*. *(A pause)* Am I right? *(Murmurs of assent)* That was the ship. And he— *(Points at Lindberg)* — shot the Captain.

*AN ERUPTION OF REMARKS.*

LINDBERG: I had my reasons!
DONNA-MARIE: Fishes! Fishes!
FRANK: I was eaten up. I remember it distinctly.
PHOEBE: This place. This bloody place.
ROSE: Oh God, it was terrible.

*A SILENCE.*

MELBA: Once I was drowned, I went walking. Walking on the bottom of the ocean.

CARYS: I chatted with a dead sailor. He was quite flirty.

FRANK: It's too much.

LINDBERG: They're just dreams. Let's keep it in proportion.

PHOEBE: Where did *you* go, Rose?

ROSE: Oh . . . looking for shells.

PHOEBE: I lost you.

DEXTER: There were cities.

LINDBERG: I saw none.

DEXTER: You don't know what you missed. Streets full of fish.

VINCE: Crabs ate my balls.

MELBA: I found an octopus. It made love to me. And you know what? I enjoyed it.

PHOEBE: I lost everybody. I was alone. The sea was empty.

LINDBERG: So we all slept in separate rooms and we dreamt the same dream. Is that so unusual? We're staying by the sea; we hear the waves in our sleep . . . it happens.

VINCE: Coincidence?

LINDBERG: Of course, coincidence.

DEXTER: Oh, come on—

LINDBERG: *(To Dexter, suddenly ferocious)* Compromise with the truth. Whatever happened—

ROSE: Dreams should be private. I mean, they're very personal.

LINDBERG: —we don't want to remember it.

FRANK: That's right.

PHOEBE: I wouldn't have remembered. *(Re: Donna-Marie)* Except for her.

CARYS: You are a cow, you really are.

LINDBERG: No arguments now. Not about this. We have to stick together. We have to . . . agree to forget.

CARYS: Wait. For a while we were in each other's heads. One mind; all of us. Isn't that a wonderful thought?

FRANK: No. It makes me feel dirty.

DEXTER: So much for brotherhood.

LINDBERG: Frank's right. It's invasive. I am who I am.

CARYS: Maybe it doesn't have to be that way.

PHOEBE: I wasn't asked. It was forced on me. If I'd been asked, well, that's a different thing. But this was totally unwarranted.

MELBA: It's probably illegal.

CARYS: Oh Mum, for God's sake.

PHOEBE: *(A beat)* We all have our little secrets. We have to respect that in each other. That's how we get on in the world, isn't it? I don't go meddling in your mind and you stay out of mine.

*BELLS HAVE STARTED TO RING, DISTANTLY.*

PHOEBE: (*Continuing*) That's how we keep control.
CARYS: Of what?
LINDBERG: Of the world.
CARYS: Is that what you think?
LINDBERG: You'll learn.
FRANK: I suggest we pack the cars and start home.
PHOEBE: Now, that's a good idea.
MELBA: Yes.
ROSE: Where's Rob?
LINDBERG: Let him find his own way back. Dexter, bring the bags down from the landing.
ROSE: What about the photograph?
LINDBERG: Let's just pay the bloody bill, and go—
FRANK: (*At the front door*) Good God.
MELBA: What?
FRANK: It's a wedding procession!

*NOISE OUTSIDE. THE BELLS ARE GETTING LOUDER.*

CARYS: It's Mr. Foss!
LINDBERG: That old bugger? Getting married?

*THE WEDDING PARTY GOES TO THE DOOR, AS THE TECHNICIANS ENTER, UNROLLING A CARPET. SEAN FOLLOWS, IN HIS BRIEFS, A TOWEL AROUND HIS NECK. HE SPREADS ROSE PETALS.*

SEAN: Out of the way! Out of the way!
PHOEBE: Quickly, before they arrive. Let's get out of here.

*THE NOISE IS LOUDER BY THE MOMENT.*

LINDBERG: It's only a wedding. What's to be afraid of?
FRANK: There's always something.

*MRS. CORCORAN HAS COME ON. ULYSSES FOLLOWS.*

MRS. CORCORAN: What on earth is going on?
SEAN: It's Mr. Lear, formerly known as Mr. Foss. He's just got married.
MRS. CORCORAN: Oh my Lord. How exciting.

*THE BELLS ARE SUDDENLY VERY LOUD, AND THE SEC-OND WEDDING PARTY OF THE PLAY ENTERS. TECHNI-CIANS AS GUESTS, ALL WEARING FALSE NOSES OF VARI-OUS SHAPES AND SIZES. EVERYBODY IS TALKING NOW. THE TECHNICIANS LAUGHING. ROB ENTERS, IN HIS JEANS, SHIRT ROUND HIS NECK. TREADAWAY FOLLOWS.*

MR. TREADAWAY: Over the threshold! Over the threshold!

*MR. FOSS ENTERS, CARRIED BY HIS BRIDE, WHO IS ENTIRELY SWATHED IN GLORIOUS LACE, A VEIL OVER HER FACE.*

*THE TECHNICIANS BRING UP THE REAR, CARRYING THE TRAIN.*

*CONFETTI FILLS THE AIR. MAYBE THE WEDDING MARCH; MAYBE SOME PUCCINI.*

*DONNA-MARIE LAUGHS AND LAUGHS. CARYS HAS TAKEN TO DANCING WITH DEXTER. THE BRIDE PUTS MR. FOSS DOWN, TO A GREAT DEAL OF APPLAUSE. EVEN THE JUFFS AND THE SKINNERS ARE CAUGHT UP IN THE EUPHORIA.*

*THE BRIDE THROWS HER BOUQUET INTO THE AIR. ROB CATCHES IT. SMILES AT SEAN. TOSSES IT TO ROSE.*

ROB: Kiss the bride! Kiss the bride!

*EVERYBODY JOINS IN THIS NOW. MORE APPLAUSE!*

*MR. FOSS PLAYS IT OUT A LITTLE; BUT HE EVENTUALLY UNVEILS THE BRIDE.*

*IT IS, OF COURSE, THE GORILLA. ON ITS OVERSIZED, CALLOUSED FINGER, MELBA JUFFS' EARRING.*

*CHAOS ENSUES AT THE SIGHT OF IT. ROSE ALMOST FAINTS. LINDBERG SHOUTS, PHOEBE STARTS TO CRY. FRANK IS DISGUSTED.*

*CARYS LAUGHS, LEARNING FROM DONNA THE EASE OF THAT RESPONSE.*

*THE FOLLOWING REMARKS OVERLAP.*

LINDBERG: This is an outrage! I shall sue!
MRS. CORCORAN: Is this some sort of joke?
VINCE: I don't think so.
MRS. CORCORAN: Isn't it illegal?
LINDBERG: Out! Out! Everybody follow me!
PHOEBE: Pick yourself up, Rose. Rose!
DONNA-MARIE: Here come the fishes! Here come the fishes!

*NOW THE LINES FOLLOW MORE AUDIBLY.*

MRS. CORCORAN: What about the bill?
PHOEBE: Donna-Marie! Come here!

*DONNA-MARIE IGNORES HER.*

FRANK: *(To Dexter)* Quickly, the cases.
DEXTER: You get them.
FRANK: Vince!
VINCE: Huh?
FRANK: Cases.
VINCE: *(Empty-handed)* I'm laden, chief.

*FRANK EXITS.*

LINDBERG: *(Taking out money, and giving it to Vince)* There! Take it all!
VINCE: I never accept small bribes.
LINDBERG: *(Throwing the money at him)* Are you mocking me?
VINCE: Perish the thought.

*LINDBERG PICKS UP THE CASES HE BROUGHT DOWN.*

LINDBERG: Come on, Phoebe!
PHOEBE: Rose!

*LINDBERG EXITS.*

ROSE: I'm coming.
PHOEBE: We're not waiting, Rose.
DONNA-MARIE: I'm a frog.
PHOEBE: No, you're not.

*SHE HAULS DONNA-MARIE TO THE DOOR.*

DONNA-MARIE: Bye bye! Bye bye!

*PHOEBE AND DONNA-MARIE EXIT.*

MR. FOSS: *(Sees cameras and chairs)* I propose a photograph, as a remembrance of this perfect day!

*HE STARTS TO ARRANGE HIS PARTY IN FRONT OF THE CAMERA ON THE SEATS SET OUT FOR THE JUFFS AND THE SKINNERS.*

ROSE: Oh, I've left my camera in there!
LINDBERG: Forget your bloody camera!
SEAN: It's starting to rain.
MR. FOSS: Just got in in time.
ULYSSES: I'd better get the chairs off the patio.

*FRANK HAS COME DOWNSTAIRS WITH THE REST OF THE CASES. HE AND MELBA MAKE FOR THE DOOR.*

MR. FOSS: Oh, are you leaving us? We were just arranging a photo-graph.
MELBA: I'm afraid we've got an appointment.
MR. FOSS: On a Sunday morning?
FRANK: This is an abomination!
MELBA: Now, Frank . . .

FRANK: Sodom!

MR. FOSS: My sentiments exactly, sir. You're a man after my own heart.

FRANK: I'm not after anybody's heart.

MR. FOSS: Then I pity you, sir. I truly do.

*EXIT MELBA AND FRANK.*

CARYS: Keep safe, Rob. *(Kisses him)*

MRS. CORCORAN: *(To Sean)* You should put a shirt on, you'll catch your death.

DEXTER: *(To Rob)* Likewise. *(Hugs him)* I'm sorry I didn't break your heart.

ROB: You'll get over it.

DEXTER: Bye, then.

MRS. CORCORAN: I knew the weather would break sooner or later.

TECHNICIAN: Look at the color of that sky.

*DEXTER AND CARYS EXIT TOGETHER.*

*OUTSIDE THE JUFFS AND THE SKINNERS ARE STILL SHOUT-ING AS THEY PILE INTO THEIR CARS. A FEW LINES CARRY.*

ROSE: That was an expensive camera!

LINDBERG: I'll buy you another one! Now will you get in the car?

DONNA-MARIE: Here come the fishes!

PHOEBE: If you mention fishes once more—

*AND SO ON. CAR DOORS ARE SLAMMED. ENGINES START.*

*MR. FOSS' WEDDING PARTY IS NOW GATHERING IN FRONT OF THE CAMERA.*

MR. FOSS: *(To Rob)* I told you I'd marry, didn't I?

ROB: What sex is . . . your . . . significant other?

MR. FOSS: I didn't ask. It seemed impertinent. It loves my nose. That's all that matters. For that I could love it, whatever it was.

*THE LIGHT IS FADING, TURNING A DUSKY PINK, AS IF BEFORE A MAJOR THUNDERSTORM.*

MR. FOSS: Significance does seem to lie in insignificant places, doesn't it? In an arrangement of clouds, in the ink stain on my thumb.

ROB: In dreams.

MR. FOSS: Of course in dreams. There most of all.

*TREADAWAY, WHO HAS TAKEN OVER AS PHOTOGRAPHER, COMES TO FETCH MR. FOSS AND ROB.*

MR. TREADAWAY: Please take your seats, or we'll never get to the Wedding Breakfast.

MR. FOSS: I hope everyone's in the mood for nuts and bananas.

*MR. FOSS GOES TO STAND IN THE CENTER OF THE PIC-TURE, BESIDE HIS GORILLA. SOME OF THE GUESTS ARE SITTING, OTHERS STANDING. MRS. CORCORAN IS THERE, AS IS ULYSSES. SEAN, OF COURSE. NOW ROB JOINS THE GROUP TOO.*

MR. FOSS: Well, here we are. Finally.

MRS. CORCORAN: You have to say a few words.

MR. FOSS: Must I?

MRS. CORCORAN: It's traditional.

MR. FOSS: Well, I'm a great believer in tradition.

*THE REST OF THE GUESTS APPLAUD. MR. FOSS QUI-ETENS THEM DOWN.*

MR. FOSS: Of course, it's all a complete mystery to me. I freely admit it. Who proposed to who. What God can possibly mean, joining us in Roly-Poly Paddle Me. But isn't that the sweetest thing, mystery? To have that is, I think, to have everything. Everything.

TECHNICIAN: Poem!

MR. FOSS: No . . .

ALL: Yes! *(They chant)* Po! Em! Po! Em!

MR. FOSS: I have nothing prepared.

ROB: Make it up.

MR. FOSS: Then you'll have to help me.

ROB: I'll do my best.

MR. FOSS: So . . . *There once was a fellow called Lear . . .*
ROB: *Whose life was . . . exceedingly queer.*
MR. FOSS: *One day, for a jape,*
 *He married an ape . . .*
ROB: *And . . .*

*EVERYBODY WAITS, BREATHLESS, FOR THE NEXT LINE.*

ROB: *And swung from a tree for a year.*
MR. FOSS: Yes! Yes! *(Applauds)*

*HE KISSES THE BRIDE.*

MR. FOSS: Yes. Oh yes. Oh yes . . . *(Quietly, to Rob)* It's all non-
  sense of course. But it brings a tear to my eye nevertheless.
ROB: Ah, love!
MR. FOSS: Ah. *Love.*

*A FLASH. THE IMAGE FREEZES, AS HANDS ARE ABOUT
TO CLAP AND TONGUES ABOUT TO MAKE WORDS. NOT
THE DEAD SMILES OF PREVIOUS PHOTOGRAPHS. THIS IS
AN INSTANT CAUGHT; FULL OF GENUINE PLEASURE.*

*THUNDER RUMBLES.*

*THE LIGHTS GO DOWN ON THE FROZEN MOMENT,
THROUGH ROSE PINK TO DARKNESS.*

*THE PLAY ENDS.*